The Making of Modern Burma

Burma has often been portrayed as a timeless place, a country of egalitarian Buddhist villages, ruled successively by autocratic kings, British colonialists and, most recently, a military dictatorship. *The Making of Modern Burma* argues instead that many aspects of Burmese society today, from the borders of the state to the social structure of the countryside to the very notion of a Burmese or Burman identity, are largely the creations of the nineteenth century, a period of great change, away from the Ava-based polity of early modern times, and towards the 'British Burma' of the 1900s. The book provides a sophisticated and much-needed account of the period, and as such will be an important resource for policy-makers and students as a basis for understanding contemporary politics and the challenges of the modern state. It will also be read by historians interested in the British colonial expansion of the nineteenth century.

Thant Myint-U is Humanitarian Affairs Officer at the Office for the Co-ordination of Humanitarian Affairs, the United Nations, New York. His publications include *Knowledge and Multilateral Interventions* published by Chatham House in 2000.

The Making of Modern Burma

Thant Myint-U

CAMBRIDGE
UNIVERSITY PRESS

PUBLISHED BY THE PRESS SYNDICATE OF THE UNIVERSITY OF CAMBRIDGE
The Pitt Building, Trumpington Street, Cambridge, United Kingdom

CAMBRIDGE UNIVERSITY PRESS
The Edinburgh Building, Cambridge CB2 2RU, UK   http://www.cup.cam.ac.uk
40 West 20th Street, New York, NY 10011–4211, USA   http://www.cup.org
10 Stamford Road, Oakleigh, Melbourne 3166, Australia
Ruiz de Alarcón 13, 28014 Madrid, Spain

First published 2001

Printed in the United Kingdom at the University Press, Cambridge

Typeset in Concorde BQ 9.5/14pt [VN]

A catalogue record for this book is available from the British Library

ISBN 0 521 78021 7 hardback
ISBN 0 521 79914 7 paperback

Contents

Acknowledgements

Most of this book was written in the period 1995–98, while I was a Research Fellow of Trinity College, Cambridge, and I would like to thank the Master and Fellows of the college for their support. Professor Victor Lieberman, Professor James Scott, Professor Michael Aung Thwin, Dr Anil Seal, Dr Tim Harper, Dr Ian Brown, Dr Patrick Tuck, Miss Elizabeth Sellwood and Mrs Zunetta Liddell all read parts of the manuscript at different stages and I am grateful for all their comments and criticisms. I would also like to thank Mrs Patricia Herbert of the British Library, Dr John Okell of London University and Dr Lionel Carter of the Centre for South Asian Studies, Cambridge University for their expert help. In Burma, I am indebted for the assistance and advice of Dr Than Tun, U Than Htut, U Thaw Kaung, U Maung Maung Tin, and to HRH Prince Hteik Tin Taw Hpaya. The late Dr Michael Aris generously spent many memorable afternoons with me in Oxford discussing Tibetan and Burmese religion, language and history. My special thanks, however, are to my former Ph.D. supervisor Professor C.A. Bayly. I could not have asked for a better supervisor, and I am deeply grateful to him for all his kind and invaluable support over the years. This book is dedicated to my parents.

Introduction: The fall of Mandalay

Late in the afternoon, on 29 November 1885, King Thibaw of Burma appeared at the steps of his summer palace, holding the hand of his queen and half-sister Supayalat. The evening before, a British expeditionary force under the command of General Sir Harry Prendergast had entered Mandalay unopposed and had ordered the king's immediate and unconditional surrender. A request to remain in the city for another day had been rejected by General Prendergast and, instead, Thibaw was given a few more hours to collect his possessions and leave his kingdom forever. And so, after a brief interview with the gentleman from *The Times*, the last of the Konbaung monarchs abdicated his throne and began his journey into exile.

Thibaw and Supayalat were accompanied by their three young daughters and other close family, as well as by several ministers of state and an entourage of servants carrying trunks full of treasure and royal costumes. Riding in an ordinary ox-drawn carriage, they slowly made their way out though the Kyaw Moe gate to the south and then towards the steamer *Thooreah* anchored in the Irrawaddy river three miles away. Several hundred British soldiers, men of the 67th Hampshire Regiment, escorted the royal party as they emerged unceremoniously from the walled city and proceeded through the thick crowds of ordinary people who had gathered to watch. As Thibaw made his way past, the townspeople seemed only then to realise that he was being taken away. Thousands prostrated themselves on the ground alongside the road to the pier. Some cried out and several stones and clumps of earth were thrown at the scarlet-coated troops marching alongside the carriage.

Nearer the river, Supayalat called on a few of the British soldiers close at hand and then favoured one by granting him the privilege of lighting her royal cigar. When they finally reached the Irrawaddy after dark, Thibaw, a white umbrella of royalty held high over his head, walked across a narrow wooden plank and onto the waiting steamer, never to set foot on Burmese soil again. Aged 28, he would spend the remaining thirty years of his life as a state pensioner and prisoner just outside the town of Ratanagiri along western India's steamy Konkan coast.

Thibaw's fate had been sealed several weeks before with a decision by the British Secretary of State for India, Lord Randolph Churchill, to occupy Mandalay. The British and the Burmese had already fought two wars, in 1824–6 and 1852–3, both resulting in decisive British victories. Assam, Manipur, Arakan and the Tennasserim were ceded to Calcutta after the first war, and the remainder of the Indian Ocean coastline was taken during the second. But the heartland of the Burmese kingdom, what the British called 'Ava' or 'Upper Burma', remained in the hands of an enfeebled Burmese monarchy, together with a collection of nearby Shan principalities. For twenty-five years, attempts were made by both sides, British India and Burma, to find a mutually agreeable system of bilateral relations. Treaties were signed which opened the country to European commerce and several embassies were exchanged.

But by the death of Thibaw's father, King Mindon, in 1878, many businessmen both in Rangoon and Calcutta were calling for the outright annexation of the remaining royal domains. Political unrest under Thibaw, allegations of frightful imprisonments and massacres of suspected opponents provided ammunition to the interventionist cause. Politicians and officials in Calcutta, Westminster and Whitehall also began considering intervention by the late 1870s. At a time when France was consolidating her hold over Vietnam, Laos and Cambodia, they feared increased French influence at the Court of Ava and eyed with suspicion the diplomatic missions of Burmese envoys to Paris and other European capitals. The Burmese had insisted on maintaining their independence in their foreign affairs, and the limits of British tolerance were soon breached.

The decision to employ military power in support of commerce and strategic concerns was certainly nothing unusual for Victorian Britain.[1] The Empire was enjoying a period of continued expansion, pushing forward colonial boundaries and enlarging spheres of influence across Africa and Asia. What were highly unusual, however, in the history of late-nineteenth-century imperialism, were the decisions taken by London and Calcutta in the aftermath of Thibaw's sudden exile. These decisions, taken primarily between December 1885 and February 1886, amounted to no-

[1] Ronald Robinson, 'Non-European Foundations of European Imperialism: Sketch for a Theory of Collaboration', in Roger Owen and Bob Sutcliffe (eds.), *Studies in the Theory of Imperialism*, London, 1972, pp. 132–7; Ronald Robinson, *Africa and the Victorians: The Official Mind of Imperialism*, London, 1961.

thing less than a complete dismantling of existing institutions of political authority and the undermining of many established structures of social organisation. The monarchy, the nobility, royal agencies, the army, all disappeared, virtually overnight. In the countryside, local ruling families, many of whom had governed their charges for centuries, lost their positions as all hereditary status effectively came to an end. The political framework which had organised life in the Irrawaddy valley for at least three hundred years vanished under the weight of new colonial policies. 'Modern Burma' was born out of this transition.

The natural course for British policy-makers would have been to place another Burmese prince on the Konbaung throne and rule indirectly through a protected native court. Working through indigenous elites and institutions was a policy with which the British were certainly familiar. Even those who favoured annexation would likely have settled for the establishment of Thibaw's dominions as a new princely state of India. Senior civil servants had called for a protectorate rather than direct rule and even the Court of Ava seemed to believe that this would be the most likely outcome of a British victory. In Calcutta, a draft treaty had been prepared for the signature of the new 'Prince of Upper Burma'. The country would have become the largest and the richest of all the Indian princely states, the royal family and aristocracy would have remained intact, and the course of twentieth-century Burmese history would have taken an entirely different path.

But instead, by January 1886, the monarchy had been abolished altogether. Important members of the royal family were exiled to disparate places in India and many others were sent far to the south, to Tavoy and Moulmein, banned from returning home until the very end of British rule in 1948. Royal lands were seized, royal slaves and hereditary servants released from their obligations and a 'Prize Committee' divided palace possessions to be sent as gifts to notables at home in England and Ireland.

A series of further decisions and events then conspired to destroy the old nobility of Ava. The high officialdom had been composed of inter-related families, strictly organised according to relative status, the most senior of whom were often in turn closely related to the extended royal family. The majority of Thibaw's ministers seemed willing and even eager to assist in setting up a new administration, British-controlled, which would work through existing agencies of government. For several weeks, attempts were made to direct policy through the Hluttaw, the Council of

State. Court grandees were reorganised under the overall supervision of Sir Charles Bernard, the chief political officer, and orders were sent to the various governors and garrison commanders up and down the valley. But this experiment soon failed and a purely British regime was established.

The nobility had lived in elaborate compounds near the royal palaces, within the walled city of Mandalay. In late 1886, their homes, which had been meticulously placed according to rank, were demolished, and the thousands of people who had made up court society, their servants and retainers, were forced to join the common population outside the great ramparts. The palace itself was turned into a British headquarters, the principal throne rooms serving as the 'Upper Burma Club' and the garrison chapel. Even worse for the nobility than the loss of their special residences was the destruction of the royal treasury. The treasury had contained all official records related to aristocratic family genealogy. They had been inscribed on palm-leaf manuscripts and were burned by drunken soldiers on the first night of the occupation. With their loss, claims to noble status could no longer be authenticated. Without a king, a court or ways of verifying aristocratic descent, the nobility as a separate class collapsed within a generation.

As puzzling as the reasons behind Britain's decision to abolish the Burmese monarchy and impose direct rule were the changes in local administration which were brought about by the new state. In many other parts of Britain's imperial realm, colonial administrators had tended to work through intermediary classes. Even where the British imposed formal control, they still, more often than not, chose to leave day-to-day government in the hands of local elites, landlords or tribal chiefs. In the Shan hills, a peripheral part of Thibaw's kingdom, this is what the British did. The hereditary chiefs or *sawbwa* were allowed considerable autonomy under the general supervision of a colonial superintendent. But in the Irrawaddy valley itself, the new state imposed bureaucratic control right down to the village level. From the village headmen, through the township officers up to the deputy commissioners and finally the Chief Commissioner, a wholly new framework of government rapidly supplanted existing institutions.

In the Irrawaddy valley, the counterpart of the Shan chiefs were the Burmese *myothugyi*, hereditary office-holders who ruled over small town-based polities of various sizes. They and other lesser office-holders and their families had comprised the gentry class which governed the countryside under varying degrees of royal direction. Often titled and granted special sumptuary privileges, these men served as intermediaries between the distant Court of Ava and the thousands of villages and hamlets scattered across the lowlands. And yet British policy-makers, rather than attempting to co-opt their services into the new regime, deliberately shunted them aside. *Myothugyi* quickly lost their dominant position. What had been a complex hierarchy of local hereditary office dissolved into a sea of undifferentiated and salaried village headmanships.

The military expedition which had been charged solely with the occupation of Mandalay and the removal of King Thibaw thus became a permanent military occupation, one which dramatically changed the social and political organisation of the country and created a new colonial state and society. The explanation most often given for the abolition of the monarchy was that there was no suitable prince whom the British could place on the vacant throne.[2] The Nyaungyan Prince, an elder half-brother of Thibaw, had been living in Calcutta and had been the obvious choice for future king. But he had died only a few months before the outbreak of the war. Another senior member of the royal family was the Myingun Prince, but he had fled British territory, first for Pondicherry and then for Saigon, and was thought by the British to be much too close to the French to be considered as a possible puppet. Several other sons of Mindon had been killed in the political executions of the late 1870s. But despite this, many other possible candidates did exist. There was, in fact, no shortage of princely contenders, including, for example, the young Pyinmina Prince, who was finally considered as a possible king, but not until more than half a century later by very different masters, the Japanese.

While at least some explanation is usually offered for the abolition of the monarchy, little if anything is ever said about the destruction of the nobility or the undermining of local elite positions. Where the *myothugyi* and other gentry leaders are mentioned at all, historians have argued that they formed the backbone of anti-colonial resistance in the 1880s and were effectively wiped out as a class. But this does not agree with the records of the fighting which took place. Where local hereditary leaders did play a role, they are usually portrayed by contemporary British observers as supporting the new authorities. In most English-language

---

[2] See, for example, D.G.E. Hall, *A History of Southeast Asia*, London, 1955, p. 681; John Cady, *A History of Modern Burma*, Ithaca, 1958, p. 120.

histories of this period, however, the nobility and gentry are not discussed at all.[3]

To a large extent this was the result of a reading of pre-annexation Burmese society which saw the political system as a sort of 'oriental despotism', a king ruling ruthlessly and absolutely over an otherwise egalitarian society.[4] The nobility and the gentry were not recognised as distinct groups, and office-holders were simply seen as clients of the king, serving at his whim. Little was known about the elaborate hereditary structures which had developed over the preceding several hundred years, and few early colonial writers were concerned with the details of local social organisation. In addition, this image of a corrupt king ruling over a mismanaged but otherwise attractive and egalitarian Burmese society fitted well with British attempts to justify the imposition of direct rule.

But while these later historians focused exclusively on the removal of Thibaw and tended towards this simple image of pre-colonial Burmese society, the discussions of policy-makers at the time reveal a much broader set of considerations which moved events in their peculiar directions.

A key reason given at the time for the abolition of the monarchy was not that there lacked a suitable prince but that the Court of Ava was simply unable to fulfil the role of a local collaborator, and that successive kings and governments had shown themselves incapable of accommodating British interests, permitting free trade or keeping out unwanted rival European influences.[5] This reason seems much closer to the truth. Despite a clear awareness by the late nineteenth century of its extremely weak international position, Mandalay had continued to resist British

[3] See, for example, J.S. Furnival, *Colonial Policy and Practice: A Comparative Study of Burma and Netherlands India*, Cambridge, 1948, pp. 70–4; D.G.E. Hall, *A History of Southeast Asia*, London, 1968, pp. 770–4; Ernest C.T. Chew, 'The Fall of the Burmese Kingdom in 1885: Review and Reconsideration', *Journal of Southeast Asian Studies* (hereafter *JSEAS*), 10 (1979), 372–81; David Steinberg, *Burma: A Socialist Nation of South East Asia*, Boulder, 1982; Michael Aung-Thwin, 'The British Pacification of Burma: Order Without Meaning', *JSEAS*, 16 (1985), 245–62; and the more recent Carl A. Trocki, 'Political Structures in the Nineteenth and Early Twentieth Centuries', in Nicholas Tarling (ed.), *The Cambridge History of Southeast Asia* (hereafter *CHSEA*), vol. II, Cambridge, 1993, pp. 119–20.

[4] See, for example, Htin Aung, *A History of Burma*, New York, 1967, pp. 266–9; H. Fielding-Hall, *The Soul of a People*, London, 1898, pp. 79–93.

[5] See, for example, V.C. Scott O'Conner, *Mandalay and Other Cities of the Past in Burma*, London, 1907, p. 26.

efforts aimed at securing a stable 'informal empire' over Upper Burma. France and other continental states were courted by Mindon's and Thibaw's ministers, royal monopolies remained over key sectors of the economy, and even on issues of protocol the Burmese would not give in to British demands for greater accommodation.

And while this poor record of collaboration had pushed many colonial policy-makers in the direction of annexation, it was the situation in the countryside during the first few months of the British occupation which settled the issue. The British knew that the area around Mandalay had been plagued for several years by banditry. But it was only during attempts to work through Thibaw's former ministers, and the royal agencies which they were supposed to control, that the extent to which law and order had broken down throughout the kingdom became clear. The writ of court mandarins no longer extended far beyond the city walls and a few garrisoned towns along the Irrawaddy. Their position had already been weak and the blow to their legitimacy resulting from the king's surrender and exile had been fatal. Governors and other provincial officials were fleeing their posts and bands of armed men up to several thousand strong held sway across the valley. By April 1886, the bandit gangs were joined by others, including men of the old royal army, Buddhist monks and even a few displaced nobles and princes. What had been a continuation of the banditry under Thibaw became an organised countrywide resistance against the new colonial regime, with calls by new royal pretenders to protect 'Buddhism and tradition' and drive the English 'infidels' into the sea.

The response of the Marquess of Dufferin, Viceroy of India, and his Burma-based subordinates was to 'pacify' the countryside through a campaign of violent suppression. Tens of thousands of villagers were forcefully relocated and suspected rebel sympathisers were summarily executed as the British army took the offensive. Over the next year, 40,000 British and Indian troops were poured into the old kingdom and harsh measures against civilians continued. Gradually, the colonial authorities gained the upper hand and, when the dust had cleared, very little of the old regime was left. The colonial state was born as a military occupation.

But this interpretation of the events surrounding the fall of Mandalay invites a whole new set of questions: why, for example, were existing political structures so brittle? And what underlay the considerable resistance to British rule? Why did the Court of Ava not become a better

'collaborator' and preserve a degree of autonomy, if not nominal independence, as did nearby states such as Nepal, Afghanistan or Siam?

This book is an attempt to answer these questions and to explore more
generally a much neglected chapter in southern Asian and in British
colonial history: the long transition in the Irrawaddy valley away from the
Ava-based imperial polity of the early nineteenth century and towards the
British Burma of the early twentieth.

The English-language historiography of this period is almost entirely
confined to specialist monographs or to chapters in more general histories
of 'Burma'. These chapters are either found at the very end of books on
'Burma before the British', or at the very beginning of books on 'modern
Burma'. Scholarly works which are set entirely within the nineteenth
century have all focused on specific themes, nearly all related to Anglo-
Burmese diplomatic relations or war.[6] The reaction of successive royal
regimes to European expansion and other contemporary challenges, in
particular the reformist programmes of Mindon and Thibaw, are thus
never placed in a broader historical context. Attempts by Mandalay in
the period 1853–85 to modernise administration are dismissed as well-
meaning but insignificant.[7] Attention is focused on the gradual consolidation of British rule in the south, and the annexation of 1885 is seen
almost as an inevitable final episode in the growth of British Indian power
across the Irrawaddy basin.

Burmese-language historiography is not very different. While the Burmese court is predictably portrayed in a kinder light, the focus remains the
same. The possibility of political and social change over the course of the
nineteenth century is similarly ignored. Within the study of local history,
much greater interest is always paid to the time of the Pagan and the early
Toungoo monarchs, than to what is seen as the sad and ignoble decades
preceding alien occupation.

---

[6] For example, Htin Aung, *The Stricken Peacock: Anglo-Burmese Relations 1852–1948*,
The Hague, 1965; Oliver Pollack, *Empires in Collision: Anglo-Burmese Relations in
the Mid-Nineteenth Century*, Westport, 1979; Charles Keeton, *King Theebaw and the
Ecological Rape of Burma: The Political and Commercial Struggle between British
India and French Indochina in Burma 1878–1886*, Delhi, 1974.

[7] For example, Furnival, *Colonial Policy and Practice*, esp. pp. 73–4; G.E. Harvey,
*History of Burma from the Earliest Times to 10 March 1824 – The Beginning of the
English Conquest*, London, 1925; Cady, *History of Modern Burma*, esp. pp. 141–4;
Frank Trager, *Burma: From Kingdom to Republic: A Historical and Political Analysis*,
London, 1966, esp. p. 38; Joseph Silverstein, *Burma: Military Rule and the Politics of
Stagnation*, Ithaca, 1977, esp. pp. 11–12.

More generally, both English and Burmese scholarship tends to assume a fairly static and passive Burmese society. The nineteenth century is viewed in terms of a political transition from Burmese to British rule over an otherwise stable 'Burma'. If one were to remove the recent Indian immigrants and the occasional European trader, civil servant or solider, the Burma of, say, the 1920s was not thought to have been very different from the Burma of a century before. Both colonial and nationalist writers saw an undifferentiated and unchanging rural landscape of egalitarian Buddhist villages and assumed little had ever been otherwise.

At an even broader level, there is hardly any questioning of 'Burma' or the 'Burmese' as a stable category. The boundaries of post-1885 Burma are viewed as 'more or less' the same as the boundaries of the various royal polities over the previous thousand years. The 'Burmese' themselves, following their immigration from some distant snowy homeland are seen as being the predominant people around which history revolves. The 'Shan', 'Mon' and 'Karen' were always 'minorities', their relative power waxing and waning over periods of 'Shan dominion' or the Burmese–Mon 'civil wars'. With British rule there then follows the 'unnatural' administrative attachment of Burma to 'India proper'.

A number of recent works on the early modern history of the Irrawaddy valley have helped to much better illuminate local society and political institutions in the hundred years or so prior to the first Anglo-Burmese War. Seminal works by Victor Lieberman, William Koenig, Than Tun and others have given us a much clearer picture of the world of the Restored Toungoo and early Konbaung kings.[8] The challenge thus remains to bridge from this world to the world of contemporary Burma and offer some explanations of the changes and continuities which took place.

Through this book, I will argue the following points: firstly, that the period 1853–85 was in fact a period of sustained innovation and attempts at adaptation to rapidly changing local and global conditions. The Ava (or Mandalay) based polity, reduced to its core territory through military

[8] Especially Victor Lieberman, *Burmese Administrative Circles: Anarchy and Conquest c. 1580–1760*, Princeton, 1984; Victor Lieberman, 'Secular Trends in Burmese Economic History, c. 1350–1830, and their Implications for State Formation', *Modern Asian Studies* (hereafter *MAS*), 25 (1991), 1–31; William Koenig, *The Burmese Polity, 1752–1819: Politics, Administration and Social Organisation in the Early Konbaung Period*, Ann Arbor, 1990; Than Tun, *Essays on the History and Buddhism of Burma*, Edinburgh, 1988.

defeats, was fully aware of the need to refashion state structures and find a place within the emergent international system.

Secondly, these policies failed, as a result of several internal and external factors, to achieve their prime objective of creating an independent and modern Burmese state. These included the loss of the Irrawaddy delta to British India, the imposition of British commercial treaties which limited state involvement in the economy, the effects of the 1870s world depression, the effects of the Panthay revolt in Yunnan and contemporaneous crises in China, and the chronic political instability at home related to the ever present threat of British intervention.

Thirdly, the net result of the interplay among British imperial policies, the reaction of Ava to changing circumstances and a host of other local and global factors was the creation of a peculiarly unrooted colonial regime, one which started (and ended) as a military occupation with little popular support. The interplay of these various actors and processes also led to significant social change. Just as new landed elites emerged under the old regime, colonial policies largely undermined their position and created a much more homogeneous and egalitarian social order.

Fourthly, local reaction to British expansion and other challenges was itself conditioned by the region's recent history, including a long era of imperial conquest from an Irrawaddy valley core and the development of patriotic sentiment tied to the Ava polity and the related 'Burmese' or Myanma identity. On the opposite side, Calcutta's policies were framed within the context of Indian interests and strategies and saw the Burmese kingdom with reference to Indian experiences, knowledge and objectives.

Finally, the end of the century witnessed the birth of Burma as we still know it today. The territorial limits of the country, the notion of who is Burmese and who is not, key social and political structures, all find their origins in this period surrounding the fall of Mandalay.

The nineteenth century in the areas in and around modern Burma is an interesting but largely unexplored episode in both British imperial and regional history. The century witnessed the gradual displacement, in the Irrawaddy, Brahmaputra and Salween river basins, of the once expansive authority of the Court of Ava by the authority of an equally aggressive British Indian state. It also witnessed quite vigorous attempts by the Court of Ava to construct a modern though territorially more modest state under the shadow of colonial encroachments. And finally the century saw the development of a strong patriotic sentiment centred on the rump Ava polity and memories of a conquering past. Burma was created out of the interaction of these processes, as well as a number of other factors, not least contemporary events in China and the impact of increasingly global markets. This book is a story of that century, of the final decades of autonomous Burmese rule at Mandalay and the making of modern Burma.

1 | Kings and distant wars

A still nameless ridge of mountains, rising to heights of over 20,000 feet, extends east from the Himalayas and separates Tibet from the headwaters of the Irrawaddy river. For more than two months each winter, temperatures fall well below freezing and fierce storms envelop the region in snow. Between the mountains, narrow and thickly forested valleys are crowded with rhododendrons, magnolias, maples, firs and tall Formosan pines, and the mountains themselves, in their lower reaches, are covered in dwarf junipers and an abundance of small evergreens and perennials.

Here, in this home of tigers, Himalayan black bears and the Asian rhinoceros, two small rivers, the Mali Hka and the N'Mai Hka, have their origin. Fed by the melting snows, they wind their way south and eventually merge to form the Irrawaddy just below the twenty-sixth parallel. From this confluence, the river rushes down, in occasionally violent torrents, through steep gorges, some only fifty yards across, before reaching the hot arid plains below.

The country which it crosses through nearly all of its 700-mile-long journey to the sea is very dry, with cool winters and scorching summers, a dusty expanse of alluvial land where temperatures climb to an average of over 100 degrees Fahrenheit in March and April and the annual precipitation in places barely reaches twenty inches. The rains, when they do come, come in a few sharp downpours, violent monsoon storms which transform waterless stream beds into dark brown torrents in a matter of minutes. Much of the region is covered in a dry scrub forest of short thorny acacias, euphorbia and cutch. Along the water lines there are taller tamarind and Indian elm trees and nearly all the cultivation is confined to these irrigated zones. An extinct volcano, Mount Popa, 5,000 feet high, dominates the middle part of this otherwise almost entirely flat plain. The only other exception is a long line of hills, the Pegu Yoma, which parallel the Irrawaddy along its middle course.

The river's valley is almost entirely surrounded by a horseshoe of increasingly high mountains. To the west are dense forests, mainly of ebony, and then series of mountain ranges – the Arakan Yoma, the Lushai and Naga Hills and others – the tallest mountains over 12,000 feet high. To the east are thick teak forests which suddenly give way to the Shan uplands, a plateau averaging 3,000 feet, in some places rising in single steps of 2,000 feet from the basin below. Often treacherous passes link the valley to its nearest lowland neighbours: Arakan, Manipur, Assam and Siam.

Only to the south is the valley free from its mountain fastness. Here, the badlands, savannah and scrub-clad hills give way to the broad alluvial plains of the delta, as the Irrawaddy spreads out like a fan, the river dividing and sub-dividing and finally spilling into the Bay of Bengal through nine smaller rivers and countless streams. This lower region is as wet as the upper valley is dry, with some parts receiving nearly 200 inches of rain a year. Much is also relatively new: the gradual silting of the river has pushed the land forward three miles each century, with many parts of the delta still below the level of the spring tides. Mangrove swamps and great tidal forests along the coast turn to marshes and grassland further inland, and dense tropical jungle covers the higher elevations just to the east and west.[1]

Bodawpaya and western campaigns

The Prince of Badon was 37 years old when he ascended the throne of Ava in 1782.[2] His reign, which lasted until his death in 1817, was to be the longest in Burmese history since the days of Pagan, the longest in over five centuries. He is better remembered today as Bodawpaya or 'the royal grandfather king', the name by which he was often referred to in court writings of the mid-nineteenth century. With 53 wives and 120 children, Bodawpaya, the fifth son of Alaungpaya, the dynasty's upstart founder, was perhaps the greatest of all the Konbaung kings. He presided over the Burmese empire at its very height, marching his armies steadily westward to the very borders of an equally expansionist British India.[3]

His first target was Arakan, a small kingdom along the Bay of Bengal

---

[1] Eugene Dobby, *Southeast Asia*, London, 1950, pp. 147–67.

[2] On Bodawpaya's reign, see Tin(Mandalay), *Konbaungzet Maha Yazawindawgyi* (Great Royal Chronicle of the Konbaung Dynasty) (hereafter *KBZ*), vol. I, pp. 525–67; vol. II, pp. 1–219.

[3] For a first-hand description of Bodawpaya, see Hiram Cox, *Journal of a Residence in the Burman Empire and More Particularly at the Court of Amarapoorah*, London, 1821, p. 90.

which was separated by a formidable mountain range, the Arakan Yoma, from the Irrawaddy valley. The Arakanese ruling class spoke Burmese, and there existed many similarities in court culture and social organisation between the two societies, but the area's principal role as a centre of Indian Ocean trade and piracy also meant that Arakan was much more exposed to Indian Ocean influences, in particular from Bengal, but also from further afield. The religion was primarily Theravada Buddhist, but with a large Muslim minority and strong Brahmanical influences. In the late eighteenth century, the kingdom was in a period of disarray and more than one of its rival palace factions appealed to the Burmese for assistance, providing Ava with a welcome excuse to invade .

The Arakan campaign was led by the new crown prince, the king's eldest son, Thado Minsaw, the Prince of Shweidaung. The Burmese invaded in four columns totalling 30,000 men, three columns crossing the Arakan Yoma mountains and the fourth coming up along the Indian Ocean coastline from the erstwhile English base at Negrais, and they occupied the Arakanese capital at Mrohaung without serious loss in early 1785. Arakan was then annexed outright as a 'kingdom held by arms' (*lethnet naingngan*) and divided into four governorships, each backed by a garrison. Revenues from the occupied towns were divided between the treasury and selected members of the Court of Ava, with all the revenues from Mrohaung itself being granted to the king's white elephant. The Shweidaung Prince brought back with him the great Maha Muni image, symbol of Arakanese sovereignty, together with 20,000 captives to populate his father's new capital of Amarapura, the 'Immortal City'.

Earlier imperial dreams had rested on the conquest of the Chao Phraya valley and had led to the bloody sacking of Ayuthaya, the Siamese capital in 1767. But now the new and vigorous regime at Bangkok ended any real hope of expansion to the east, and it was an entirely new empire, to the west, which would now provide fertile ground for royal ambitions. In 1817, Bodawpaya died and was succeeded by his grandson (his son having died earlier) in the smoothest of all the Konbaung successions. The new king, Bagyidaw, though not nearly as capable as his grandfather, proved an even more ambitious imperialist.

Manipur, which had given so much trouble to the last Toungoo kings, had been the first object of Burmese aggression under the new Konbaung rulers. By the early eighteenth century, their nascent state, set in a small valley to the west of the Chindwin, had come under the influence of

Vaishnavite Hinduism and a process of 'Sanskritisation' encouraged by immigrant Bengali Brahmans. Their king, Garib Nawaz, had been the first to convert to the new faith and pursued a policy of repression of indigenous religious beliefs as well as of rival Hindu sects.

The first Konbaung invasion of Manipur in 1758 wreaked havoc on the small kingdom and was followed by an even larger and more devastating invasion in 1764.[4] Thousands of Manipuris were forcibly deported to the Burmese capital and the combination of war, flight and deportation left Manipur virtually empty for years. Many of these captives were boatmen, smiths, weavers and artisans who became hereditary crown servants at Ava, and for generations they, their descendants and later Manipuri deportees formed an underclass in the valley, acting as domestic servants, menial labourers and agricultural workers for the Burmese royal family and nobility. They also formed the new Cassay Horse, an elite cavalry regiment, a few gaining fame as the best polo-players of their generation.

In 1813 the Burmese, having moved their forward bases up the Chindwin into the adjacent Kabaw valley, decided to consolidate their position in Manipur, and Prince Marjit Singh, a member of the local ruling house, was installed on the throne at Imphal. Marjit Singh had spent much of his youth at Ava and the Burmese believed he would make a pliant tributary. But by 1819 he had proved much too ambitious for the Court of Ava's liking, asserting his autonomy and refusing to attend the coronation of Bagyidaw, Bodawpaya's grandson and successor. This then led to the final conquest of the Manipur valley and a change in Burmese policy from a simple demand for tribute to indirect administration through a puppet prince. A permanent garrison was stationed, backed by a long supply line up the Chindwin river.

From their most northern forts along the Hukawng river, the victorious and confident Burmese army pushed yet further west, to Assam.[5] The kings of Assam, with their capital at Rangamati, ruled over the Brahmaputra valley, from the descent of the great river in south-eastern Tibet to its entry into the plains of Bengal. A narrow valley hemmed in by high mountains, Assam had come under the rule of the originally Tai-speaking Ahom royal house in the thirteenth century. This old and distinguished family had led the mainly Tibeto-Burman-speaking peoples of the valley

---

[4] Gangamumei Kabui, *History of Manipur, Vol. I: Pre-Colonial Period*, New Delhi, 1991, pp. 194–291.

[5] S.L. Baruah, *A Comprehensive History of Assam*, New Delhi, 1985, pp. 220–369.

in a series of defensive wars against the Mughal empire and had gradually, like the Manipuris, come under increasing Sanskrit and Hindu cultural influences. By the 1790s, however, the power of the Ahom court had begun seriously to decline, as intra-dynastic disputes combined with a widespread uprising by followers of the neo-Vaishnavite Moamariya movement. Rival groups turned to both Ava and Calcutta for assistance, leading to an initial British expedition in the winter of 1792–3 which aided in the quelling of the rebellion.

But by 1817, the situation in Assam had again reached a point of considerable instability, as the leader of one of the court factions appealed to Bodawpaya to intervene against the incumbent ruler or *swargadeo* of Assam, Chandrakanta Singh. Bodawpaya had already been looking to invade the Brahmaputra valley in support of the Moamariyas and in support of his own imperial aims. A well-equipped force of 8,000 men was marched north, swelled along the way by thousands more Jingpaw and Shan levies from the Hukawng valley and then, in an amazing logistical feat, was brought across the Himalayan passes along the Patkai ridge, and into the valley at its eastern end. The Assamese were decisively defeated at the battle of Kathalguri and the pro-Burmese premier Badan Chandra was installed. Chandrakanta Singh was allowed to remain as the nominal king.

Several years then followed of local intrigue and Burmese intervention, Assamese princes constantly switching allegiances and Ava becoming convinced of the need for tighter control. In 1821, a huge army of 20,000, including 10,000 Jingpaw levies, under the command of General Thado Maha Bandula again crossed the snow-clad mountains and began a pacifi-cation campaign intended to consolidate Ava's permanent hegemony over the country. In 1823, with the back of Assamese resistance largely broken, Thado Maha Bandula established his forward base at Rangpur and extinguished the Ahom court. He then began his initial forays into Cachar and Jaintia, and planned to march on Bhutan.[6]

Domination of this vast area, now sandwiched between British Bengal and Burma, was to have two profound effects. The first was the import-ation to the Court of Ava of many of the often Sanskrit-educated elites of these occupied states, a process which will be discussed in chapter 4. The second was to whet the Burmese appetite for further expansion, into the

---

[6] Baruah, *History of Assam*, pp. 361–8.

heart of India, a course of action which would lead directly to the First
Anglo-Burmese War in 1824.

The British and the Burmese

The first two hundred years of Anglo-Burmese relations had revolved
around occasional attempts by the British East India Company to establish profitable trade ties with the Court of Ava. Small branch offices were
set up at Syriam, Ava and Bhamo in the mid-seventeenth century but
these had soon closed, mainly for lack of business. Another attempt was
made to resume trade relations in the 1750s and a fortified settlement was
established at Negrais along the coast. But the unwillingness of the British
to intervene on the side of the Burmese had aroused suspicions in Alaungpaya's court and he ordered the settlement destroyed in 1759. When
contact resumed almost forty years later, the British and Burmese had, for
the first time, a common border, between Bengal and Arakan. As this
frontier expanded northwards and westwards, mutual mistrust and fears
over security on both sides increased.

By the turn of the century, Amarapura had become deeply concerned
with the growth of British power in India. Spies were sent to the Tipu
Sultan in Mysore, to the Marathas, to Nepal and to the imperial court in
Delhi as well as to British Bengal. Interest in the East India Company even
led Bodawpaya to employ an Englishman, or perhaps a Eurasian, named
George, to teach English to several of his sons.[7] Muslims and Armenians
at the court had warned Burmese officials of the coming British threat.
One intelligence report announced that 'only the East India Company flag
flies along the Coromandel coast'. Another compared the English to a
Banyan tree, which first leans on others while growing, only later to kill
them when strong.[8]

The main point of tension between Calcutta and Amarapura was to be
Arakan. The Burmese occupation of that country had been extremely
repressive, with constant demands for men and material. In 1795 a levy of
20,000 men to help expand Meiktila lake, south of Amarapura, set off the

---

[7] Than Tun, ed. *Royal Orders of Burma 1598–1885*, part 9, Tokyo, 1989 (hereafter *ROB*),
3 March 1810.

[8] Tin (Pagan), *Myanma Min Okchokpon Sadan* (Documents Relating to the
Administration of the Burmese Kings) (hereafter *MMOS*), 5 vols., Rangoon, 1931–3,
vol. III, pp. 70–1.

first wave of refugees into British territory and the beginnings of an Arakanese insurgency. In 1811, a new royal levy for 40,000 men sent another huge exodus of refugees towards Chittagong, adding impetus to the local guerilla resistance which soon defeated the Burmese garrison and took Mrohaung. The guerilla leader Chin Byan had offered to hold Arakan as a vassal of the East India Company, and this increased Amarapura's suspicions of Calcutta's motives, especially as his bases were located well within Company territory. British troops had prevented the Burmese from pursuing his men across the Naaf river boundary and cross-border relations quickly soured.

The second arena of contention was in the far north, in Manipur and in the Himalayan states of Assam, Jaintia and Cachar, where Ava's forward policy was meeting with growing British influence and concerns over the security of Bengal. The Burmese occupation of Manipur had driven large numbers of refugees into Cachar and the raja of Cachar in 1823 invited Ava to help restore order in his country. The Burmese occupation of the Brahmaputra valley and its probing moves into the adjacent high grounds were clearly intended to place pressure on Bengal. The British, worried about losing this buffer and with expansionist designs of their own, unilaterally declared Cachar and neighbouring Jaintia as protectorates and sent a force to halt the Burmese advance. Clashes soon developed between the two armies in Cachar and this, coupled with a worsening situation along the disputed Arakan border, led Fort William, on 5 March 1824, to declare war on the Kingdom of Ava.[9]

The First Anglo-Burmese War turned out to be the longest and most expensive in British Indian history. It lasted nearly two years, cost the British exchequer 5 million pounds, and led to the deaths of 15,000 British and Indian soldiers as well as tens of thousands of Burmese. At the onset of the war, the confident Burmese forces, under the command of their well-tried general and governor of Assam, Thado Maha Bandula, made a spirited attempt to break through British lines and march simultaneously on Syhlet from the north and Chittagong from the east. Bandula, a very tall man with a violent temper, had little time for precedence and protocol in a country obsessed with both. He was reported once to have decapitated by his own hand one of his senior officials for counselling retreat

---

[9] George Bruce, *The Burma Wars: 1824–1880*, London, 1973, pp. 1–127; Htin Aung, *History of Burma*, pp. 194–217; *KBZ*, vol. II, pp. 369–425.

and had been one of the main proponents at Bagyidaw's court of an offensive policy against Calcutta. He believed that a decisive victory could gain them eastern Bengal as well as allow them to consolidate their gains in their new western empire of Arakan, Assam, Jaintia, Cachar and Manipur.

But despite a few initial victories against British Indian border units, the Burmese were quickly thrown on the defensive. As the rains approached, Bandula, having crossed the Naaf, paused with his army of 40,000 on the road to Chittagong, only to receive urgent news that a British fleet had reached Rangoon. This was a possibility the Burmese had not taken into account. Bandula was then forced to wheel his divisions around quickly and march them over the Arakan Yoma at the height of the monsoon while keeping most of his army intact. But then, even with fresh troops from Amarapura and levies from throughout the Irrawaddy valley totalling 60,000 men the general was unable to re-take Rangoon.

With the coming of the cold weather, and reinforced and resupplied by sea, the British then managed to break through Burmese lines and begin their march up-river. At Danubyu, Bandula tried to make a stand, massing 60,000 at that small delta town, including 35,000 musketeers and Ava's best cavalry. He had continued walking among his troops under a gilt umbrella marking his rank, despite the obvious danger, and was killed by an exploding shell. In disarray, the Burmese, under heavy bombardment, retreated north.

The British Expeditionary Force was led by General Sir Archibald Campbell, a veteran of the Peninsula Wars where he had fought the French under the Duke of Wellington. He pushed his army north along the Irrawaddy and then halted for a second rainy season at Prome. A faction at the court, led by the Prince of Tharrawaddy advised the king to open negotiations. The prince, who was the king's younger brother, was a military man. He had been Bandula's deputy at Rangoon and Danubyu and had seen first-hand the enemy's superiority in arms. The king, however, decided to try his luck and fight on, sending down thousands more hastily raised and improperly equipped levies.

The British resolutely pressed on despite Burmese attacks both on land and on the river. The *Diana*, a steamer recently arrived from Calcutta and the first ever used in battle, was deployed to counter the huge teak war-boats which had been the pride of Amarapura's armed forces. These were one hundred feet long, with up to sixty oarsmen and thirty musketeers and were fitted with six- or twelve-pounder guns, and it was the defeat of this river fleet, as well as a decisive British victory at Pagan, which finally led to a Burmese request for negotiations in early 1826. On 24 February at Yandabo, a small village along the Irrawaddy forty-five miles from the capital, a peace treaty was signed between Campbell and the Myoza of Lègaing, a senior minister.[10]

Under the Treaty of Yandabo, the Court of Ava agreed to cease interference in the affairs of Jaintia, Cachar and Assam and to cede to the British their provinces of Manipur, Arakan and the Tennasserim. They also agreed to allow for an exchange of diplomatic representatives between Amarapura and Calcutta and to pay an indemnity, in instalments, of 10 million rupees or 1 million pounds sterling. The British would withdraw to Rangoon after the payment of the first instalment, and withdraw from Rangoon after the payment of the second.[11] After much delay, the second instalment was paid, the British left Rangoon, and in the steamy towns and forests of the Tennasserim and Arakan began their creation of 'British Burma'.

The end of empire

The kingdom's inglorious defeat was a profound shock for the Court of Ava. But Bagyidaw held on to his crown and his government remained essentially the same as before the war, dominated by those who had counselled against negotiation until the very end. His closest and most powerful advisor was his queen, Mè Nu, who was intensely disliked by many in the aristocratic establishment because of her common origins and autocratic manner. She had ensured her position by having her brother, the Myoza of Salin, raised to princely status and made the *de facto* head of the Council of State. The two together established a huge patronage network throughout the country, appointing loyal followers to key offices both in the provinces and at the capital, and amassing a substantial private fortune. Mè Nu schemed to marry her only child, a daughter, to the crown prince, Bagyidaw's son by his deceased chief queen.[12]

The king himself changed in personality after the war, shunning all of

---

[10] For a translation of the relevant portions of the Konbaungzet chronicle, see Anna Allott, *The End of the First Anglo-Burmese War: The Burmese Chronicle Account of How the 1826 Treaty of Yandabo Was Negotiated*, Bangkok, 1994.

[11] *ROB*, 31 August 1824.   [12] On Bagyidaw's reign, see *KBZ*, vol. III, pp. 220–545.

his foreign friends except for the Spanish merchant Don Gonzales de Lanciego, who translated for him the Calcutta newspapers and was thought by the British to be pro-French. Described by the American missionary Judson as 'mild, amiable, good natured and obliging . . . fond of shews, theatrical exhibitions, elephant catching and boat racing', he was said to be 'inordinately devoted to technical researches and experiments'. Understandably weary from the endless rituals and intrigue of court life, Bagyidaw was also reported to be 'particularly desirous of discovering the secret of rendering himself invisible at will'.[13]

Up until the early 1830s, the Burmese government harboured considerable hope that with the final payment of indemnity, Calcutta would hand back Arakan and the Tennasserim. The Viceroy, Lord William Cavendish Bentinck, sent as the first British Resident to the Court of Ava Henry Burney, a career company-man who had just spent several years as Political Agent in Bangkok, and a Burmese embassy headed by Mingyi Maha Sithu visited India in 1830 in return. But when the last payment was made and it was clear to Amarapura that the annexations were final, relations began to deteriorate. This worsening of ties coincided with a decline in Bagyidaw's health, the king sinking into a severe manic-depression and increasingly unable to fulfil any of his official functions.

A regency was formed, headed by his full-brother the Prince of Tharrawaddy and including the queen, Mè Nu, her brother, the Myoza of Salin, and two half-brothers of the king, the princes Thibaw and Kanaung. This was a coalition. During most of this time, Tharrawaddy kept a low profile, spending time with a circle of courtiers described as including 'the most saucy set of fellows in Ava'.[14] Mè Nu and Salin, on the other hand, became very active and tightened their grip on power, much to the dismay of the rest of the court, and eventually provoked an open split between them and the royal family. On 21 February 1837, Salin ordered the arrest of the Pagan Princess, Tharrawaddy's sister, on suspicion of hoarding arms, and Tharrawaddy, fearing he would be next, first fled the capital, and then, after weeks of fighting and attempted diplomacy, defeated Salin's forces and seized the throne. Bagyidaw was spared and died a natural death in 1846, but both the ex-queen and her brother were soon executed together with dozens of their followers as the new king moved to secure his throne.

The British had hoped that relations would now improve. But neither

[13] Political and Secret Correspondence with India, Bengal Secret and Political (vol. 341), 5 August 1826.   [14] Quoted in Pollack, *Empires in Collision*, p. 16.

under Tharrawaddy nor under his son and successor Pagan did the Burmese court display the sort of deference Calcutta now expected. By the early 1840s, British policy-makers grew fearful that Ava, having crushed an uprising in the delta and having reorganised the army, would launch a surprise attack on British Moulmein. Tharrawaddy's sons were given military commands in the south in Rangoon, Bassein and Toungoo and the king himself in 1841 sailed down-river at the head of an enormous flotilla of war-boats to pay homage at the Shwedagon Pagoda. Tharrawaddy knew that the British were preoccupied in China and Afghanistan and had hoped that his sabre-rattling would compel the British to negotiate the return of lost territory. But it seems he also knew that his armed forces were still no match for the East India Company and was careful not to be overly provocative.

Amidst this bellicose atmosphere, Tharrawaddy began to show signs of the same manic-depressive affliction which had debilitated his brother. Increasing the number of his wives and concubines from the sixteen he had when a member of the Regency Council to over one hundred probably aggravated his condition. A new cycle of intra-dynastic intrigue then began with several of his many sons jockeying for position. One of these, the Prince of Prome, rebelled against his father in 1845, supported by a number of grandees. Another son, the Prince of Pagan, was then made head of the government. He moved fast to end the rebellion and to purge the court of his brother's supporters. Tharrawaddy himself was placed under restraint as his condition worsened. When the king died in November 1846, Pagan ascended the throne.

Pagan's rule was not to last long. Once secure in power he entrusted many of the day-to-day affairs of state to one of his Privy Councillors. Initially, the king concentrated on his religious obligations and undertook numerous merit-making projects. He abolished livestock slaughter during certain parts of the year, freed caged animals, built pagodas and monasteries and searched far and wide for a new white elephant. His government, however, was directed towards managing relations with the British, in particular the large and vocal business community in Rangoon, where an unbending Burmese administration combined with profit-hungry British traders and ambitious missionaries to create a volatile atmosphere. Pagan's officials raised port charges, increased shipping regulations, opened incoming mail and restricted the movement of Burmese women, all measures which led the expatriates to call for a tough British response.

Calcutta was indeed frustrated that the Court of Ava, after such a resound-ing military defeat, had not adopted a more subservient attitude. Once the Company's hands were freed from other far-flung engagements, the Governor-General, Lord Dalhousie, began actively to consider a new war, one which would impress upon the Burmese the need to recognise British superiority.

In December 1851, the governor of Rangoon fined the captains and crews of two British ships 1,000 rupees for reported customs violations. Lord Dalhousie immediately dispatched two vessels of the Royal Navy with an ultimatum that the Burmese government rescind the fine and that the governor be immediately removed. The surprised Pagan and his minis-ters, fully aware of the consequences of a new war, accepted the terms. Nevertheless, the British naval officer in command at Rangoon, Com-modore Lampert, went ahead and blockaded the coastline. Though Dalhousie reprimanded Lampert for his actions, Calcutta decided hostil-ities were inevitable and sent a new ultimatum, demanding 1 million rupees to cover the costs of having had to prepare for war. Without waiting for a reply, joint British naval and ground forces quickly seized Rangoon, Bassein and Martaban.

Burmese forces were commanded by the Myoza of Tabayin, a son of the great general Thado Maha Bandula and a career military man, who had served as colonel of the Marabin Artillery and as captain of the Eastern Gate. But thirty years of advances in military technology and planning on the British side, and little innovation on the Burmese side, meant that the king's forces could offer only a limited defence. In April 1852, the Myoza of Tabayin himself was killed in the defence of Rangoon, and Pegu was taken in November despite spirited resistance.[15] In December, Dalhousie declared the newly occupied territory as a new province of British Burma. Two months later, a palace coup overthrew Pagan. His half-brother Mindon, leading a peace party, became the new king and Burmese forces were withdrawn northwards of the annexation line.

[15] Hmawbi Saya Thein, *Myanma Wungyi Hmugyi Mya Akaung*, Rangoon, 1967, p. 151.

2 | The Irrawaddy valley in the early nineteenth century

The early-nineteenth-century realm of the Burmese monarchs stretched from the Himalayan mountains in the north to the Andaman Sea in the south and from the plains of Siam in the east to British Bengal in the west. But the writ of the king and his ministers only penetrated sections of this vast territory. Much remained under the cover of dense jungle or within the effective authority of tributary chiefs. In Arakan, Burmese governors, backed by elephants and musketeers, barely controlled more than the main towns of Mrohaung, Ramree, Cheduba and Sandoway, as the peoples of the marshy countryside and the adjacent hills held out against their grasp. Ava's occupation lasted only forty years and throughout this time rebellions and cross-border raids by Arakanese insurgents continually challenged a precarious presence.

In the small northern and eastern principalities nearby, local rulers accepted or resisted Burmese sovereignty but never lost their autonomy. The Shan and other *sawbwa* were required to attend regular homage ceremonies, bring tribute of gold and silver and provide daughters for the king's western apartments. Burmese troops were posted at selected garrison towns and the largest was at Mong Nai. But these soldiers were there to suppress outright rebellion and were not part of a more general structure of government. These lesser states were viewed by the regime as their principal tributaries, a vast arc of dependent polities. In areas close to Ava, there existed strong cultural and often personal ties between the Shan-speaking and Burmese-speaking courts. Marriage tied the Ava aristocracy to all important tributary princely clans and the sons of Shan rulers often spent their formative years as pages to their paramount ruler. But further away, Ava's authority was negligible, and the more distant states, such as Chiang Hung across the Salween, were all but independent.

The Burmese initially sought a similar tributary relationship with the states to the north-west. Indeed, the term *sawbwa*, from the Shan *saohpa*, 'lord of the sky', was normally applied to the rulers of these predominantly non-Tai-speaking principalities and kingdoms. But chronic instability, continued resistance to any tributary relationship and expansive Burmese ambition eventually led to attempts at a more permanent occupation and Ava's direct administration. This was, however, to be very short-lived and the first British war ended the Burmese presence throughout the Brahmaputra basin.

In between all these lowland polities were the extensive upland regions. Here, with the exception of slave raids and occasional trade, the Court of Ava showed little desire to impose her authority. Only in the far north was there any official interest: the aggressive drive of Jingpaw-speaking peoples into the upper reaches of the Irrawaddy valley had begun to harass the rear bases of Ava's Himalayan campaigns, and royal patrols attempted, usually in vain, to check their southward movements.

It was only the Irrawaddy valley that the Burmese kings really controlled. The overwhelming proportion of their subjects lived in a narrow strip of land on either side of the Irrawaddy and its principal tributary, the Chindwin. Quite a large proportion lived within the environs of the royal city itself. This relatively densely populated region was the core of the local state, as it had been during the heyday of Pagan. It measured approximately 400 miles north to south and about 200 miles across. The boundaries of the region were almost exactly those of the dry-zone, thus creating a political and ecological unit which remained at the heart of the kingdom until its final demise.

Directly to the south, the delta and the Tennasserim littoral was a frontier region, one which was firmly tied to royal power, but still sparsely settled and not yet fully Burmese-speaking. By the early nineteenth century, the language and culture of the royal courts were only just pushing south, displacing older traditions centred on the Mon language and memories of autonomous Mon-speaking rule. Rangoon emerged as the second most important city in the kingdom and the rice-growing economy of the delta became an important part of the overall economy. Under the early Konbaung kings, administrators worked to pull the delta and the Tennasserim littoral firmly into the orbit of Ava's government, a process, half-finished, which was to be interrupted by the annexations of 1853.

People and population

Exactly how many people lived in the valley is not known. The earliest extant royal census dates from 1783 and lists a total of 282,000 households while a slightly later census of 1802 lists only 178,000 households. If the average number of people per household was seven, this would work out to 1.97 million and 1.25 million people respectively.[1] These censuses included all the registered households reported by local officials to royal agencies from the entire valley as well as some of the Tennasserim littoral and settlements along the Shan escarpment. They did not include Arakan and more peripheral parts of the kingdom. Local officials often under-reported the number of households in their charge in order to minimise the amount of revenue or labour later demanded. In addition, people living away from royal authority such as forest monks or bandits, itinerant traders and entertainers, as well as the slaves and the retainers of the larger and more important households, were probably not reported at all. Thus, there were perhaps somewhat over 2 million people in the Irrawaddy valley in the early nineteenth century, a figure similar to that reached by several contemporary European observers.

This population was very unevenly distributed. A majority of people lived close to the Irrawaddy river itself, from around Shwébo in the north to Prome in the south. This is an area of only about 40,000 square miles compared with a total area for present-day Burma of 238,000 square miles. A large proportion of these people lived in and around Ava and as much as 10 per cent of the valley population lived either in the royal city or nearby along the Irrawaddy–Chindwin confluence. Ava and Amarapura were both, at different times, reported to have been home to over 100,000 people. Few other places reached even a tenth of that figure, including major towns such as Alon or Salin. Other areas were very sparsely popu-lated, including the delta, which was only just beginning to recover from the devastation of the mid-eighteenth-century wars. Even along the middle valley, large tracts of scrub forest separated the mainly riverine communities.

Population trends are even more difficult to estimate, but it is possible that overall population grew very gradually over the early modern era, say from the sixteenth century onwards. Population certainly rose and fell to an extent. War, disease, famine and forced relocations could all turn fairly densely inhabited areas back to desert or jungle in a short space of time. On the other hand, long periods of internal stability, such as the peace

---

[1] On population, see Lieberman, *Burmese Administrative Circles*, pp. 20–1; Lieberman, 'Secular Trends' pp. 3–12; H. Burney, 'On the Population of the Burman Empire' (1842), reprinted *Journal of the Burma Research Society* (hereafter *JBRS*) 31 (1941), 19–33.

which the dry-zone enjoyed from the final expulsion of Mon-led forces during the civil war in 1752 to the turn of the century, were periods of demographic expansion. In the late eighteenth century, natural population growth was also supplemented by the large-scale importation or immigration of peoples from the surrounding uplands, Manipur and Siam.

Most of the people of the valley spoke Burmese as their mother tongue. Many were descendants of the earliest Burmese-speakers of the valley but many others were descendants of speakers of other languages, such as Pyu, Thet or Kadu, who gradually came to adopt Burmese and assimilate into the majority society. Others were recent arrivals. These included recent captives, as well as Armenian, Jewish, Chinese, Persian, Bengali, Tamil and other south Asian traders. They also included the descendants of Portuguese and Muslim mercenaries from the Deccan, and peoples imported after earlier military victories. Some had ancestors from quite far afield. In 1758, for example, a French warship was seized towards the end of the civil war. Its crew were marched north, enlisted into the king's army as hereditary gunners and given land near the capital. There they joined the descendants of earlier European mercenaries, Dutch, Spanish and Portuguese. Their leader, the *chevalier* Pierre de Millard was made head of the royal bodyguard and granted a suitable noble title. A few small Roman Catholic villages remain to this day, and their inhabitants are aware of their European ancestry. But in every other way they are virtually indistinguishable from their neighbours. For the Theravada Buddhist Lao, the Siamese and others, assimilation was doubtless even faster. While names such as 'Vientiene Hill' or 'Manipuri village' remain, very few are aware of the great mix of backgrounds which went into creating the modern Burmese.

Kinship and social organisation

The vast majority of people in the Irrawaddy valley were organised into small descent or kinship groups. These groups were normally associated with a particular place. People generally married within these descent groups and lived together with other group members. Peoples' livelihoods and their relationship to political authority rested on their group membership and their group position. Larger villages and towns might contain members of more than one group but smaller villages might consist exclusively of a single group of extended kin. Some groups were part of larger formations with constituent descent groups scattered across a region. From the royal family itself to a group of slaves attached to a small village pagoda, these descent groups formed the basis of social organisation and of political control throughout the king's realm.[2]

People lived in very distinct clusters of settlements along the Irrawaddy river. Some of the settlements were fortified, and these were called *myo*. Some also had a moat as well as a wall and a permanent market, or *zay*, and were usually the site of a shrine to a local deity, or *nat*, where a festival would be held once a year. There would be one, or perhaps several, Buddhist monasteries which served not only as religious centres but also as local schools, places of rest for travellers and places of refuge for stray animals. Many of the houses were built of simple materials, bamboo and thatch, but the more important people of the *myo* – its rulers, rich traders and representatives of the king – lived in large wooden compounds, their doors sometimes painted vermillion, the colour of minor nobility. An army garrison might be stationed within the walls, but more likely a number of local men would be given the right to bear arms and they would act as police and as a military reserve in times of need.

Other settlements, which were not fortified were known as *ywa*. A *ywa* was generally smaller than a *myo* and was often just a collection of houses, perhaps a few dozen, built closely together near the fields, where most of the inhabitants worked. The houses themselves would be simple constructions of bamboo and thatch and were raised for protection from floods and snakes. Mango and tamarind trees were often planted for shade and the entire settlement would normally be surrounded by a protective wall of tall thorny hedges.[3] At the edge of the *ywa*, there would invariably be a small shrine to the village *nat*.

A *myothugyi*, the chief of the *myo*, was the hereditary ruler of his town and its hinterland, the *myo-nè*. Some of these chiefs had other names, but all were the leading members of the area's dominant descent group and served as the primary link between their communities and the Court of Ava. They were supervised to varying extents by the royal governors, quite senior officials who set up headquarters in the largest and most strategi-

[2] On Burmese kinship and village organisation in the immediate post-colonial period, see Manning Nash, *The Golden Road to Modernity: Village Life in Central Burma*, New York, 1965; and Melford Spiro, *Marriage and Kinship in Burma: A Cultural and Psychodynamic Analysis*, Berkeley, 1977.

[3] O.H.K. Spate, 'The Burmese Village', *Geographical Review*, 3(4) (1945), 23–43.

cally placed *myo* and acted as agents of the crown. In addition to the governor and the local chief, the third important figure within the rural towns was the *myo-za*, literally the 'eater' of the town. These were members of the Ava aristocracy, normally members of the royal family or serving high officials, to whom the crown alienated its customary income from a given town. They also had other rights, including some judicial authority, but this varied from place to place and time to time. They normally lived in the royal city and so were represented at their *appanage* by their representative, the *myo-kaing*. Together these three august personages, the governor, the chief and the eater, dispensed justice, collected taxes, presided over religious and state ceremonies and led their men in war. Between themselves, they shared the power and divided the surplus wealth of their local community.

Most people lived with their extended families. The word for 'kinsman' or 'relation' is *a-myo*. Confusingly, though *myo* meaning town and *myo* meaning kin or descent are spelled the same in English, they are distinct in Burmese, being of different tones. They are entirely different words. The root of the words for kinsmen and descent group is a cognate of the Tibetan *'bru*. Both mean 'seed'. In Burmese *myo* has come to imply a shared origin or a common descent. It also has come to have a more general connotation of 'sort' or 'kind' and may be applied to people and animals as well as inanimate objects. The Burmese saw the word as equivalent to the Pali word *jati*, which in English is usually translated as 'caste'. Descent was reckoned biologically, that is both the mother's and father's relations were regarded as the individual's *a-myo*.

Marriage tended to be endogamous, within the circle of one's *a-myo*. Cross-cousin marriages in particular were encouraged and incest rules extended only to parents, children and full siblings, marriages to half-siblings being far from unknown. Marriage outside of one's group was permitted, but often actively discouraged, both by royal decree and probably as well by local custom. Various rules were established to then determine the position of children in a 'mixed' marriage, the general principle being that male children were recognised as members of the father's group and female children as members of the mother's group. Residence was neo-local, that is to say newly married couples moved away from their respective parents and into their own homes.

Throughout the early modern era, periodic war and famine and attendant displacements of people led to frequent abandonment and recolonisation of villages, particularly in less productive areas. In addition, the low density of population in all but the most intensely irrigated places, and places close to the main river-ways, meant that new communities were constantly being formed by immigrants. These immigrants included settlers from nearby upland areas such as Maru, Jingpaw or Mizo speakers of related Tibeto-Burman languages.[4] Others were immigrants from overseas, or war captives who were settled in newly colonised land by the crown.

Within these small single-*myo* villages, there would be a line of chiefs. This was known as the chiefly *yo*, or bone. *Yo* is a cognate of the Tibetan *rus-pa*, and in Tibetan means clan or family.[5] In Burmese, however, the word means 'lineage', normally a patrilineage in which office descended from father to eldest son. This was the most common inheritance system in general, the eldest son having the special position known as *oratha*, which granted him not all his parent's property, but the largest share. In some villages, the *yo* might descend from father to youngest son, or even from mother to daughter, but these systems of inheritance were relatively uncommon. Most chiefs were known as *thu-gyi*, literally 'the big person', and he would be the head of his lineage, the head of his descent group, and the chief of his village.

Over time, outsiders would arrive at these new settlements and apply for permission to live. They would normally be accepted, given the acute labour shortages in most parts of the valley. They were known as *kappa*, and would be assigned land or other duties by the chief. If they married into the local *myo*, their children were known as *ala*. This sense of difference between 'locals' and 'outsiders' was very important and was traced through many generations of descent, with clearly marked categories for varying degrees of 'outsideness'. The members of the original descent group would propitiate the same deity, perhaps an ancestor of the ruling family. This would be their ancestral or *mizain-pazain nat*.[6] Outsiders would bring their own *nat* worship, and, over time, a small village might have one dominant *nat* cult with a small number of subsidiary ones as well.

As these settlements grew in times of peace and prosperity as well as in the older, larger walled towns, the founding descent group would come to

---

[4] *ROB*, 2 April 1647 refers to the settling of upland immigrants.

[5] G.H. Luce, *Phases of Pre-Pagan Burma: Languages and History*, Oxford, 1985, vol. II, chart T.   [6] Richard Temple, *Thirty Seven Nats*, London, 1906, pp. 7–8.

see itself in a position apart from newer, subordinate *myo* who had arrived later. Whatever the truth of people's actual descent, even in centuries-old towns, the dominant *myo* was seen or saw itself to be the *myo* of the original colonisers of the locality. The chief, who might enjoy a noble style, would be of the chiefly lineage of the 'founding' descent group. Being of the 'founding family' or of the 'original family of chiefs' was a key claim to local elite status. Below them, all other inhabitants would be ranked in an hierarchy.

The Burmese legal literature clearly divided all people into four general social classes.[7] The first was the *min-myo*, the rulers. The second was the *ponna-myo*, the ritualists who were 'learned in the Vedas'; the third, the *thuhtay-myo*, the bankers and rich merchants; and the fourth, the *sinyètha-myo*, the 'poor people' or commoners. These reflect the Indian *varna* system which was known to the Burmese at the time and in which descent groups were classed as *Ksatriya*, *Brahmin*, *Vaishya* or *Sudra*. The Burmese used their single word *myo* as a synonym for both the Indian derived *zati* (*jati*) and *wunna* (*varna*).[8] Indeed, the Burmese explicitly link each of their four classes to one of the four *varnas*. But the difficulty of the fit is seen in the addition, especially in the legal literature, of a number of other categories and sub-categories.

For example, a distinction was made between the ruling class and the 'noble' or 'official' class. The first was said to refer mainly to the royal family, but also included a few very senior ministers, generals and other 'exalted persons'. The second, the *amat-myo*, included the families of all office-holders, both those who held local office by hereditary right and royal office-holders who were, nominally at least, selected by the king. The first group was said to rank above the *ponna*, whereas the *ponna* ranked above the ordinary nobility. In addition, the legal literature often makes reference to the *konthè-myo*, the 'trading class', which ranked somewhere in between the richer merchant-bankers and the ordinary 'poor people'. Finally, below the normal 'poor peoples' class was the much lower class of

---

[7] D. Richardson (ed.), *The Damathat or the Laws of Menoo*, Moulmein, 1847, p. 91 and *passim*; John Jardine, *Notes on Buddhist Law*, Rangoon, 1882, *passim*; see also Kala, *Maha Yazawindawgyi*, pp. 13–14; Andrew Huxley, 'The Village Knows Best: Social Organisation in a 18th century Burmese Law Code', *Southeast Asia Research*, 5 (1997), 2–15.

[8] *Pali-Myanma Abhidan*, vol. VIII, Rangoon, 1974, p. 217; *Pitaka Kyan-hnyun*, vol. I, Rangoon, 1972, p. 519.

hereditary pagoda slaves, beggars and those who dealt with burial, the *sandala-myo*.[9]

These divisions were important to daily life in that an individual's classification determined his or her legal status. Inheritance rights as well as other civil and criminal cases involving two parties were judged with these classifications in mind. Different sets of laws, for example, pertained to assault by a trader against a noble than by a noble against a trader. In another example, divorce laws between two people of the banking class were different from those between a banker and a wife who was of royal descent.

A person's class was inherited and could not be changed except by royal order. But there were no customary prohibitions of inter-class marriage. Occasionally, there might be royal edicts encouraging people to marry 'their own kind' or even banning marriage outside one's descent group, but these were uncommon and had no standing in customary law. Polygamy was allowed and was perhaps quite common, given the likely skewed gender balance, a product of war and the large male celibate Buddhist order. Indeed, many Burmese laws deal with property, inheritance and divorce rights for men of each social class who had married several different women of different class backgrounds.

Overarching these four main social classes were two primary grades: 'superior' (*myat*) and 'inferior' (*yoke*). Rulers, nobles, *ponna*, bankers and big merchants were 'exalted' and the rest were 'inferior'. This divide also informed much of early modern law and determined many day-to-day practices, such as the custom by which those of 'inferior' status had to make way on the road to those classed as 'superior'. It also determined one's place in the sumptuary order.

As important as this fourfold class division was the twofold division of all the king's subjects into those who owed hereditary labour service to the royal court, and those who did not. People who were members of descent groups which owed labour service were known as crown servants or *ahmudan*. *Ahmudan* literally means a 'carrier of an obligation'. Perhaps as many as 40 per cent of people living along the middle Irrawaddy and lower Chindwin, the area of tightest crown control, were members of these groups. Many were groups within military regiments such as the Marabin Artillery or the Shan Horse. Soldiers, ex-soldiers, their wives and children,

---

[9] See *ROB*, 30 November 1635 for an early reference to their status.

were all members of the regiment. A particular village, for example, might be a village of the Tavoy Guards. The hereditary obligation of members of this group would be to supply a certain number of men to the Household Division as part of the Tavoy Guards regiment on a rotating basis.

Others were groups within what were known as 'soft' civilian regiments. These included groups of hereditary cooks, washermen, musicians, weavers and others. In the same way as their military counterparts, they would live together in a village or town, and supply the royal city with a specified number of people for their hereditary occupation, over a given period. These descent groups were usually known as *asu*, meaning simply a 'group' or 'collection'.

Those who were not *ahmudan* were known as *athi*. They too lived in their own closely knit communities, but paid taxes rather than provide labour to Ava. As royal agencies were not particularly concerned with their internal organisation, unlike the organisation of crown servants, we have much less information about the various types of *athi* groups. They might be mobilised in times of war or used as corvée labour, but they had no specific hereditary labour obligation.

The third cross-cutting social division was that between slaves and non-slaves.[10] 'Slave' is a very unsatisfactory translation of the Burmese word *kyun*, as *kyun* can refer to a number of different legal positions. The vast majority of *kyun* were redeemable slaves, that is people who were bonded to an individual but who might buy their freedom back in time. Financial debt and the inability to repay a loan was the most common cause, and once the loan was repaid, the person's bonded status would end. Other slaves, a much smaller number, were irredeemable and were thus hereditary slaves. These included pagoda slaves, descendants of people donated to a religious establishment, as well as most people captured in war. Slaves could perform a variety of functions, but most were used to work the land. Slaves were also bought as concubines for the well-to-do.[11] A mountain of legal literature exists to define categories of slavery and the rights and obligations attaching to each. Again, slavery cut across class lines. A trader, for example, could become the slave of a

[10] On Burmese slavery, see Michael Aung-Thwin, 'Athi, Hkyun-daw and Hpaya-kyun', in Antony Reid (ed.), *Slavery, Bondage and Dependency in Southeast Asia*, London, 1983.

[11] Toe Hla, 'Moneylending and Contractual Thet-kayits', Ph.D. dissertation, Northern Illinois University, 1987, p. 241.

common cultivator. Whether or not members of the *ponna* class could become slaves was a matter for debate. Only members of the royal family were protected by law, and could never fall into slave status regardless of financial or other indebtedness.

The last social division which might be mentioned was between men and women. On the one hand, women enjoyed a variety of legal rights, in the areas of property ownership, divorce and inheritance, which placed them on an even par with men. Women also played an important role in trade and often occupied key, if not all, places in the local market. But they were entirely excluded from political office above the rank of the extremely rare village chief. There may have been entirely female lines of chiefs, but if these did exist they would have been only at the very local village level and in more remote places. What was more common was for a woman who was related to the main patriline to be exceptionally granted office over less competent male contenders. Mi Shwé-U, for example was made chief of the village of Kwingauk, near Henzada in the delta, in 1807 and was permitted to select men for all subordinate local offices.[12]

But on the whole, women remained well outside any significant political role. And while they ran many ordinary businesses, they were never granted a place in the court banking system. The army and the Buddhist Sangha, key pillars of the social order, were all-male. There had been a women's Buddhist community, the *Bikkhuni Sangha* at one time, but this was said to have died out by the late Pagan period and the rise of neo-conservative Buddhism. A woman's place within the class structure was based upon her parents' place or her mother's place if her parents were of different *myo*. Thus a woman from a trading descent group would remain a trader in the eyes of the law whether she married a common cultivator or a prince. More generally, all women were seen as lacking the inherent dignity or *pon* of men and, for example, sat separately and in subordinate places at religious and other ritual events.

The gentry

The Burmese gentry (*akyi-akè myo* or *thugyi-myo*) of the early nineteenth century were a class apart from both the nobility at Ava and the ordinary people of the countryside. They held the important offices of rural govern-

---

[12] *ROB*, 4 October 1807.

ment by hereditary right and provided the critical connection between the royal courts and the general population. They enjoyed special sumptuary privileges and titles, and were among the very few who moved regularly between the gilded world of the palace and the more prosaic world of the common villager. They were the backbone of Burmese administration; through civil wars and changes of dynasty, the same families ruled their charges for hundreds of years.

The actual office-holders normally succeeded to their positions through rights of primogeniture. The names of the offices were varied. The most common was *thugyi* for an ordinary chief or *myothugyi* for the chief of an entire township. In the far north, near the China border, the local office-holders were often called *shwé-hmu* or *ngway-hmu*, meaning 'supervisor of gold' or 'supervisor of silver', a reference to the gold and silver mines in their localities. Many other enjoyed military designations. A senior hereditary military officer, for example, might be the leader of a collection of kinship groups, all of which provided soldiers under his charge. As these groups lived in neighbouring villages, he, living in the main walled town, would be the effective, if not nominal, ruler of the entire region. For example, along the west bank of the Irrawaddy, about fifty miles south of Ava, nearly all the inhabitants were men of the 'Shwaypyi Yanaung' cavalry regiment or members of their families. Each group of fifty or so men and their families lived under the charge of their *myinsi* or cavalry officer. The entire regiment was under their commander, the *myingaung*, the holder of the senior 'bone'.

The greatest of the gentry office-holders were the above-mentioned *myothugyi*, the chiefs of the townships. They were members of the dominant lineage in large *athi* communities. While some had charge of only a few isolated settlements, others maintained substantial courts and presided over more than one hundred villages and towns. Beneath these *myothugyi* were often a host of other lesser officials, some of whom held these lesser offices by hereditary right while others were appointed directly by the *myothugyi*. These included town clerks, criers, irrigation officers, land supervisors and the holders of a variety of possible military-style offices.

The most elaborate of these local administrations was that of Pagan. As the rulers of the most important of all the former royal capitals, the hereditary magnates of Pagan enjoyed the particularly grand style of *mintha* or 'prince', a title otherwise reserved for members of the royal family. There were four princes of Pagan, from inter-related families, and they in turn presided over a myriad of hereditary officials: the *pyizo*, who handled day-to-day administration; the *sachi*, or writers; the *sokay*, or constables; as well as brokers, fishery officers, ferry operators, toll station officers and revenue collectors. All held their positions by hereditary right as the holder of the senior lineage among their group.[13]

Other local administrations were much more modest. In general, the local *thugyi* was policeman, tax collector, judge and jury. He (very rarely she) decided the apportioning of revenue or corvée demanded by royal officers, allocated civil and military duties and was generally in charge of all aspects of local government, holding judicial and executive powers. All members of the local gentry, as well as their personal retainers, were exempted from taxation and demands for labour. Though some large communities had specific hereditary police officers,[14] in most places the local chief would simply call on all the armed men under his charge to suppress any criminal activity.[15] In Amyint, a fairly typical town to the north of Ava, the chiefly family was divided into three primary lineages: the Eastern Four Hundred, the Ponnya and the Western Four Hundred. In addition, there were seven other gentry office lineages, including lineages of the hereditary land surveyor, broker, merchant and ferry operator.[16]

In addition to the Pagan gentry, two other regional elites were particularly prominent. The first were the *thugaung* of Salin. They were a class of a few dozen inter-related families who together governed the rich irrigated area centred at Salin, along the lower reaches of the Irrawaddy. Their chiefs were organised into four lines of descent and members of these chiefly lineages, the Badda Raza, Taungzin, Hkaingza and Maha Thaman lineages, all traced their ancestry back to the late Pagan era, and to the original granting of hereditary rights in this area to their families.[17] They controlled the best agricultural land under their charge and sat at the apex of an agrarian financial system through which they dominated the local economy. The other important regional elite were the *twinzayo* of Yénan-

[13] F.N. Trager and William Koenig (eds.), *Burmese Sit-tans, 1724–1826: Records of Rural Life and Administration*, Tucson, 1979, Pagan *myo* sittan 1765.

[14] *Ibid.*

[15] J.G. Scott and J.P. Hardiman (comps.), *Gazetteer of Upper Burma and the Shan States*, 5 vols. in 2 parts (hereafter *GUBSS*), Rangoon, 1900–1, vol. II, p. 105.

[16] *ROB*, 21 July 1786.

[17] Ohn Kyi, 'Salin Thugaung Thamaing (Akyin)', in *Bama Thamaing* (Studies in Burmese History) by colleagues of Dr Than Tun (mimeo.).

gyaung. Yénangyaung ('Stinking Water Creek') was a large town on the middle Irrawaddy which was home to the main oil wells in the country. *Twinzayo* means 'Lineage of the Well-Eaters' and they owned the wells which supplied lighting oil for the whole kingdom. Like the *thugaung* of Salin, they married almost exclusively within their own ranks, forming a closely knit gentry clan. Through hereditary control of local office, they were the political as well as the economic elite of the region until the great changes of the mid-nineteenth century.

In most areas, the gentry's economic position was perpetuated through three related activities: revenue collection, control of land and irrigation, and money-lending. Revenue collection and the control of land and irrigation were prerogatives of local office. Taxation by these local hereditary office-holders varied greatly from place to place, depending on local custom. There was very little if any direct taxation on agricultural production other than rent on land constituting crown estates. Most taxes were in the form of fees for judicial and other services performed, licences, local tariffs on trade, transport and virtually every kind of economic activity.[18] In theory, all of this income was shared between the local office-holder and the royal treasury through long-standing arrangements, but in practice, many local office-holders hid as much income as possible while royal agents, in turn, were constantly in search of better information and as big a share for themselves and their king as possible.

Myothugyi and other rural magnates also profited from control of irrigation and control over the best land under their charge. In many places, landed estates were passed down as part of the local office, thus preserving their integrity. Land was seldom 'private' in the sense of being alienable, but was land which belonged either to the incumbent lord or to the family as 'ancestral land' (see below). Office-holders also enjoyed the right to assign vacant lands and arbitrate in inheritance and other disputes over land and water usage.

Revenue collection and land control meant that senior gentry members often had more cash than other members of their community. As in many poor agricultural societies, Irrawaddy valley cultivators in the early nineteenth century were seasonally in need of cash to see them through the year's harvest. As money-lenders, some members of the gentry loaned money at interest, either from their own private funds or from money they

---

[18] On local Burmese administration, see Mya Sein, *The Administration of Burma*, Oxford, 1938; Trager and Koenig (eds.), *Burmese Sit-tans*.

in turn had borrowed from their even richer cousins in the royal court.

However much money the gentry were able to accumulate, their spending was carefully prescribed through customary sumptuary rules and regulations, and the *myothugyi* in particular enjoyed a number of privileges which clearly marked him apart from his subjects. These normally included the right to wear certain types of dress or ride horses. In his 1764 *sittan*, for example, the Myothugyi of Wuntho stated:

> my retinue is comprised of two swordsmen on the right and two on the left, seven vermillion drums, one slightly smaller drum, one great horn and smaller horn. My house has a three tiered cemented roof with horns and interior partitions painted vermillion. The windows are part gilt and two parts vermillion and there are four gates to the wall of the compound . . . [19]

Another clear way in which office-holders and their wives were separated from those of subordinate classes was by their names. The Burmese attached great importance to their names and titles, but did not have anything like the system of surnames as in parts of contemporary western Europe or China. Instead, personal names were almost always descriptive Burmese words, with meanings such as 'gold' (Shwé), 'famous' (Kyaw), 'pleasant' (Tha) or 'First' (U), and were determined in part by the day of the week of one's birth. Within a small community, people often called one another by a familial term, such as 'elder brother' (*ko*) or 'aunt' (*daw*), whether or not there existed a known tie of kinship, and a person outside of his or her immediate small community was addressed by his or her name, prefixed by *nga* for a man and *mi* for a woman, or *maung* and *mè* respectively for those of more notable birth.

Gentry lineages, however, often had lineage names, such as the Maha Thaman *yo* or the Tharay Ponnya *yo*, the names of the chiefly lineages of Pahkangyi and Ahmyint respectively.[20] In addition, most if not all office-holders received a fitting title. The titles were similar to those used by the court aristocracy, but were less grand. Gentry titles were usually easy to distinguish from those of the nobility and royal family, and did not contain key court appellations, such as *min* or *maha*. They did, however, very often include the title *thamada*, which implies that the holder was someone who ruled by popular consent. The word may be translated as 'elected', and today the word is used for both 'president' and 'republic'. Other

---

[19] Trager and Koenig (eds.), *Burmese Sit-tans*, Wuntho *myo* sittan 1764.
[20] *ROB*, 30 November 1635.

than administrative elites, individuals holding local banking offices might also be granted permission to assume a noble style. Buddhist monks as well, upon entering the order, would discard their personal name and take a wholly new Pali name. As entrance into the Sangha was only open to adult men who were not slaves or bond servants, not in debt and not in the king's service, this would broadly leave the well-to-do in the countryside, other than those from military lineages.[21] Thus all the most important people in a local community, the chief, the banker and the local monks, perhaps all related, would enjoy grand Pali-Burmese titles rather than the simple vernacular names of the common folk.

We have already mentioned the most important gentry clans. Among other, less ancient families, were many crown service families who held hereditary military office. An example was the Lèzin family, who were the hereditary *myinsi*, or cavalry officers, of villages near the town of Alon in the lower Chindwin basin. The area had been selected by the Restored Toungoo and early Konbaung kings as a primary recruiting ground for the Household Guards. The Lèzin family, together with two other related families, dominated much of the countryside, holding all the important administrative and judicial offices and slowly building up sizeable landed estates. The three families were in turn related to nearby chiefly families.[22] Through money-lending and the buying of land from indebted farmers, this gentry family acquired more than 600 acres outright during the early nineteenth century and controlled the land of over one hundred other families in the area who had mortgaged their holdings. As a result of endogamous marriage, by the reign of King Thibaw, the Myinsi of Lèzin was descended from all three dominant land-owning lineages.

As recently as the sixteenth century, the valley was home to many more powerful local families: the ruling houses of Prome, Toungoo, Martaban and Sagaing, for example, had maintained provincial courts rivalling those of the greatest Ava grandees, if not the royal family itself. For this very reason, they had been removed from their positions, and many of their descendants organised into groups within the palace, as will be described in the next chapter. Governors, appointees of the incumbent monarch, were placed in their stead, removing possible rivals outside Ava's walls. Thus, the families who remained in hereditary rural office were only the second level of gentry clans who had once existed. Theoreti-

---

[21] *Ibid.*, 30 March 1810.
[22] Toe Hla, 'Moneylending and Contractual Thet-kayits', pp. 156–60.

cally, the remaining gentry were still included in the reckoning of the king's 80,000 *amatya*, his 80,000 nobles. They were part of the more general *amat-myo* which included the nobility at the capital as well. Even more generally, they were part of the *min-myo*, the ruling or *ksatriya* class together with the king himself.

But as differences in power and wealth between the remaining gentry clans and the aristocracy at Ava grew, they were increasingly treated as a class apart. While they had once been referred to primarily as *min*, as 'rulers', they were increasingly known only as *thugyi* or 'headman'.[23] Through the early modern period and into the nineteenth century, administrative and commercial processes would combine to widen the gap between the centre and the hinterland. This would take on new twists and turns in the late nineteenth century as we will see. By the colonial period, the British would see only village notables, not great rural magnates, ruling over an otherwise undifferentiated social landscape.

Markets, merchants and money-lenders

Then, as now, the staple Burmese diet was rice with fermented fish or shrimp paste and whatever vegetables or other condiments the consumer could afford, and practically all the food which was consumed in the valley was locally produced. Rice was the principal crop in the south and in irrigated areas, while in drier regions a number of other crops were grown – especially cotton, tobacco, sesame for cooking oil, wheat and onions – as well as some rice where possible. Tenures were regulated by custom rather than any set of codified rules, and differed considerably from place to place. This was in part due to differences in local economies and in part to the intricacy and varied nature of local social organisation. Very generally, however, there existed four main classes of land – crown land, ancestral or allodial land, glebe land, and official or prebendal land.[24]

Crown land (*nanzin ayadaw-myay*) was the personal land belonging to the king. This consisted of scattered but substantial estates which he had inherited from his ancestors or had acquired by marriage, and which were worked by a special class of labourers known as *lamaing*, or crown serfs.

[23] *MMOS*, vol. II, pp. 141–2.

[24] J.S. Furnival, *An Introduction to the Political Economy of Burma*, Rangoon, 1931, p. 83; *MMOS*, vol. V, pp. 19–30.

Certain other types of land could also become crown property, such as lands which were difficult to assign to any one person or group, for example the small islands in the Irrawaddy near the capital which disappeared beneath the surface of the river every year, and then, on reappearing, could not easily be identified. The right of collecting rent from such land was the responsibility of the Superintendent of Crown Property, the *Ayadaw-ok,* who was allowed to dispose of them as he thought most profitable, while gaining some sort of commission for himself. Land confiscated for criminal acts (*thein-myay,* or 'confiscated land') and land which reverted to the crown because the original owners had left no heirs (*amwe-son-myay,* or 'end of lineage land') were also supposed to become crown land if deemed valuable. Thus the king was the default landowner of his realm.

While the king was the largest single landowner, the majority of land was probably allodial or *boba-baing-myay.* This literally means 'father's and grandfather's land' and it was not private land in that the holder did not have full rights to dispose of the land as he or she saw fit. Land which was cleared by an individual and kept within the family was classed as allodial in this way. Land was often mortgaged and some may have been bought and sold, but fully private, or *pudgalika,* land did not appear as a distinct category until colonial times.

Other land belonged to religious establishments, monasteries and pagodas. They were crown lands or allodial lands donated by the king or other notables in perpetuity; their integrity was meant to be scrupulously maintained. In fact, glebe land tended to shrink over time, as lapses in record-keeping allowed cultivator-tenants or other local people to claim bits of the estate as their own. Land donations were often accompanied by donations of slaves to work the land. Those who did, the *hpaya-kyun,* were irredeemable slaves. Even though they were common cultivators in every other way, they came to occupy the lowest rung in the Burmese social ladder, as low as those who dealt in death. For ordinary people, they were beyond the pale and no social interaction was allowed.

The last and most complicated category of land was *min-myay* or prebendal land. *Min* means 'ruler' and in a village setting might refer to the local chief. *Min-myay* in this case was the 'chief's land' and was part of his patrimony, his inheritance as head of his lineage. More generally, the phrase might refer to all land seen as belonging to the chiefly clan. But this phrase was also used to categorise land granted by a king to his crown servants in return for military or other obligations. In the most simple case, the king, in establishing a new army regiment, might grant the officer in charge of the regiment an estate near the capital. The officer would then parcel out the estate among his men and their families, setting aside land for their residence (*nay-myay*), their personal cultivation when not on duty (*loke-myay*) and for extra income (*sa-myay*). He would doubtless keep the best parts for himself. As office was hereditary, these grants also tended to become hereditary and such land was treated little differently from allodial land, despite constant crown attempts to ensure the integrity of these estates and the continuity of their prebendal status. Often crown servants in debt would mortgage or even sell their land and thus the original connection of the land to service would be lost.

This distinction between different types of prebendal holdings and between prebendal and allodial land was clear only in theory. In practice, failures of royal information, coercion or will, meant that land nominally attached to office came under the control of the local gentry. For example, confiscated land which should have reverted to the crown might have remained unreported. Instead the land might have been taken quietly as part of the local chiefly estate. At the core of much of the vagueness was the substantial gap between the idea that the crown controlled land and could assign land at will, on the one hand, and local realities, on the other. This vagueness, manageable and perhaps even desired under old norms and practices, would become problematic with the approach of colonial rule and attempts to rationalise land-holding and revenue administration.

Though overwhelmingly important, agriculture was far from being the only component of the valley's economy, and large numbers of people were employed in other industries. These included, for example, the production of cotton and silk cloth,[25] the making of lacquerware and other household products, the construction of religious buildings, and the manufacture of Buddhist images and other religious objects.[26] Among

---

[25] Michael Symes, *An Account of an Embassy to the Kingdom of Ava, sent by the Governor-General of India in the Year 1795*, London, 1800, vol. I, p. 279; vol. II, p. 187; W.R. Winston, *Four Years in Upper Burma*, London, 1892, p. 37; *GUBSS*, pp. 363–76; Tun Wai, *Economic Development of Burma from 1800 till 1940*, Rangoon, 1961, p. 14.

[26] V. Sangermano, *A Description of the Burmese Empire*, reprint, London, 1966, p. 215; J. Crawfurd, *Journal of an Embassy from the Governor General of India to the Court of Ava in the Year 1826*, London, 1834, p. 426; J. Nisbit, *Burma under British Rule and Before*, London 1901, vol. II, p. 300; G. E. Harvey, *British Rule in Burma:*

other important industries in the early nineteenth century were the oil industry, located at Yénangyaung, a sprawling community along the west bank of the Irrawaddy,[27] and shipbuilding, increasingly important as a source of foreign exchange in the country's southern ports.[28]

While many of the patterns of consumption and production as described above had probably changed little over the previous several centuries, the local economy was far from static. Looking at the very long term, we have already seen that the early modern era was likely to have witnessed a degree of demographic growth. Almost certainly, the fifty years from the civil war in the 1750s to the very beginning of the nineteenth century saw an increase in population in the Irrawaddy valley, both as a result of relative peace and stability, and as a consequence of large-scale importation of war captives. The famine of 1805–07 may have been the result of a prolonged drought, but may also have been linked to overpopulation relative to production capacities in some parts of the country.

This demographic growth was a likely factor in a growing commercialisation of the valley's economy, as cultivators and others began producing for bigger and more distant markets.[29] The focus of this increased commercialisation was the periodic fairs, or *pwè*, and the permanent markets, or *zay*, of the larger towns. The smaller *pwè* would normally rotate between five large villages and were markets held in conjunction with the visit of travelling entertainers. More substantial ones might take place in conjunction with a religious occasion. Customary revenue from a periodic market or festival was given to the person holding the office of *pwèza*, or 'broker'. The larger, permanent markets in towns and in the capital were much more impressive exchange sites where a number of customary office-holders derived income from sales, licences, the use of standard weights and measures and currency exchange.[30]

Rice was in part distributed through these locally regulated markets, or sold by small-scale traders who exchanged rice for other easily portable

---

1824–1942, London, 1944, pp. 341–2; Tun Wai, *Economic Development*, pp. 12–20.

[27] Crawfurd, *Journal*, p. 55; Cox, *Journal*, pp. 34–5, 43; Henry Yule, *Mission to the Court of Ava in 1855*, reprint, Kuala Lumpur, 1968, pp. 21–2; Fritz Noetling, *Report on the Petroleum Industry in Upper Burma from the End of the Last Century to the Beginning of 1891*, Rangoon, 1892, p. 59.

[28] Sangermano, *Description*, pp. 219–20; Symes, *Account*, vol. I, p. 254; vol. II, p. 218; Tun Wai, *Economic Development*, pp. 11–12.

[29] On the long-term commercialisation and monetisation of the economy, see Lieberman, 'Secular Trends', esp. pp. 13–21.   [30] *ROB*, 26 October 1872.

commodities.[31] But rice was much too important a commodity to be left to a free or gentry-controlled market-place. Instead, the firm hand of the state directed the flow of the Burmese staple food from the irrigated rice-producing regions of Kyaukse, Yamèthin and around the capital, to the royal granaries, and from the royal granaries to the army and other crown servants, the Buddhist monasteries and, in times of need, to rice deficit regions around the country. Through taxation, rice was also brought north from the once rice-exporting areas of the delta. By the early Konbaung period, successive royal governments maintained or tried to maintain a complete ban on the export of rice overseas. This was an effort to ensure adequate food supplies, especially in the politically important but drought-prone region around the capital and this prohibition on exports by 1800 supports the picture of a growing food deficit in the dry-zone.

With a growing commercialisation of the economy came an increasing monetisation of market transactions, and a more monetised economy meant a growing role for bankers and banking, both professional and amateur. The movement of silver as currency was influenced by two related structures. The first was local and royal taxation which moved silver into the hands of gentry and noble office-holders. Second were the financial enterprises of these office-holders and their banker associates which lent this money to ordinary cultivators at interest. As in any commercial agrarian economy, cultivators needed loans with the start of each planting season and many people probably borrowed money for expensive life ceremonies.[32]

The role of money-lending as a possible income-earner for gentry office-holders has also been mentioned. But this was only part of an intricate and country-wide financial system which is little understood. The king himself lent silver to his most important subjects, including tributary *sawbwa* and *myoza* and they in turn probably lent money to their own charges. A system of indebtedness may thus have roughly paralleled political structures, the king standing at the apex of a lucrative lending machine which recycled money from the agrarian economy at a profit.

---

[31] On the redistribution of rice at Amarapura in the 1850s, see D.G.E. Hall (ed.), *The Dalhousie–Phayre Correspondence 1852–56*, London, 1932 (hereafter *DPC*), 18 March 1854.

[32] Crawfurd, *Journal*, p. 434; *GUBSS*, vol. II, p. 165; Tun Wai, *Burma's Currency and Credit*, Bombay, 1962, p. 24; Toe Hla, 'Moneylending and Contractual Thet-kayits'.

This picture of a political-financial elite is complicated by the important position of professional bankers, the *thuhtay*, of the early modern era. They are the least known of all the country's social classes. Unlike the *min-myo* – kings and noblemen – the *thuhtay-myo* figured little, if at all, in the chronicles and in the other literature of the age. We know the names of only a very few *thuhtay*, and next to nothing about their business organisation. Many were titled and in this way were clearly separated from the commoner class. These titles sometimes included the word *dana*, meaning 'donation', such as in the style Maha Danaraza, but they more often included the word *thuhtay* itself, which is a Burmese corruption of the Pali *setthi*, also meaning 'banker' or 'rich man'.

Their place in palace society will be discussed in the next chapter. Their place in rural society, however, is much less clear. As we have seen, the *thuhtay-myo*, was a recognised social division. Today, being a *thuhtay* simply means that one has wealth or property above what is common. But in early Konbaung society, *thuhtay* was both a royal designation and an inherited position. To be a *thuhtay*, to be ennobled and enjoy a fitting style, was the gift of the crown and could be revoked at any time. Usually a person becoming a *thuhtay* also entered into a contractual relationship with his sovereign. In return for the title, the royal protection the designation offered and the specific trade privileges which were granted, the *thuhtay* would agree to pay a fixed amount of silver each year. These bankers were also thus monopolists. In 1798, for example, a banker titled Yanaung Kyawhtin, was granted the position of 'Broker for River-borne Trade' (*Thinbaw-kon Pweza*). He was given a monopoly of trade in all imported maritime goods to the greater Ava area in return for 100 viss of silver per year and was placed under the responsibility of the Master of Granaries and the Commander of the Main Cavalry Regiments, an indication of the numerous business links which all senior members of the Court of Ava enjoyed.[33]

While the actual office of *thuhtay* was, at least nominally, a crown appointment, being of the *thuhtay-myo*, the banking class, was hereditary. Maung Kala, the great eighteenth-century historian, for example, was of the Singaing *thuhtay-myo*, Singaing being a village near Ava. Even if a member of a *thuhtay* descent group was impoverished, he or she would still be seen, as least in the eyes of the law, not as a 'poor person' but as the

---

[33] *ROB*, 21 September 1808.

lowest of the various internal groupings within the *thuhtay* class. One small step below the *thuhtay* were the *thugywè*, a Burmese word meaning 'full' or 'wealthy' person, an inferior grade of the same general class. One large step below both were the *konthè*, the traders. They were part of the commoner class and were not seen as 'noble'. Yet they enjoyed some legal distinction from other commoners and were thus placed between the lowest *thugywè* and the bulk of the *sinyètha*, the 'poor'. Thus the great divide between noble and common took place within the trading or business population.

Being recognised as a *thuhtay* or *thugywè* was also a licence to spend. Strict sumptuary regulations meant that spending on most things was highly restricted, and conspicuous consumption occurred only with royal approval. Many *thuhtay* became great religious donors. A pagoda near Ava built by one of my great-great-great-great-grandfathers in the eighteenth century still stands today. He was a member of the Dabessway *thuhtay-myo* and made his fortune from financial dealings across the Kyaukse area. But like many others of the moneyed classes, he also profited handsomely from long-distance trade, across the Bay of Bengal, and up through the Shan hills to the markets of China.

The early Toungoo kings and their predecessors at Pegu had benefited from the great rise in intra-Indian Ocean trade at the beginning of the early modern era, and in the fifteenth and sixteenth centuries a number of port towns along the Arakan, Pegu and Tennasserim littoral had been important entrepots of regional commerce. Imported mercenaries, horses, muskets and cannon as well as a variety of consumer goods had dramatically changed local politics as well as local lifestyles; Burmese ships and sailors travelled to distant ports and Pegu was home to a diverse mix of western Europeans, Persians, Armenians, south Asians, Mons, Burmese and others.

From the seventeenth century onwards, however, following the move of the capital from Pegu to Ava, the importance of maritime trade as a source of goods and state revenue declined. In part this may have been related to the general decline in trade around the Bay of Bengal. But it was also likely to have been related to local demographic growth which in turn led to food shortages and the royal prohibition on the export of rice. By 1800, the Court of Ava followed what might be considered a 'mercantilist' policy, with strict prohibitions as well on the export of precious metals. Otherwise, a 6 per cent *ad valorem* tax was levied on exports with 5 per cent going to the treasury and 1 per cent to local office-holders. Remaining exports included ivory, pepper, cutch, teak, other timber, and lac – as well as some gold and silver despite the prohibition. Imports, which included firearms, textiles and various manufactures, were taxed at $\frac{1}{2}$ per cent, with 10 per cent going to the treasury.[34]

By the early nineteenth century, however, China loomed very large on the horizon. Various local polities and Chinese-speaking empires had, of course, been in varying degrees of contact for a very long time. As early as the Han dynasty, Chinese armies based along the Yellow river were able to project military power across the Yunnan Plateau right up to Burma's modern borders. But this was an ephemeral and tenuous projection and it was only in recent times, as the autonomous kingdoms and chieftanships of Yunnan fell to Peking's control, that the Chinese empire emerged on the country's very doorstep. We have mentioned the likely demographic rise in the Irrawaddy valley in the eighteenth and early nineteenth centuries. But the demographic rise in Yunnan was far more dramatic, and it accompanied a rapidly changing ethnic composition.[35]

Over the course of the eighteenth century, the population of Yunnan is believed to have more than doubled, from approximately 4 to 11 million people, creating a population density in parts of the plateau far higher than anywhere on the Irrawaddy plain. Dali itself had a population of 300,000 in 1750, at least twice that of the Ava area. For the Burmese kingdom, a stronger Chinese presence to the north-east at first led to war in the 1760s, but then to rapidly increasing trade and friendly diplomatic relations. From here on, events in China would have an enormous impact on the valley, at times suddenly and almost absent-mindedly wreaking havoc on the Middle Kingdom's much smaller south-western neighbour.

Cotton was Burma's big export to China, and in return China provided raw silk for the Burmese weaving industry and, importantly, gold and silver which provided liquidity for Burma's trade and agriculture and enriched the upper classes. From across the border also came highly prized silk, copper, sulphur, zinc, cast-iron pots and pans, paper and various and exotic foods.[36] While cotton was estimated as only half of the

[34] Crawford, *Journal*, p. 440.
[35] James Lee, 'Food Supply and Population Growth in Southwest China', *Journal of Asian Studies*, 41 (1982), 711–46; Susan Naquin and Evelyn Rawski, *Chinese Society in the Eighteenth Century*, New Haven, 1987, pp. 199–205.
[36] Yule, *Mission*, pp. 148–50. See also *GUBSS*, vol. II, pp. 354–60.

valley's exports to China in the late eighteenth century, it had become the only significant export by the mid-nineteenth century. The only other significant export was tea, which came not from the valley itself but from the Shan plateau, especially the Palaung principality of Tawng Peng, with some of the tea passing through the royal customs post at Bhamo. The export of tea to China was such an important part of the local economy that Burmese officials told a visiting British delegation in 1855 that they thought 'preposterous' the idea that tea was grown in China.

The religions of the Irrawaddy valley

The religion of the vast majority of people living in the Irrawaddy basin in the early nineteenth century was an amalgam of Buddhism and the worship or propitiation of a variety of indigenous and non-indigenous deities and spirits known as *nats*.[37] According to the Burmese chronicle tradition, Buddhist teachings were first introduced to the country by the two missionaries Sona and Uttara, and the chronicles claimed that the pair were sent by the great Mauryan Emperor Asoka who flourished in the third century BC. Whether or not this was the case, Buddhism had certainly arrived in the valley by the early centuries AD with the rise of urban centres at Sri Ksetra and along the coast. This included Buddhism in all its many contemporary varieties – including the conservative Staviravadins and later the Theravadins, as well as the various schools of the newer Mahayana movement. Tantric or Vajrayana Buddhism had emerged by the latter half of the first millennium AD as an offshoot of the Mahayana movement, about the same time as Hinduism in its medieval form, in particular the devotional cults centred on Siva and Vishnu. In the Irrawaddy basin, these religious developments also found their mirror as Buddhist and Hindu ideas and practices were transplanted to new towns along the coast and in the interior. Possibly, coastal areas, exposed to trade and travel from south India, became more strongly attached to the great Buddhist centres at Amaravati and Narjunikonda along the Krishna river, while the interior, including early Pagan, was more influenced by

---

[37] On Buddhism and Buddhism in Burma, see Richard Gombrich, *Theravada Buddhism: A Social History from Ancient Benares to Modern Colombo*, London, 1988; Winston King, *A Thousand Lives Away: Buddhism in Contemporary Burma*, Berkeley, 1964; Richard Robinson and Willard Johnson, *The Buddhist Religion: A Historical Introduction*, London, 1997; Pannasami, *Thathanawuntha*, reprint, London, 1952.

overland contacts with Bengal, Tibet and Yunnan. These latter areas were all strongholds of Mahayana and Tantric Buddhism, with the university at Nalanda in Bengal being perhaps the most prominent of all the contemporary centres of Buddhist learning.

Alongside Buddhism, the worship of *nat* was the most important constituent element in the dominant religion of the Irrawaddy valley.[38] *Nat* is a generic word for any 'spirit' or 'deity' and they are seen as potentially malevolent and in need of constant propitiation, usually through the ritual offering of food and water. At the centre of the *nat* faith were the thirty-seven Nats, a royally patronised pantheon of *nat* which dated back to eleventh-century Pagan. Deities of Indian origin were easily incorporated into *nat* worship. Brahmanical gods and goddesses were given 'Burmanised' names, for example Sarasvati becoming 'Thayèthadi', Siva becoming 'Paramizwa' and Vishnu becoming 'Withano'. Indra, or Thagya Min in Burmese, was the chief of all the *nat*.[39]

To an extent, this mix of differing Buddhist, Hindu and indigenous religious notions and rituals survived until the early nineteenth century and even survives to this day. But through the early modern period this eclecticism would come under sustained challenge from a great renewal of orthodox or neo-conservative Buddhist beliefs and eventually the rise of what might be termed a fundamentalist Buddhism. The history of this renewal was intimately tied with the history of Buddhism in the not too far away island of Ceylon. There, an extremely conservative Theravada school, the Maha Vihara school, had flourished under royal protection, and then survived the Cola invasions. Links between Pagan and Ceylon had been strong and there had been a considerable exchange of monks and Theravada texts, including the Pali canon, and also the later Singhalese commentaries and the works of Buddhaghosa, the great south Indian cholastic. In the fifteenth century, Dhammazedi, the king of Pegu undertook a sweeping reform of the local Sangha, closely tying the monkhood to Singhalese forest-based religious lineages. From then on, Mahayana and Vajrayana beliefs and practices slowly declined as Ceylon-derived

---

[38] On Burmese *nat* worship, see Temple, *Thirty Seven Nats*; Melford Spiro, *Burmese Supernaturalism*, Philadelphia, 1967, pp. 40–63; Yves Rodrigue, *Nat-Pwe: Burma's Supernatural Sub-Culture*, Edinburgh, 1992; Htin Aung, 'The Thirty-Seven Lords', *JBRS*, 39 (1956), 81–101; and Shway Yoe (George Scott), *The Burman: His Life and Notions*, reprint, Edinburgh, 1989, pp. 231–42.

[39] Temple, *Thirty Seven Nats*, pp. 10–11.

conservatism triumphed, first at Pegu and then at Ava and throughout the countryside.

Greater emphasis was placed on knowledge of Theravada texts, on the Canon and related commentaries, and on much closer observance of *vinaya* rules of monastic discipline. Practices by monks such as participation in local feasts in which large quantities of meat and alcohol were consumed were ended and, in general, a more puritan ethic came to pervade at least parts of Burmese society.[40] Drinking of alcohol was replaced to an extent by the consumption of stimulants such as pickled tea and betal nut and the smoking of opium, and even the killing of large animals became a capital offence.[41] By the nineteenth century, the Court of Ava also undertook measures against homosexuality and transvestitism. Deviation from the new orthodoxy became less tolerated, religious sects opposing support for monks and monasteries were suppressed by royal order, and both Christians and Muslims experienced some persecution.[42]

But despite these neo-conservative trends, elements of Mahayana and Tantric Buddhism remained deeply embedded in popular thought. Many believed that the next Buddha, the Maitreya Buddha, would appear when the teachings of the historical Buddha, the Gautama Buddha, were forgotten, or that the disappearance of Buddhism would come at a time of general decline, the world lapsing into conflict and anarchy. Burmese kings often harnessed these popular ideas and aspired to the role of *Setkyamin* (in Pali, *Cakravatti*) or 'Universal Monarch', a sort of *Boddhisatta* who would rule over an enlightened Buddhist society, and various signs and symbols such as possession of a white elephant were seen as marks of this status. Sects which were closer to Tibetan Buddhism were known collectively as *pwè-gyaung*, and experienced varying degrees of discrimination, losing influence to the Theravada orthodoxy over the course of the nineteenth century.[43]

Alongside this majority Buddhist and *nat*-worshiping tradition was Islam, the second largest non-indigenous belief system in the Irrawaddy valley.[44] Islam had arrived in the country only a few centuries after

---

[40] Than Tun, 'Mahakassapa and His Tradition', in *Essays on the History and Buddhism of Burma*.   [41] Sangermano, *Description*, pp. 84–5.

[42] *Ibid.*, pp. 111–12. On the persecution of Muslims in the 1840s see Henry Gouger, *Personal Narrative of Two Years' Imprisonment in Burmah*, London, 1860, p. 97.

[43] *ROB*, 23 July 1813.

[44] On the history of Muslims in Burma, see especially Moshe Yeager, *The Muslims of Burma: A Study of a Minority Group*, Wiesbaden, 1972; Ba U, *Mandalay Centenary: History of Burmese Muslims*, Mandalay, 1959.

Buddhism, and before the growth of the Singhalese Theravada. Chinese travellers described Muslim Persian-speaking communities along the present Burma–Yunnan border as early as 860, the period of Nan Chao dominance, and the valley was mentioned by Persian writers around the same time. There were certainly Arab and Persian merchants and noblemen at the Pagan court and the earliest Europeans arriving in Pegu and elsewhere referred to sizeable Muslim communities by the sixteenth century. During the Restored Toungoo period, the arrival of firearms and artillery was complemented by the importation of Muslim soldiers, primarily from the Deccan, and these men and their families were settled around Myèdu and Yamèthin, and in lesser numbers near Sagaing and in Kyauksè. These mercenaries formed the core of the later Burmese-speaking Muslim population, as opposed to more recent Pathan, Bengali, south Indian, Panthay-Yunnanese, central Asian and other arrivals.

By the early nineteenth century, Amarapura was home to a large number of Muslims, perhaps as many as eight or nine thousand. While the majority were Sunni Muslim descendants of Deccani musketeers and gunners, others included grand merchants from around the Persian Gulf and even Samarkand and Bokara. There were forty mosques in all, most being crowded into the Kala quarter, and they were the religious centres for not only Muslims of foreign descent, but also a growing community of *Zerabadi*, Muslims perceived to be of mixed Burmese and foreign origin; *Zerabadi* is a corruption of the Persian *zir-bad*, or 'below the winds', a reference to south-east Asia.[45]

Bodawpaya, the most religiously minded of all the early Konbaung kings, took an interest, at least for a while, in this second religion of his growing empire. This coincided with the arrival at Ava of a Naqshbandi Sufi named Abhisha Husseini, who had come from Aurangabad in western India. Abhisha Husseini was welcomed by the royal court and appointed the religious head of all the country's Muslims. The *ponna* establishment was then ordered to translate all of his written works, a task one suspects they performed somewhat reluctantly.[46] There was also a small Christian community by this time, almost entirely limited to the Portuguese-speaking settlements along the Mu river north of Ava and composed of men and women descended in part from French and Portuguese soldiers who had retained their Roman Catholic faith.

[45] Henry Yule and A.C. Burnell, *Hobson-Jobson*, London, 1903, see entry for Zerabadi.
[46] *ROB*, 17 November 1807, 16 December 1807.

In general, the Irrawaddy valley in the early nineteenth century, in the years just prior to the English wars, remained a society of divers forms of local social organisation and cultural norms, but was also one slowly being tied together by webs of growing commercial and religious connections, as well as by the centralising power of the Court of Ava.

3 | The Court of Ava

The Burmese kingdom on the eve of the First Anglo-Burmese War was at the very height of its powers. The imperial formation over which the Court of Ava presided was the most expansive in its people's history. Burmese soldiers, following their mounted chiefs, had marched, almost unchecked, from the frost-covered foothills of the Himalayas to the malarial jungles of the Malay Peninsula. Though their hold on many of their new possessions remained tenuous, their newest campaigns, in the west, were meeting with growing success.

At home, along the banks of the Irrawaddy, the Court of Ava's authority was stronger than ever before. Building on core institutions which reached back to Pagan, increasingly bureaucratic royal structures peeled away the autonomy of local magnates and established a more direct administration. The gentry came under tighter control and the area under the sway of appointed provincial officers began to stretch beyond the neighbourhood of garrison towns and into more outlying areas. Within the walls of the royal city, a generation of relentless conquest had produced a cosmopolitan society and a cultural renaissance. Titles became grander and internal differences more marked. Food and entertainment became richer and more varied. A new capital was built and was named Amarapura, 'the Immortal City'. The king of Ava, styling himself 'The Master of the White Elephant' and 'The Lord of All Umbrella-Bearing Chiefs', came to see himself as an equal of the emperor of China and more than an equal of the newly arrived and somewhat inscrutable English governors of India.

But while the territory over which it ruled grew over the years, and while its hold over the villages along the Irrawaddy increased, the basic functions and resources of the Court of Ava remained much as they had been for the previous 200 years or more. The administrative reorganisation which had taken place following the restoration of the Toungoo dynasty had set in place key elements of government. These remained largely unaltered. The principal institutions of the early modern state, such as the Council of State, the Privy Council, the *appanage* system, and provincial governorships date back to this formative period. The restored

Toungoo kings, in turn, probably drew upon their knowledge of earlier royal governments, at Pegu and at Pagan. Burmese administration in the early nineteenth century thus grew out of a long tradition, and the Court of Ava, despite being under a wholly new royal house, approached change conservatively and with a keen and constant eye towards precedence.

Royal government revolved around the exemplary administration of the capital, the supervision of the countryside and the occasional expansion of empire. Supporting the religion, providing for the royal family and the nobility, ensuring domestic tranquility, mobilising men, taxing trade and making war: these were the day-to-day concerns of kings and courts in the early years of the nineteenth century.

The Golden City

In the same way that 'country' in English can mean the rural hinterland or the country as a whole, *pyi* in Burmese could refer to the royal capital or the entire realm. The *Myanma-pyi*, the place of the Burmese, maintained this dual meaning, a sign of the overriding dominance the royal city held over the rest of the surrounding valley. For over two hundred years, the royal city had been located, without interruption, close to the confluence of the Irrawaddy and Chindwin rivers, first at Ava then at Amarapura, an enormous, perfectly square enclosure, with walls over a mile long, surrounded by a wide moat and then by numerous supporting towns and villages. The population of the city and its immediate environs was likely to have been no less than 150,000 people, or as much as a tenth of the population of the entire valley. No other place from Bengal to Bangkok was even a tenth of the size. All roads, by water or by land, led to Ava. The capital was the pre-eminent political, religious, cultural and trading centre and was without rival.

The close, detailed management of the city and its immediate neighbourhood was the first and oldest aim of government. The city contained not only the royal palaces, but also other government buildings and the residences of the nobility and other crown servants. High officials lived in their own, often considerable, residential compounds, complete with slaves and retainers. The city was seen as an example to be followed by other, lesser communities, and its careful regulation was painstakingly overseen. The placing of residences, the style of the buildings, the dress of the inhabitants, the riding of horses and elephants, the size of aristocratic retinues, the colour of personal umbrellas, all were organised and assigned according to rank and precedent. Everyone, depending on their exact place in the hierarchy, had his or her special dress and relative place. In ceremony after ceremony, religious and cultural, no one was ever at a loss as to what to wear or where to sit.[1]

Around the city were the town and various smaller satellite communities. Many, if not most of the population were hereditary crown servants, *ahmudan* units living among their own kind and under their own chiefs: masons, carpenters, tailors, artisans, smiths and other craftsmen as well as soldiers grouped by army regiment. A large number of those in the lower status occupations, as well as slaves and soldiers, were Manipuris, people from the Imphal valley who had been brought as war-captives or were their immediate descendants, and by the mid-nineteenth century they were said to form perhaps as much as a quarter of the population or at least 25,000 people. They were Ava's underclass and nearly all domestic servants and many ordinary workers were from this displaced community.[2]

Many others in the town around the city were Buddhist monks. As Defender of the Faith, the king, as well as the entire ruling class, lavished considerable patronage on the many monasteries which sprang up around the fort. They were the most important monastic schools in the land and many, such as the Bagaya and Parama monasteries, were distinguished by their education of many future kings and ministers. Bright young novices from provincial monasteries came here to complete their studies in the religion, as well as readings in law, history, mathematics and astronomy; often they ended up in the king's service. One in ten people, or one in five men at the capital were monks in the mid-nineteenth century, and the proportion was not likely to have been any less in the past.

There was also a mercantile community, divided mainly along ethnic or religious lines: Chinese, Armenians, Europeans, Muslims and others lived in their separate quarters, the Chinese and Muslim presence being particularly strong. Some of the Chinese were from families which had arrived, indirectly, from the south-eastern coastal provinces of China and who were linked with the wider Chinese trading world of south-east Asia.

[1] See Yule, *Mission*, pp. 150–61 for a detailed description of Amarapura in 1855. For an earlier description of Ava, see Sangermano, *Description*, pp. 82–3. For a description of Mandalay city, see Herbert White, *A Civil Servant in Burma*, London, 1913, p. 120.

[2] Yule, *Mission*, pp. 153–4.

Most however were overland traders, Yunnanese Chinese, including a number of Muslims. In addition to these Yunnan Muslims there was a significant population of other Muslims, as mentioned, immigrants from across south, west and central Asia, together with their descendants.

The government of this extremely heterogeneous mix of people at the very centre of the Ava polity was in the hands of a number of different high officers of state. They included two *myowun*, governors of the town, as well as the four justices of the Eastern Court. The Eastern Court, backed by a constabulary, was responsible for all criminal matters, as well as the even greater responsibility of fire-prevention. As there was an enormous sprawl of wooden, bamboo and thatch buildings across a rain-parched plain, fires were a constant problem and a perennial preoccupation. Shortly after the establishment of the British residency in the late 1820s, for example, one of the first Burmese requests, after a request for English gardeners, was for fire-engines.[3]

The Lord of All Umbrella-Bearing Chiefs

The focal point of the city was the king himself. Known as the *Min Ekarit* the 'Ruler and First Lord' he was the fount of all honours and privileges. Theoretically, all others in the ruling classes, ministers and chiefs, governed in his name. He was always the son of a king through a senior wife who was also a member of the royal clan. His right to the throne was founded first and foremost on his hereditary claim.

The ideology underlying kingly rule, however, stemmed from a system of Indian, especially Indian-Buddhist thought which dealt with the role of government and the organisation of society.[4] Government was viewed as arising through a social contract: the first king (*Maha Thammada* or 'The Great Elected') was described as popularly chosen in order to create a peaceful ordered society conducive to religious activity. The incumbent king held his position, ideally, because his accumulated merit, through many incarnations, made him a 'future Buddha' (*Hpaya laung*) or at least placed him in a more meritorious state than all his subjects. He deserved

---

[3] Burney, 'Population of the Burman Empire', pp. 300–1.

[4] S. J. Tambiah, *World Conqueror and World Renouncer: A Study of Buddhism and Polity in Thailand Against a Historical Background*, Cambridge, 1976, pp. 73–101, esp. pp. 93–4.

his position because of his past good works and was now the leading defender and patron of the religion.

In a second and related myth, the first law-giver (Manu) was said to have been a former minister, who lost his position because of a poor legal judgement, retired to the forest, gained knowledge of an absolute moral law and returned to provide renewed service to the government. The king ruled because he was an upholder of this received moral law, the *dhamma*, and as a 'righteous king' (*dhamma-raza*) governed according to timeless moral precepts. His was not an arbitrary or violent rule, but one which acted through established parameters and in conformity with Buddhist ethical ideals. The great Mauriyan emperor Asoka, who was said to have converted to Buddhism while at the very height of his powers, was seen as the model for all Buddhist rulers to follow.

An important function of the king, as patron of the religion and as a righteous ruler, was to preside over the many and varied spectacles which dominated palace life. The most significant of these were His Majesty's own *abhiseka* consecrations, which could be held at various times throughout his reign, and also grand ceremonies which were held to mark numerous Buddhist and Hindu occasions. Every month offerings were made to Burmese *nat* as well as Hindu gods, among the more important being the offerings made to Ganesh and later to Skanda. Lavish affairs were also organised around the life-ceremonies of members of the royal family. The 'cradling' ceremony for new-born princes and princesses, the ear-boring ceremony for adolescents, and countless royal marriages and funerals were usually attended by the king in person; many occasions involved gifts or the exchange of gifts between the sovereign and his principal subjects.

Enveloped in a world of queens, chamberlains and Officers of the Guard, the daily routine of the reigning monarch was theoretically subject to detailed regulation. Ostensibly, the king's daily schedule was a carefully constructed affair, as set down by age-old precedent. According to one source, the day began fairly prosaically at 5.30 a.m., when his majesty awoke, listened to the news, washed and shaved. He then granted a brief audience to his queens who came to pay their respects, dealt with some official business at eight, and ate his morning meal. In the late morning, he met with members of the royal family and then retired to the library to read learned works. At one, he attended a meeting of his senior generals, then his Privy Council, followed by a midday meal at four, more meetings and a general conference of all his ministers at six. Only then did the king return to his private apartments.[5]

In fact, the life of a Burmese king was often much less circumscribed. Tharrawaddy for one was extremely fond of billiards, becoming practically addicted to the game, and apparently threw traditional scheduling to the wind. Captain William McLeod, a member of the British Residency at the time, wrote:

> His Majesty was yesterday from 12 to 5 playing at billiards. He afterwards regaled his friends with a dinner in the Billiard Room. A chest of beer was ordered to be produced, but the Royal Steward reported that the Princes had drained His Majesty's cellar. The Ministers are sometimes vexed at his Majesty's frivolous amusements.[6]

While perhaps Tharrawaddy's fondness for beer and billiards was unusual for a Konbaung monarch, his predilection for somewhat unkingly amusements illustrates the substantial gap which must have existed between the theory of kingship found in Burmese texts of the period and the more sobering reality. Certainly there were great differences between the kings themselves in how they used their positions and employed their time. The early kings of the previous dynasty, up to Singu, were great generals. Alaungpaya had conquered his kingdom by force of arms, and his elder sons, Naungdawgyi and Hsinbyushin, followed in the martial tradition, personally leading their men into war. Singu himself disliked war but liked hunting, though one suspects more for the post-hunting entertainment. Bodawpaya, though an imperial expansionist, never took to the battlefield himself and as king preferred to concentrate on matters of religion. For years he personally supervised the construction of what would have been the largest pagoda in the world at Mingun and also directed the building of smaller pagodas in 230 towns and villages around the country.[7] In strong contrast his successor Bagyidaw was known for having no interest in Buddhism at all. Instead, he spent most of his time on horseback, enjoying the vogue in polo-playing and other equestrian sports which had swept the court, and feeding his favourite horses himself.

What all the kings of Ava had in common, however, right up to Thibaw

[5] Ba U, *Myanme Okchokyay Pyinnya*, Mandalay, n.d., pp. 64–5.
[6] Secret Correspondence with India, India Secret Consultations, vol. 20, McLeod's Journal, p. 1614.
[7] *KBZ*, vol. II, pp. 102–4; Hall, *History of Southeast Asia*, p. 627; Koenig, *Burmese Polity*, 81.

who was the stark exception, was that they had, and spent much of their day with, their many wives. Fathering a bewildering number of children, often over a hundred, was an unwritten task of the Burmese monarch, and, by the mid-nineteenth century, the House of Alaungpaya, the royal *myo*, was a small society in itself.

The last royal family

By the ascension of King Mindon to the Konbaung throne in 1853, the descendants of Alaungpaya numbered in the hundreds, if not thousands. The founder himself had fathered at least six sons by two wives. Three of his sons, Naungdawgyi, Hsinbyushin and Bodawpaya, one of his grandsons, Singu, two of his great-grandsons, Bagyidaw and Tharrawaddy, and two of his great-great-grandsons, Pagan and Mindon, would follow him as king. Thibaw was a fifth-generation descendant of Alaungpaya. Many of these and other descendants were extremely procreative, each with dozens of, if not over a hundred, offspring. The men were allowed to take many wives, and many did, and widows were allowed to remarry. The royal house might have populated an entire city within a hundred years if it had not been for two attenuating factors: the extremely high rates of infant and child mortality and the occasional fratricide which led to entire lineages being exterminated. Well over half of Alaungpaya's descendants who can be traced died in infancy and childhood, most likely from smallpox and other unchecked diseases.[8] Singu and all his descendants were killed when he was overthrown and this sort of royal blood-letting continued irregularly up until the infamous massacres of 1789 when eighty-three princes and princesses were executed.

The family itself, until they provided the kingdom's Lords of the White Elephant, were of relatively modest origins. They traced their ancestry back to cavalry officers who had been given land north of Ava in return for service in the fifteenth century. Their particular lineage held the office of *kyedaing* in Moksobo, a *kyedaing* being a village official considerably beneath a *myothugyi* in rank.

Nonetheless, in their home territory the Moksobo family had been very much part of the local ruling class. As the lord of his village, Alaungpaya, then titled Bala Nanda Kyaw, was closely related to gentry families

[8] Arthur Phayre, 'A Historical Memorandum on the Burma Hunters Family from Beginning to the Present 1866 AD', British Library, Oriental Manuscript, OR 3470.

throughout the Konbaung region and these allied families had provided him the support he desperately needed during his initial campaigns. The early marital ties of the new royal house continued to be with these local gentry, as well as with selected high official lineages from Ava, and with members of the old dynasty. Their closest marital allies were the family of Min Thiri of Yandaza, whose formidable clan provided wives for three generations of Konbaung princes. By the early nineteenth century, the dominant pattern had changed, and the royal house had become fairly endogamous. Kings themselves made strategic partnerships with a number of noble and tributary families, and the minor royals did as they chose. But the upper-level princes and princesses married each other, almost without exception.

Like all other groups at the Court of Ava, the royal family was carefully ranked. Princes, sons and grandsons of the reigning monarch, were divided into nine major grades and many more lesser grades. They enjoyed the style *mintha*, and were alone in having the title *minyè* as part of their name. The grander princes, like their royal father, were also styled *dhamma-raza*, 'righteous king'. They could expect a share of a town's income as their *appanage* and were granted lavish sumptuary rights, including the rights to ride an elephant and have a golden umbrella held over their heads. They were sometimes called into the business of government, but more often were idle or were plotting to ensure that they were not among the next victims of a princely purge.

Equivalent in power and influence, if not in formal rank, to the princes were the king's women. A sizeable progeny was an important royal goal and much kingly energy was apparently devoted to this aim. The women were ranked, generally by background, with the most senior positions being taken by daughters of the previous monarch, that is the king's half-sisters. They were one of the four to six 'chief queens' and were known as the queen (*mibaya*) of one of the several palaces. Next were the junior queens, known as the queens of one of the various royal apartments. There then normally followed a host of other lesser wives and concubines. These were other members of the royal family, daughters of noblemen, generally grandees of the court, as well as daughters of important members of the gentry. Daughters of tributary princes were also well represented. They were known as the *thami-kanya*. The concubines of the early Konbaung kings included the daughters of many Shan *sawbwa* as well as real and fictitious princesses from distant lands. Together they formed the 'Western Court', with their own elaborate rules and regulations. Middle-ranking male officials assisted the senior queens in the orderly running of this society. There were also officials, who may have been eunuchs, known as *mainma-so*, or 'superintendent of the women'.[9]

Below the princes were other male members of the royal family, descendants of Alaungpaya removed from the dominant line. Most if not all, together with their immediate families, were placed into *thwé-thauk*, which were palace-based associations which grouped together men of similar rank and descent. The most important were associations known as The Royal Forty or The Royal Fifty. Like all such groupings in Ava, they were methods of keeping track of people, keeping them from causing trouble, and keeping them on standby in case of need. The extended royal clan, as a whole, was placed under the authority of a minor prince known as the *swaydaw-ok*, the 'supervisor of the royal clan'. Images of dead kings and queens were kept at the *Zetawun-saung*, the 'Hall of Ancestors', and obeisance ceremonies, led by the reigning monarch and attended by the entire Konbaung family, were held three times a year.[10]

After a few generations, some of these members of the extended family lapsed into obscurity. Others, however, gained high office as ministers and noblemen in their own right. A good example was Maung Shwé Tha, a grandson of Alaungpaya through his minor son the Prince of Malun. Born in the 1780s, he was eventually appointed to a number of high-level positions and was granted his father's old *appanage* of Malun, as its *myoza*. Though holding an official rank equal to other court grandees of non-royal birth, his style, Thado Minyè Raza, indicated his connection to the Konbaung house, *Minyè*, as mentioned, being a title reserved for princes of the blood. He eventually was made a senior minister, or *wungyi*, and was the first *wungyi* to be posted in Rangoon, just after the end of the First Anglo-Burmese War, as part of Bagyidaw's abortive attempt to handle his relations with the British away from the capital.[11] Too distant from the main line to be a contender for the throne, he made his name as a minister rather than as a prince.

The immediate royal family lived a lavish lifestyle and were provided ample income by the reigning monarch through the *appanage* system. All

[9] *ROB*, 24 October 1808.
[10] Aung-Thwin, *Pagan: Origins of Modern Burma*, pp. 52–3.
[11] Hmawbi Saya Thein, *Wungyi Hmugyi*, p. 151.

queens, many other wives and concubines of the king, and all princes and princesses above a certain age were granted a town, village or other locality as a source of income. In part because of the great length of Konbaung titles, royals (and noblemen) were commonly known by these *appanages*, for example as the Myoza of Syriam or the Prince of Prome. The Salin princess, at her 'cradling ceremony' (*pahket-mingala*) in 1853, was granted the towns of Mohkaing, Thonzè and Alon as her *appanages*. She was also given other landed estates south of the capital, a personal barge, two baby elephants, two adult female elephants, thirty oxen, a host of personal retainers and a select group of 'royal playmates' (*kasataw*), chosen from among the children of blue-blooded nobles.[12]

Though royals no longer resided in their appointed *appanages*, in many cases they clearly continued to take a strong interest in the affairs of their towns and villages. To a large extent, this interest was related solely to income, but in some cases involvement by members of the royal family in local administration remained. For example, in 1807, a daughter of Bodawpaya who had been granted the town of Kyaukmaw as her *appanage* applied successfully to the Hluttaw for permission for the local hereditary chief, the Myothugyi of Kyaukmaw, to be given extraordinary powers to deal with crime. Specifically, she asked that the chief, Wuttana Zeyya, be permitted to govern the township alone, without interference from centrally appointed officials, in order that he might take severe measures to combat banditry in the area. Leaving aside what those measures actually were and why he needed special powers, this case demonstrates the special relationship which often developed between the *appanage* holder and the people, especially the ruling class, of that community.[13]

A second and perhaps equally important source of income was money-lending. As *appanage* holders, members of the royal family accumulated silver which they could then lend out, through bankers, to the cash-starved population. The king himself was also involved in the business of money-lending, occasionally extending cash loans, for example, to his tributary Shan chieftains.[14] As relatively cash-rich members of society, others in the Konbaung family probably followed this lead and endeavoured to profit from financial dealings themselves. Special officers were appointed to look after their money-lending businesses. For example, one

[12] *KBZ*, vol. II, p. 174.   [13] *ROB*, 13 November 1807.
[14] Toe Hla, 'Moneylending and Contractual Thet-kayits', p. 133.

such official, Kyawhtin Nanda Sithu, handled all financial affairs for the Kutywa, Nyaungyan and other princes at the turn of the century.[15]

In addition to private bankers, such as Kyawhtin Nanda Sithu, princes and princesses maintained large personal courts. Many of these courts were staffed with officials and servants who belonged to a class of people known as the *kyundaw-yin*, hereditary royal retainers. *Kyundaw* literally means 'royal slave' and all the king's subjects were often referred to in this way. But the *kyundaw-yin*, the 'close royal slaves' were members of lineages which had personally served the Alaungpaya family since their capture of Ava, or perhaps even before as servants of the family at Moksobo. They were the trusted, close aides of the family. Over the years, they produced a number of illustrious officials. Possibly the greatest *kyundaw-yin* lineage was that of the Myoza of Syriam.

Maung Kyaw Hlaing had been born a hereditary retainer to the royal family around the turn of the century. Both his parents had been servants in the private court of Bodawpaya when the latter was still a prince and he had grown up with many of the royal children. After a spell at a local monastic school, he followed an exemplary official career successively serving as the Chief of the State Palanquin Bearers, Captain of the Kaunghan Guards, Commander of the Left Household Brigade, Senior Minister of the Hluttaw, Governor of Toungoo, Governor of Bassein, Privy Councillor, and finally Master of the Royal Granaries. Through much of his later career he had also been Myoza of Syriam and enjoyed a portion of the income from that port.

With his rise to power, he was able to secure for both his sister and his daughter the position of lesser queens with their own *appanage*s. His daughter held Meiktila as one of her *appanage*s, and his brother-in-law was appointed the town governor, ensuring their hold over the town. Among his own brothers, the most eminent was his younger brother Maung Kyaw Shwé, who eventually also became a senior minister, only to be killed at Rangoon during the English War. Other brothers held a variety of army posts. The Syriam family continued to enjoy important places in the Court of Ava for at least another two generations, the daughter of Maung Kyaw Shwé, for example, becoming the Myèdu Queen in the 1830s.[16] When this man, born a royal servant, died, he was allowed

---

[15] *Ibid.*, p. 129.   [16] Hmawbi Saya Thein, *Wungyi Hmugyi*, p. 150.

the funeral of royalty itself, with a white umbrella held over his palanquin *en route* to his cremation.[17]

The royal household

Hereditary royal retainers also dominated the 'royal suite'. The royal suite consisted of a large number of *aides-de-camp*, equerries, pages and chamberlains. In the mid-nineteenth century, this inner group of royal retainers numbered over a thousand.[18] They protected the king's person and attended to his daily needs. Those who were not hereditary retainers were the sons of noblemen or tributary princes, most of whom were enlisted into the royal suite at an early age, as part of their entrée into the world of the palace. Just beyond these closest servants were the rest of the royal household, which included a vast army of *ahmudan*, hereditary cooks, cleaners, tailors, dancers, musicians and others who provided their specialised skills.

While the protection of the king was the responsibility of his personal bodyguard, the protection of the city as a whole was placed under the charge of the Household Division. This was the core of the king's armed force and was headed by two brigade commanders, or *windaw-hmu*. Heading the 'inner' and 'outer' brigades, they each commanded six Guards regiments, the composition of which changed slightly over time. They were in charge of all movement in and out of the city. The commanders and their musketeers provided the bulwark against any possible insurrection or princely coup.

Other denizens of the inner courts included the *ponna*, the primary court ritualists, about whom much more will be said in the next chapter. Assisting the king in very different matters were the *thuhtay*, the royal bankers, who aided the king in his financial dealings and who acted as intermediaries between the privy treasury and the world of trade. The royal household as a whole was under the charge of four trusted Privy Councillors, or *atwinwun*, as will be described below.

The early Konbaung kings were thus surrounded by a mixed world of hereditary family retainers, officers of the Guard, queens and princesses, ritualists and the occasional favourite monk. Many also chose to keep close foreign friends. Bagyidaw, for example, was said to have been very

[17] *Ibid.*   [18] *KBZ*, vol. II, p. 161.

fond of a Spaniard known as Don Gonzales de Lanciego. Educated in Paris, this man had been shipwrecked in Rangoon where he settled and married the daughter of the Rangoon port-master Joseph Xavier de Cruz. De Cruz, himself of Portuguese descent, had long been in royal service and was the father of Bagyidaw's wife the Danubyu Queen. Lanciego married de Cruz's other daughter and was thus closely related to the king by marriage. Though he was temporarily imprisoned during the 1824–6 war, he later regained Bagyidaw's trust and became Collector of Customs.[19] A generation before, the Frenchman Pierre de Millard, erstwhile Myoza of Tabè and Captain of the Royal Artillery, had been a companion to a succession of early Konbaung kings.

The royal agencies

Government was increasingly an affair between the reigning monarch and his ministers and not a shared family responsibility. Princes in the past had held high office, at Ava or as important regional governors, but by the early nineteenth century, while the influence of senior queens remained considerable, male members of the immediate royal house seldom held administrative positions. Instead, power shifted between kings and grandees depending upon the character and circumstances of the king and his interest or willingness to involve himself in day-to-day government. The grandees themselves, the senior ministers and generals of the court, formed a political elite, enjoying great privilege and authority. Often related to the royal family by marriage, they and other lesser office-holders at Ava constituted the noble class (*amat-myo*), an inter-related and somewhat closed social grouping which stood between the House of Alaungpaya above and the gentry and common people below.

The most important of these office-holders were the four *wungyi*, literally the 'Great Burden Bearers' of the realm. Always four in number, to represent each of the four cardinal directions, they each held no particular portfolio but instead shared joint responsibility for all affairs concerning the kingdom's administration. The *wungyi* were thus the senior ministers of the king and enjoyed a status below only His Majesty himself and the higher-ranking princes. Collectively, they chaired the Hluttaw, literally the 'Royal Place of Release', the place

[19] R.B. Pemberton, 'Journey from Munipoor to Ava, and from Thence Across the Yooma Mountains to Arraccan', *JBRS*, 43 (1960), 98–103.

where royal orders to servants and subjects were formulated and from which they were sent. The Hluttaw is often referred to as the 'Council of State'.

These senior ministers of the early Konbaung dynasty were often men of considerably literary and scholarly accomplishment, and the tumultuous but highly productive career of U Paw U illustrates the multifaceted world of the highest court grandees. Unlike many other senior officials, he had been born into an undistinguished local family in the small village of Tasè near Myèdu. After a very successful monastic education, he became an expert in the Buddhist Tripitika as well as the Vedas and Burmese law, joining Bodawpaya's court, and rising to become a Privy Councillor and the Myoza of Yaw. He was later stripped of his office and titles for opposing the expenditure of 800,000 rupees on precious stones for the king's great-grandson and exiled to the Shan state of Theini, close to the Chinese border, spending his time there writing the series of poems for which he is renowned. In one of these poems, he argues that money from taxation should only be used in the interests of the country as a whole and not for war and extravagant expenditure. The king, hearing the poem read, then recalled him to royal service. Under Bodawpaya's grandson and successor Bagyidaw, Paw U finally became a *wungyi* as well as Minister for War. He lived to see defeat in the first English war and died at the end of the Burmese century, in 1838, aged 84.[20]

The balancing organ of the Hluttaw was the Byèdaik. The word is Mon, literally meaning the 'Bachelor Chambers', and is often translated as the 'Privy Council'. Its function was to serve as a gateway between the king and the Hluttaw, and between the king and all other royal agencies, handling the inner affairs of the royal court, while the Hluttaw handled the government of the country. The four heads of the Byèdaik were called *atwinwun*, literally 'Inner Minister'. The word is also translated as 'Privy Councillor'. While the *wungyi* and other ministers often came up through the official ranks, these Privy Councillors were usually intimates of the reigning monarch, members of his private princely establishment who followed his rise to the throne.

Below this highest level of officialdom – *wungyi* and *atwinwun* – were a multitude of other grandees who ran departments and headed crown service groups, such as the *athi wun*, the minister in charge of corvée

---

[20] Hmawbi Saya Thein, *Sasodawmya*, Rangoon, 1967, pp. 313–17.

labour and mass mobilisation for war, and the *myinsu-gyi wun*, the 'Chief of the Main Cavalry Regiments', the highest regular army position.

Another step down were a host of other high-ranked noblemen. They included the important *shwedaik wun*, the privy treasurer, who was in charge not only of treasure in precious metals, but also of treasure in information; he was the palace's chief archivist who kept accounts of all noble and gentry family genealogies and census reports. Among others were the four *wundauk*, deputies to the four *wungyi*, who assisted them in the running of the Council of State. Rounding out the upper echelon were four 'justices' (*taya-thugyi*) of the Eastern Court, who dealt with all law-and-order matters for the royal city. All these men wore elaborate costumes with high peaked or conical hats, enjoyed the style *mingyi*, or 'great lord', and were followed though the streets of Ava by a considerable retinue dressed in distinctive white coats. A golden umbrella, an emblem of upper nobility, was held over their heads.

Many middle-level officials dealt primarily with information. They were known by a variety of titles, but most included the words 'royal voice' (*thandaw*) or 'royal ear' (*nahkandaw*). They acted as intermediaries between state organs as well as between the king and his ministers. They collected, sorted and interpreted reports, read proclamations at official gatherings and transmitted orders to provincial courts.[21] A formal intelligence establishment also provided the court with information from within the city and from the countryside. Those who openly provided the king and ministers with information about goings on in and around the royal city included a number of former monks. Others were selected from among the fairly large group of palace stewards (*asaungdaw-myè*), including at least one who was sent as a spy to India at the turn of the century. Secret agents included monks, nuns, court officials and members of the royal family, in particular women members. Masseurs were also prized as spies, presumably because they often found themselves privy to indiscreet conversation.[22]

The middle ranks of the court were also held by a multitude of writers or secretaries, known as *sayay*. The Hluttaw establishment included dozens of secretaries of different grades, headed by chief secretaries, or *sayay-gyi*. Others of middling rank included the numerous crown service heads. Many of these held military office, as the captains and colonels of

---

[21] *MMOS*, vol. IV, pp. 7–8.   [22] *Ibid.*, vol. III, pp. 76–7.

various regiments. Others were head of 'soft' groups (*asu-nu*) such as the Chief of the Royal Tailors, the Master of the Glassworks, or Head of the Royal Cooks. The rank and file of these groups, military and civil, provided the ordinary working class of the royal city. Serving on a rotating basis, they ate, slept and worked in their cells, and then, after a period, returned to their home villages, cultivating the land that was their right as crown servants, their places at Ava taken over by near relatives.

Methods of recruitment varied and were never completely systematised. Generally, a person assumed office through an hereditary claim or after a long period of apprenticeship. The other possibility, of a direct appointment without an apprenticeship, was said to be very rare.[23] Occasionally, a son might inherit his father's office as well as his *appanage*, but he would almost always have already been in government service.[24] Connections made through an *appanage* holder were also important in obtaining appointments. For example, one of Bagyidaw's senior ministers, born Maung Ta, was not of a noble family and had been born in the fairly remote though important town of Taungdwingyi. When the wife of one of the king's sons had held Taungdwingyi as an *appanage*, he had been selected to serve the princess at Ava, as a member of her private establishment. He then worked his way up and out of the princess's court and into mainstream royal government.[25] In general, the lower the rank of the office, the more important the hereditary principle. Senior ministers and other high officials were all appointed by the reigning monarch and though he might take family background into consideration, other factors such as competence and loyalty were likely to be much more important. Lesser officials, however, could often count on their family backgrounds and connections to secure them posts, similar to their fathers, in due time.

The Burmese nobility

The exemplary nobleman of the early Konbaung dynasty was the Myoza of Myawaddy, also known by his personal name, Maung Sa. His father had been an officer of the Household Cavalry and he was from the town of Alon, an important recruiting ground for Konbaung soldiers. His mother was from an older and grander Ava lineage which traced its descent from Bannya Kyandaw, a minister of King Thalun in the early seventeenth

---

[23] Ba U, *Myanma Okchokyay Pyinnya*, pp. 107–8.   [24] *ROB*, 22 July 1824.
[25] Hmawbi Saya Thein, *Wungyi Hmugyi*, p. 51.

century. Maung Sa was schooled at the Parama monastery near Ava, later marrying within the Ava aristocracy to Mè Aye, the daughter of a retired minister of state. He was first noticed by the future king, Bagyidaw, when, while still crown prince, he was bringing together a circle of innovative young artists in his private court and when Maung Sa was already gaining a name as an accomplished musician.

He soon rose quickly through court offices but became much more famous for his great works of music and drama, especially his translations of the Javanese epic *Enao* from Thai and his many songs influenced by the Ayuthaya style. As an official, he had been a financial secretary to the crown prince and later followed him into the main palace establishment as a minister, gaining the noble style Thiri Maha Zeyya Thura and being granted the town of Myawaddy as his *appanage*. But like many Konbaung officials, he was also a soldier, commanding four companies in the Manipur campaign of 1813, and serving as the 'Commander of the Left' in the first English war under Thado Maha Bandula on the Arakan border. After the war he was raised to the rank of *wungyi*, but unwisely became involved in the machinations surrounding Bagyidaw's final days, was sentenced to death for treason, and then was granted a royal reprieve just before his execution. He continued to compose music and poetry and he lived just long enough to see the British annexation of Rangoon in 1853, dying later that year, aged 92.[26]

The career of the Myoza of Myawaddy was exemplary in several respects. The first was that he was of noble birth. The Burmese nobility was an office-holding nobility in that noble status depended, in one way, upon crown recognition. This in turn was granted, with very few exceptions, to those men who held royal office. They would then be given a fitting title and a *salway*, the principal marks of noble (*amat*) status, the latter being a collection of silk cords which was worn around the person's outer coat. The office, title and *salway* could all be revoked upon order of the king, and this did on occasion take place. With the gentry, and with the tributary princes, crown recognition of office and its accompanying marks were, to a much greater extent, a mere formality; members of the nobility were much more dependent upon active crown support.

But nobility at the Court of Ava also had a much broader and no less important meaning. Within the Indian-inspired fourfold social division,

---

[26] *Ibid.*, p. 155.

nobles would be grouped into the ruling *min-myo*. But they also made up part of their own *amat-myo* sub-division, separate from royalty and the gentry. A person could be raised to this sub-division or class. If a man, born of a lower order, achieved a position in a royal agency, he would be ennobled and would be seen as a full member of the *amat-myo*. But a person born of noble parents, or a son born of a noble father, was a noble by birth. Unless, for some reason, the crown ordered him to be reduced to a lower status, he would enjoy the legal position of being a nobleman regardless of whether or not he eventually held office.

In fact, nearly all office-holders were members of this more broadly defined noble class, that is they were noblemen (and women) by birth. This is similar to the way in which office-holding rural chiefs were members of the broader gentry class. The only difference was the degree to which the hereditary principle was important. For rural chiefs, the prime qualification was being of the local chiefly lineage. At Ava, being of a noble lineage was only one of several factors taken into account. The civil war of the 1750s and the fall of Ava to Pegu had devastated the old noble class. Alaungpaya's seizure of power through force of arms, and without any substantial help from the old nobility, led to an influx of many outsiders, self-made men, into the restored Ava court. A few of the officials in the very early years of the Konbaung dynasty were holdovers from the last. The Ywaza of Inyon, for example, the author of the *Lawka Byuha Kyan*, was kept on as an advisor on administrative practices by Alaungpaya, having been a minister in the old regime.[27]

Certainly by the 1820s the nobility had re-emerged as a distinct class in local society. This was done in part through increasingly endogamous marriage practices which came to link much of the ruling class by blood. While there was no formal bar to non-nobles attaining office, the key mechanisms of selection made sure that commoners would find entrance into palace service very difficult. This is another way in which the Myoza of Myawaddy's career was exemplary. He had started his career as a royal page, a sort of apprenticeship only open to members of the nobility. This was a training ground for future office-holders and was entirely restricted to sons of families already in palace circles. These were early ties which lasted a lifetime. In a major land dispute in 1826 between the Sawbwa of Kalay and the Teinnyin Town Officer, for example, both had used the

27   *Ibid.*, p. 145.

palace connections they had made as royal pages to try to influence the arbitration.[28]

Office-holding noblemen were allocated among a hierarchy of grades.[29] A royal order of 1826, for example, lists a total of 132 senior officials, sorted into their different grades, attending the king's coronation.[30] The most important divisions were reflected in what was known as the individual's place or *naya*, a reference to his seating position at a royal audience. Places were grouped into *taw, du, atwin, pyin bawaw* and *sanee naya*, with each *naya* coming with its own sumptuary privileges and funeral rights.[31] More generally, all office-holders were classed as 'senior' (*pyadan-gyi*) or 'ordinary' (*pyadan-yo*). Grades were also reflected in names.

Except for the king's closest intimates, members of the nobility, once they had received their coveted titles, were never referred to by their old personal names. Indeed, the first title received by a newly ennobled official was known as his *ngè-mi hpyout bwè*, literally meaning 'the title which does away with his name in youth'. Replacing one's personal name with a royally granted style was only the first step in a very carefully designed ladder of titles which marked each person's exact position within the Court of Ava. The simplest way to determine a nobleman's relative position was the length of this title, the longer being the better. In general, a core title, such as Thinhkaya, was maintained throughout, and a series of additional titles, in Pali or mixed Burmese and Pali were added on, each addition being accompanied by a ceremony, sometimes attended by the king himself, in which the official was presented with his new name inscribed on a sheet of gold. After having achieving a simple title, the next highest title was a title containing the name 'Shweidaung', followed in turn by ones containing the names 'Nawrahta', 'Naymyo', 'Naymyo Min', 'Min' (without the 'Naymyo'), 'Maha', 'Mingyi', 'Thado', 'Thettawshay' and finally 'Thudamma'. These titles do not, taken together, have any definite meaning. Each of the words does have a meaning, 'Naymyo' for example meaning 'of the race of the sun' in Burmese and 'Maha' meaning 'great' in Pali.[32]

[28] Toe Hla, 'Moneylending and Contractual Thet-kayits', pp. 232–3.
[29] *ROB*, 8 March 1826.   [30] *Ibid.*, 8 August 1826.
[31] For the earliest reference to these divisions, which apparently changed little over more than two hundred years, see *ibid.*, 26 September 1605.
[32] Ba U, *Myanma Okchokyay Pyinnya*, pp. 110–11.

This elaborate and precise hierarchy of titles did not achieve its final form until well into the nineteenth century. In the early and mid-eighteenth century noble titles were very different. Late Toungoo ministers were styled Nanda Thuriya or Maha Tarbya.[33] By the mid-nineteenth century, there were eleven very specific grades of titles. In fact, it was probably immediately after the First Anglo-Burmese War that the system described above became fully fixed. If we look at a list of Bodawpaya's ministers around the turn of the century, for example, we find that many are still styled 'Naymyo', a very middling title in a later period when every single minister enjoyed the much grander 'Mingyi' or 'Great Lord' as part of his name.[34] The wives of noblemen also had their own parallel places in court society. The wife of a high official was known as his *kadaw*. The wife of a more junior official or other titled person was known as his *maya*.[35]

All of these are assigned ranks, the assignments depending upon royal favour and the day-to-day politics of the court. A more subtle hierarchy, however, existed alongside, one which prized ancient noble lineages over the shallow lineages of relative newcomers to Ava.[36] The origins of noble families were varied. By late in the Konbaung period, and perhaps late in the previous dynasty as well, many were actually minor royal lineages, descendants of sons by concubines. Many were descendants of the former ruling families of Prome, Toungoo, Martaban, Tavoy and other principalities which were now under royal administration.[37] After losing their family seats to royal appointees, they were organised into elite crown service groups which merged into palace society.[38] Others were descendants of captive royalty. The blood of the Ayuthaya, Pegu, Arakan, Chiang Mai and other royal lines was often claimed by Burmese aristocrats in the later Konbaung period. One of the last Burmese noblewomen, for example, the Htayanga Princess, wife of the Pyimina Prince, both of whom lived until the 1950s, was a direct descendant of the last kings of Ayuthaya.[39]

The income position of the nobility was very similar to that of the royal family. The most important source of income was the *appanages* granted by the king. At the upper end of the nobility, these *appanages* were entire

[33] Inyon, The Ywa of (Thiri Uzana), *Lawka Byuha Kyan*, Rangoon, 1968, pp. 200–15; also see lists in *Lawka Byuha Kyan*, pp. 200–15.

[34] Hmawbi Saya Thein, *Wungyi Hmugyi*, p. 152.   [35] *ROB*, 26 April 1838.

[36] *MMOS*, vol. II, p. 147.   [37] *ROB*, 2 June 1679.

[38] See *ibid.*, on the creation of these service groups.

[39] Damrong Rajanubhab, *Journey Through Burma in 1936*, Bangkok, 1991, p. 129.

townships or villages. But they could also be tollgates, markets or small landed estates. There appears to have been no set system for choosing *appanages*. A particular town, for example, did not automatically become the *appanage* of a person holding a particular office. In general, it is possible that the crown attempted to limit the ability of families to develop powerful local bases of support by constantly rotating *appanages*, and selecting an *appanage* away from a nobleman's actual home area. But this was certainly not always the case. In at least one case, a son inheriting his father's middle-ranking position at court, was allowed to inherit his *appanages* as well.[40] The nobility were also heavily involved in finance, in much the same way as their gentry and royal cousins, and in partnership with the great bankers of the court.[41] As a result of these formal as well as informal sources of income, many of the great men of the court were, by any standard, very rich. The Myoza of Bassein, for example, was said to be able to expect 100 viss of silver a year from his *appanage*, in the early nineteenth century worth 15,000 rupees.[42] In the mid-nineteenth century, the estate of the Myoza of Magwé was worth no less than 1.2 million rupees in silver. When compared with average wages later in the century of a few hundred rupees a year, these were princely sums.

Monks and bankers

Ava and Amarapura were not only the centre of secular power, but also the centre of Burmese Buddhism. The Burmese Community of Monks, or the Myanma Bhikku Sangha, organised around varying degrees of allegiance to the texts of the Singhala orthodoxy, was headquartered outside the king's city in the great monastic colleges which were examples for the thousands of village *kyaung* scattered throughout the realm. The overall head was called the Thathanabaing, a fairly new office, the establishment of which accompanied the rise of neo-Singhalese Buddhism. The word means 'Controller of the Religion' and the office was a royal appointment which ended at the end of a royal reign.

Provincial heads were known as *gaing-ok* and local heads as *gaing-gyok*. The *thathanabaing* and leading members of the royal monasteries near the capital were expected to maintain discipline throughout the

[40] *ROB*, 22 July 1824.
[41] Toe Hla, 'Moneylending and Contractual Thet-kayits', pp. 133–6.
[42] *MMOS*, vol. IV, p. 202.

Sangha and often enjoyed a close relationship with the king and his ministers.[43] Monks who were advisors of the king were styled *sayadaw* or 'royal teacher', though by the mid-nineteenth century this had become a title applied to almost any distinguished monk. Several lay officers assisted the Thathanabaing and the Sangha leadership in their administration of glebe lands and their relations with secular authority.[44] Various kings in the nineteenth century tried different policies, all wishing in some way to support religious activity and encourage monastic organisation and discipline while also being wary of permitting too strong an alternative structure to the state.[45]

The other titled group at court which enjoyed high status were the royal bankers, the *thuhtay*. The formal office of *thuhtay* was a royal appointment. In the mid-nineteenth century there were approximately a dozen *thuhtay* and the same number of *thugywè*, a similar but lesser designation. Many acted as personal brokers (*pwèza*) for the king and more generally as financial middlemen between the cash-rich court and the agrarian countryside.[46] This was, at times, an ephemeral designation, and not a lifelong contract. One unfortunate merchant, for example, who had lost his position after several years, tried to regain the status of *thuhtay* through a series of bribes. He was found out and executed, leaving behind a sizeable estate of 40,000 rupees.[47] Others were much luckier and died in office. On these occasions, the position, title and relationship to the crown sometimes passed on together to his heir, as in 1847, when the son of the prominent *thuhtay* Thiri Thuhka Anadabain inherited his father's place and style as well as all his property.[48] The weightiness attached to this office, to the position of the banking elite, was represented most clearly in royal consecration ceremonies, when a selection of bankers and their daughters played key ritual roles.[49] Noblemen connected the king to gentry, and monks to the village monasteries. But bankers made the king rich and ensured that he was, besides all other things, the chief financier in his realm.

[43] Donald E. Smith, *Religion and Politics in Burma*, Princeton, 1965, pp. 3–31.
[44] *GUBSS*, vol. II, p. 10, *passim*.
[45] E.M. Mendelson, *Sangha and State in Burma: A Study of Monastic Sectarianism and Leadership*, Ithaca, 1975, p. 84.   [46] *ROB*, 11 November 1854.
[47] Cox, *Journal*, pp. 341–3.   [48] *ROB*, 20 April 1847.
[49] See for example, *KBZ*, vol. III, pp. 399–400.

Governing the countryside

The rulers of Ava drew a firm distinction between *pyi-yay*, the 'business of the capital' and *ywa-hmu* 'the affairs of the villages'. While the business of the capital was the business of the king and his ministers, the affairs of the villages called for only occasional attention. Many royal edicts, with an air of finality, simply called on the people of the countryside to live in peace and prosperity under their hereditary chiefs. While strengthening the capacity of royal governors to intervene in village life, the aim was still for intervention to be unnecessary: men, rice and silver were to be sent according to customary arrangements and the gentry left to keep order amongst themselves. Ava would concentrate on making the capital grander still and on enlarging the boundaries of empire. There was certainly an understanding as to the limits of the royal courts' ability to directly administer even the lowlands. While outright rebellion could easily be crushed and dacoity kept within bounds, not all problems of governance could be dealt with by decree. A recurrent directive to newly appointed ministers was to 'make large issues small and small issues disappear', a clear appreciation of the limits of the early modern state. As we have seen, the detailed management of the capital city itself was the clear responsibility of royal government. But as distance from the capital and from the Irrawaddy grew, so did any pretence at day-to-day administration.

Beyond the immediate environs of Ava, the Irrawaddy valley was divided into several dozen provinces and each was headed by a governor.[50] These governors were known as *myowun*, literally meaning 'minister-in-charge of the town'. Their tenures never lasted very long, as they were men of quite senior rank in court who would soon retire or be promoted to the very top echelon of royal service. A number of senior ministers such as Thado Maha Bandula and the Kinwun Mingyi spent time as provincial governors before moving on to the Hluttaw.

Newly appointed *myowun* were often allowed to appoint a completely new set of provincial officers to serve as their local court.[51] This included the *sitkè*, the commander of the local army garrison, as well as revenue officers, the provincial treasurer and clerks. More elaborate provincial courts included those of the port towns such as Rangoon, where the local governor would be aided by the *shah-bandar*, the port commissioner, as

---

[50] *MMOS*, vol. IV, pp. 109–16.   [51] *ROB*, 15 March 1807.

well as several customs officers. All of the *myowun* supervised the local hereditary elite. The area under a governor's charge would normally overlap with the jurisdictions of several *myothugyi* and dozens of other gentry office-holders. The *myowun's* court, the *myo-yon*, was thus the point of interface between the irregular and varied forms of rural government, and a systematising royal administration.

Beyond the main riverways and into the surrounding hills, even nominal jurisdiction passed from the hands of these court officials and into the hands of tributary princes, the *sawbwa*. The word *sawbwa* is derived from the Shan *saohpa* meaning 'lord of the sky' but it became a generic Burmese term for all tributaries and was applied to Palaung, Jingpaw, Manipuri and other dependent chiefs as well. Ava's partial hold over their territories was based in part on its ability to project military forces in the event of a breakdown in customary tributary arrangements, and a *sitkè*, or military commander, was based at Mong Nai in the southern Shan states, backed by a substantial garrison. Sons of *sawbwa* were often educated at court and served for a time as royal pages.[52] Leading Shan families intermarried with the Burmese aristocracy.

If the key aim of the Court of Ava for its hinterland was the maintenance of peace and stability, other principal objectives included the mobilisation of manpower and the expropriation of surplus food and silver. Manpower, as we have seen, was organised in large part through the *ahmudan* crown service system. Military and other service communities supplied labour on a rotating basis; Ava's command over the armed villages it had settled across its hinterland was at the very heart of the monarchy's power. Under the *athiwun*, the remainder of the population were also often mobilised for war and other grand Konbaung projects, a manpower demand mediated through gentry elites. The importation of thousands of captives from conquered territories doubtless lightened the burden on the valley's indigenous inhabitants. But this proved an ephemeral relief, and by the early nineteenth century, the royal court was again attempting to muster yet more local men for the new campaigns to the west.

Food and money were extracted from the economy in part through customs posts, port tariffs, rent on crown lands, and royal ownership of several silver mines in the north. Ava also expected, and usually received,

---

[52] *MMOS*, vol. IV, pp. 116–24.

a share of gentry-administered taxes, a customary proportion set aside for the king's agents. Some of this was deposited directly, in silver or in kind to the provincial treasury. Some might have been presented in person by the *myothugyi* or *sawbwa* at a tribute ceremony. Much more was decentralised through the *myoza* or *appanage* system already discussed. Rather than the still fairly small bureaucracy becoming involved, the task of extracting income from sometimes distant communities would fall on the *appanage*-holding nobleman, prince, princess or queen. In this way, the burden on royal agencies was lightened, and otherwise idle and potentially troublesome aristocrats and wives were brought into the business of the early modern state.

Royal agencies relied on information to help maintain their hold on the country. Periodic inquiries, including two countrywide censuses in 1783 and 1805, were held to ascertain precisely the number of households in the kingdom and the hereditary obligations to the state of each individual, community and hereditary office-holder. Births and deaths were required to be reported to the provincial court and important family genealogies from throughout the valley were regularly updated by the Shwédaik, or privy treasury. *Nakhan* or reporters were posted in every provincial office and at the capital and communicated local proceedings directly to the Hluttaw.[53] In addition, networks of covert spies were kept by the king.

By the early nineteenth century, the writ of Ava's monarchs was strong to an unprecedented degree. In the area around the capital, many villages and towns were inhabited mainly by crown servants, and as the Hluttaw's control over service families tightened, so did the Court's overall authority in the area. In Kyauksè, the richly irrigated region just to the south-east of Ava, the positions of the nine hereditary *myothugyi* gave way to a host of crown officers who supervised royal lands and royal irrigation works. The forts at Myittha and Mekkaya, seats of old ruling families, slowly turned to ruin and a more complicated administration, directly from the capital, took root.

In general, outside the capital area, the Burmese state in the early nineteenth century was one where increasingly bureaucratised central agencies were grafted upon much older structures of government run by gentry elites. The military basis of much of royal authority remained intact and the transition away from direct rule by the king and his battlefield

---

[53] *Ibid.*, vol. IV, pp. 7–14.

comrades-in-arms to government by palace mandarins had only just begun. The political authority, and thus the extractive capacity of the state, varied greatly from region to region, mainly as a result of distance from the capital or major garrisoned towns, but the direction was certainly one of greater integration and strengthened royal supervision over local hereditary leaders. The Burmese state was well suited to the early modern environment in which it arose – harnessing manpower and dealing with threats from conspiring princes, nobles and headmen. A whole new environment, however, would soon emerge.

4 | Empire and identity

Defeat had made the Court of Ava anxious for the future of the kingdom. Until the First Anglo-Burmese War, the men of the Golden City, buoyed by a generation of virtually unchecked military expansion, had entertained grand schemes for further conquest. Their home was the centre of an expanding empire, and their king a universal monarch, a *chakravatti* over many subject peoples. Within months their world had come crashing down. As the army of the East India Company sailed up the Irrawaddy, the extent of the new English threat became clear for the first time. The defeat, the annexations and the indemnity, the sudden awareness of their inferiority in science and technology, threw the Burmese ruling class into confusion. One of their first responses was to write a new book of history, the *Hman-nan Raza-windaw-gyi*, 'The Glass Palace Chronicle'.

History and origins

In the summer of 1829, King Bagyidaw ordered that a new royal chronicle be composed. A committee of scholars – 'learned Brahmins, learned monks and learned ministers' – was assembled and began meeting in the front chamber of a small glass-mosaic-covered palace near the king's own private apartments. There they met every day for months, with their secretaries, reading decaying palm-leaf manuscripts and examining even older stone inscriptions. They drew heavily on a number of existing chronicles, scrutinising apparent contradictions, adding their own commentaries and cross-checking sources, and brought the narrative up to Bagyidaw's own coronation. Their stated desire was to analyse the many discrepancies between existing historical works and to arrive at a definitive interpretation. They wished to 'adopt the truth in the light of reason and the traditional books'.[1]

This was to be one of the last of the great royal chronicles and represented the culmination of at least three hundred years of local historiography.

---

[1] Pe Maung Tin and G.H. Luce (translated), *The Glass Palace Chronicle of the Kings of Burma*, Rangoon, 1910, p. ix.

Increasingly secular in orientation, these historical writings had gradually moved away from religious themes and towards narratives of the reigns of Burmese kings.[2] The earliest extant Burmese history is the *Maha Thamada Wuntha*, otherwise known as the *Razawin Gyaw*, written in 1530 by the monk, poet and Pali scholar Thila Wuntha. The *Razawin Gyaw* or 'Celebrated Chronicle' is largely a history of Buddhism in India and Ceylon, with only the very last portion listing the Burmese kings of Pagan and Ava and, in some instances, mentioning their works of merit. The vast majority of the information is drawn from the Singhalese *Maha Vamsa*, the seminal chronicle of Ceylon.

The first complete history of the Irrawaddy valley appeared only later, in 1730, and was written by the historian Maung Kala.[3] His father was a well-to-do banker named Dewa from the small town of Singaing just south of Ava. His mother, Mani Awga, was of mixed Shan and Burmese noble descent.[4] Called the *Maha Razawindaw-gyi* or 'Great Royal Chronicle', his work has formed the basis for all subsequent histories of the country, including the earliest English-language histories of Burma written in the late nineteenth century.

Maung Kala prefaced his chronicle with an apology for its writing, noting that Buddhist scriptures considered the writing of history to be inimical to religious development. He justified his work by explaining that the study of past events would help to demonstrate the impermanence of all things, including political authority, and that meditation on this theme would actually promote religious insight.[5] His work is based on a compilation of all existing historical material with the exception of lithic inscriptions, which he apparently did not consult. His history begins with the earliest local dynasties in the Irrawaddy valley and continues through the Pagan period to the modern day.[6]

[2] For an analysis of a similar development of Thai historiography, see Charnvit Kasetsiri, 'Thai Historiography from Ancient Times to the Modern Period', in Anthony Reid and David Marr (eds.), *Perceptions of the Past in Southeast Asia*, Singapore, 1979, pp. 156–70.

[3] For a discussion of his work, see Victor Lieberman, 'How Reliable is U Kala's Burmese Chronicles? Some New Comparisons', *JSEAS*, 17 (1986), 236–56.

[4] Hla Pe, *Burma: Literature, Historiography, Scholarship, Language, Life and Buddhism*, Singapore, 1985, p. 38; Kala, *Maha Yazawindawgyi*, vol. I, introduction.

[5] On early modern Burmese historiography, see also Michael Aung-Thwin, 'Prophecies, Omens and Dialogue: Tools of the Trade in Burmese Historiography', in David Wyatt and Alexander Woodside (eds.), *Moral Order and the Question of Change: Essays on Southeast Asian Thought*, New Haven, 1982, pp. 78–104.

The writing of history received new impetus under the young Konbaung kings. Bodawpaya, in particular, was keen on reading history, and ordered a collection of inscriptions from throughout the kingdom. These were brought to the capital and were examined by the scholar and writer Maha Sithu, a nobleman, and a one time superintendent of the Twinthin region. Based in part on these sources, and together with material from the royal library, Maha Sithu composed the *Razawin-thit*, the 'New Chronicle' towards the end of the eighteenth century. Other historical writings around this time include a number of other royal chronicles; *thamaing*, or local histories of individual towns and pagodas; and stories written in verse about the exploits of former kings and princes.

In many of these histories, the origins of the Burmese royal lineage are eventually traced back to the quasi-legendary founder of the Pagan dynasty, Pyuminhti. He was said to be the product of a union between a Sun spirit and a Naga princess. But by the early nineteenth century, an even grander if slightly less exotic lineage was devised for the somewhat upstart Konbaung family. Alaungpaya's genealogists had already contrived a suitably royal pedigree for their new king by linking him, somewhat spuriously, to the Pagan royal house. But now the kings of Pagan, in turn, were shown not merely to be descended from a long noble line beginning with Pyuminhti, but to be 'Sakiyans', members of the Sakya clan of the Gautama Buddha himself. In a long digression from the principal narrative, the authors of the Glass Palace Chronicle carefully dissect the legends surrounding Pyuminhti's mythic origins and conclude their improbability. In place of the founder's birth from the union of the Sun and the Naga princess, they argue that he was simply a scion of the Sakiyan house, the same house which had provided rulers in the Irrawaddy valley since long before Pagan's construction. Burma's kings were *Ksatriya*, and looked to the Ganges valley, the home of Buddhism, as their place of origin.[7]

According to Bagyidaw's post-bellum historians, the first kingdom in the Irrawaddy valley was the kingdom of Tagaung, along the upper river. Tagaung was said to have been founded by a Sakiyan prince, named Abhiraza, in the early first millennium BC. This prince was a refugee,

[6] Tet Htoot, 'The Nature of the Burmese Chronicles', in D.G.E. Hall (ed.), *Historians of Southeast Asia*, London, 1961; Tin Ohn, 'Modern Historical Writing in Burmese', in D.G.E. Hall (ed.), *Historians of Southeast Asia*, London, 1961.
[7] Pe Maung Tin and Luce (translated), *Glass Palace Chronicle*, pp. 30–9.

having left after a violent conflict in his north Indian homeland. Other Sakiyan immigrants followed. They and their descendants were portrayed as members of the valley's one true royal line. The line extended backwards in time, past the time of the Gautama Buddha, to the very first 'king of the world', Maha Thammada. Through him, the Burmese *Ksatriya* still claimed ultimate descent from the Sun, and styled themselves *naymyo*, 'of the solar race'. The line then went forward in time through the kings of Pagan to Alaungpaya himself and finally to his Konbaung successors. Purity of this special race of kings was said to be best preserved through strict endogamy. By the 1820s the presence of dozens of young princes and princesses made this possible. Half-sibling and first-cousin marriages became the rule. And so in the years just after Ava's most humiliating defeat, the formerly quite humble gentry clan of Moksobo became, officially, the true heirs of the greatest of all possible royal lines.

This rendering of the Burmese royal house as Sakiyans from the Ganges basin does not, however, mean that early-nineteenth-century scholars believed the ordinary people of the Irrawaddy valley migrated from the west. Instead, the Glass Palace Chronicle mentions a number of different people as inhabiting the Irrawaddy valley in the first millennium, without any discussion of other origins. The Pyu, the Kanyan and the Thet are mentioned as three 'divisions' among the people of the Irrawaddy valley in the first millennium. The Myanma, or Burmese, are described as the product of a later division from among the same mix. They appear for the first time about halfway through the narrative, or early in the first millennium. There is no mention of migration, other than that of the Sakiyan princes and even they were said to have arrived long ago. The ordinary people are all 'native' people, arising and disappearing, in appropriate conformity with Buddhist notions of constant change. But the overall picture is one of change within continuity, the continuity of the Sakiyan lineage, and continuity of the Irrawaddy valley as a Buddhist land, a place of refuge for Buddhism and for Buddhist princes from their homeland across the Brahmaputra.

And to all this must be added mention that members of the royal court did not necessarily believe all that they read. Bagyidaw himself was a sceptic. He once remarked to the English Resident that 'histories, being human compilations, are unreliable, and interpolations are often made to please the reigning sovereign'.[8] But the general notion that the rulers

---

[8] Burney, 'Population of the Burman Empire', pp. 300–1.

of Ava shared a common heritage with ancient Buddhist rulers of the Magadha seems to have been a part of received historical knowledge at the court, at least in the mid-nineteenth century. It was also generally accepted that Buddhism had been displaced in north India, and the culprits were seen as Muslim invaders from the west as opposed to a Brahmanical revival or new Hindu faiths. The Europeans, as 'westerners' like the Muslims, are, in a way, viewed as part of the same invading tradition. In a private meeting with Sir Arthur Phayre in 1855, Mindon, explaining his Ksatriyan lineage, remarked 'Our race once reigned in all the countries you hold. Now the Kalas have come close up to us.'[9]

A Burmese country?

By the mid-nineteenth century, the Court of Ava had begun referring to its kingdom almost exclusively as the Myanma *Naing-ngan*, the 'Burmese Kingdom', and to their king as the Myanma *Min*, the 'Burmese King'. These had come gradually to replace older terms. In the mid-eighteenth century, Alaungpaya, in writing to the East India Company, had referred to himself as the king of Tampradipa and Thunaparanta, of Ramannadesa and of Kamboza, old and imprecise names for parts of the Irrawaddy valley and its eastern tributaries. He also styled himself the 'Lord of the White Elephant' and the 'Ruler of All Umbrella Bearing Chiefs'.[10] This was all very much in the local tradition of kingship, which viewed the monarch as a universal sovereign over many and varied peoples. 'Myanma *Naing-ngan*', however, clearly implies an ethnic-based polity. Was the Irrawaddy valley becoming more 'Burmese'? And what did this mean?

The word 'Mranma' or 'Myanma' first occurs, somewhat surprisingly, in a Cham inscription and refers, presumably, to the people of the Pagan, with whom they apparently traded. The Myanma or Burmese language itself appears slightly afterwards, in a late-twelfth-century inscription. This inscription, commemorating a religious dedication by a Prince Rajkumar, is likely to have been a very early attempt to reduce the language to writing. There follows a brief period of orthological trial and error and then written Burmese assumes more or less its present form. This all occurs very late in the Pagan era.

Other languages were also present at Pagan: Pyu, Mon, Pali and

---

[9] Yule, *Mission*, p. 107.
[10] A. Dalrymple, *Oriental Repertory*, London, 1808, pp. 10–11.

Sanskrit were all known, and a vast spectrum of other indigenous languages and dialects must have been spoken across the valley and in the
surrounding uplands. The origin of Burmese itself remains obscure.[11] The
language is quite closely related to Yi, a group of languages now spoken in
remote parts of northern Burma as well as in much of western Yunnan
and southern Sichuan provinces, in China, and more distantly to Tibetan.
Yi is likely to have been the language of the Nan Chao ruling class, Nan
Chao being the kingdom based in what is today western Yunnan, which
dominated the upper Irrawaddy valley in the eighth and ninth centuries. If
so, languages immediately ancestral to Burmese may have arrived together with the Nan Chao invasions of the ninth century and perhaps a
related spread of cultural influences from Yunnan. There needs to have
been no large-scale migration of people, only a diffusion of Burmese-Yi
languages accompanying the push of Nan Chao political power into the
lowlands. 'Myanma', as a new language accompanying Pagan's rise to
regional greatness, may have been a sort of creole, a dialect of the formerly
occupying Nan Chao forces which was locally adopted and which took on
aspects of existing native tongues, such as Pyu.

The emergence and diffusion of the Burmese language from what
appears to have been its original core around Pagan was the principal
cultural transition of the early modern period, together with the rise of
neo-conservative Buddhism. In the early Pagan period, we know that
Mizo-Chin languages were spoken along the Chindwin river, Sak-Kadu
languages just to the north, as well as Pyu everywhere in the upper and
middle valley. By the eighteenth century, only pockets of other indigenous
languages remained. In Arakan as well, a dialect of Burmese displaced
existing, possibly Indo-European languages and became the language of
the Mrohaung aristocracy. In the delta, Mon still dominated but Burmese
was making inroads as far south as the Malay Peninsula by 1800. Around
this time there also existed an increasing linguistic uniformity within the
Burmese language itself. Burmese spelling books and other attempts to
standardise the written and spoken language first appeared in the early
modern era.[12] A vast vernacular literature had already emerged and nu-

---

[11] On the early development of Burmese, see Luce, *Phases of Pre-Pagan Burma*, vol. I,
pp. 98–108.

[12] Anna Allott, Patricia Herbert and John Okell, 'Burma', in Patricia Herbert and
Anthony Milner (eds.), *Southeast Asian Languages and Literatures: A Select Guide*,
Whiting Bay, n.d.

merous texts circulated, together with religious commentaries written in Burmese interspersed with Pali.

Pyu, as an important local vernacular and the Pyu as a people appear to have disappeared almost completely by the immediate post-Pagan era. Traces of people professing this identity remained, however, into the twentieth century. Writing in the 1930s, the then Yamèthin settlement officer wrote that the 'last of the Pyu' were living in Kaing-galay village, about thirty of them altogether. He wrote that they dressed the same as the others, but were all American Southern Baptists and were 'regarded with contempt' by their Burman neighbours.[13] Other languages and peoples such as the Mizo-Chin also disappeared from the lowlands but remained in large numbers in surrounding upland areas.

The Burmese language received a further boost at the hands of the early Konbaung kings who were themselves exclusively Burmese-speaking. The civil war which had preceded the establishment of their dynasty had taken on vaguely 'ethnic' overtones, with Burmese-speakers in the north being set against largely Mon-speakers loyal to the new Pegu-based regime. The Konbaung conquest of the delta was followed by a quite ruthless campaign of repression against Mon-speakers, and included an active discouragement of the Mon language.[14] Over the next several decades, thousands of Mons either migrated eastwards to the Tennasserim or to Siam, or changed their identities by speaking Burmese, adopting Burmese dress and hairstyles and taking Burmese names. Thus, by the early nineteenth century, nearly the entire Irrawaddy valley for the first time spoke a common language.

But was this increasing linguistic unity a sign of more general cultural integration as well? One important area of cultural change was religion. Buddhism had been present in its various forms since at least the middle of the first millennium AD, perhaps since much earlier. The Buddhism of Sri Ksetra and other Pyu polities at this time was likely to have been most influenced by the Pali Buddhism of south India, a precursor of the later Theravada tradition. Other influences may also have been present and by the turn of the millennium aspects of the Mahayana movement, originating in north India, had begun to take root.

As we have seen, however, by late in the Pagan era, there was a growing shift towards a renewed Buddhist orthodoxy and ever closer links with the

[13] R.S. Wilkie, *Burma Gazetteer – Yamèthin District* (hereafter *Yamèthin Gazetteer*), 2 vols., Rangoon, 1934, vol. I, p. 8.   [14] Koenig, *Burmese Polity*, p. 61.

Mahavihara Theravada school of Ceylon. While the chronicle tradition traces the neo-Singhalese revival to Anuiruddha's capture of Thaton in 1066, the rise of Theravada orthodoxy is more likely to have developed through contacts between Dhammazedi's court at Pegu and the kingdom of Kandy in the late 1400s. Over the next three hundred years, Theravada Buddhism would go from strength to strength, benefiting from vigorous royal patronage, spreading north to Ava and replacing more hetero-geneous recensions. Explicitly Mahayana schools were marginalised or suppressed and new internal conflicts, largely on matters of monastic discipline, occurred within the new conservative framework.

By the time of Bodawpaya, the royal courts worked to strengthen Sangha organisation at the higher levels and end internal conflict, inter-vening vigorously to solve inter-sect disputes. Bodawpaya himself ap-pointed his personal tutor as *Thathanabaing*, or 'Primate'. Through all these merit-making efforts, he supported growing attempts to arrive at a more 'authentic' Buddhism, a Buddhism of greater textual accuracy, one which was believed to be closer to that of the religion's founder. In 1817, a royal inquiry was established to study the discrepancies between Pali texts recently acquired from India and Ceylon and existing Burmese commen-taries, and Buddhist monks were sent with court Brahmins on religious fact-finding missions to Benares and Kandy.[15]

It must be said, however, that the king himself was sceptical at some of the new ideas being acquired. He questioned the value of collected relics of the historical Buddha to be enshrined at new pagodas, asking why, if the great Buddhist monarch Asoka had considerable problems in locating such relics two thousand years before, was the Burmese court able to find so many? As he grew older he attenuated his religious zeal with increasing tolerance and ruled that Mahayana traditions, which he said were older among the Burmese than Theravada Buddhism, needed to be permitted though not encouraged.[16] Nevertheless, the early nineteenth century saw no important reverses in the general long-term trend towards an ortho-doxy based on the Theravada canon and its Singhalese interpreters.

There also existed a common political tradition. The later chronicles themselves are clear in seeing a long political tradition stretching back to Pagan, Sri Ksestra and to Tagaung, the 'first' Sakiyan kingdom in the Irrawaddy valley. Tagaung is generally dismissed by modern historians as

---

[15] *ROB*, 22 March 1817.   [16] *Ibid.*, 8 November 1807, 7 August 1812.

'mythical' though it is considered the ancestral polity by both the Ava and the various Shan-speaking courts to the east. We know little about the Sri Ksestra polity and even less about the relationship between Sri Ksestra and early Pagan. But we do know that Pagan extended its sway through much of the valley for over two centuries and that memories of a unified monarchy lived far into the politically more fractured period which followed. The extent of institutional continuity between Pagan and the various successor states, whether based at Pegu, Pinya, Sagaing, Ava, Toungoo, Prome or elsewhere is a matter of debate. But the idea of a grander valley-wide polity surely remained, informing kingly rituals and local ambition.

Pagan also bequeathed a common legal heritage which not only survived its decline but developed considerably through the early modern era. Benefiting from the rise in literacy which seems to have accompanied more textually inclined religious study was a mushrooming of writings on civil justice and governance.[17] The Irrawaddy basin possesses one of the oldest legal traditions in the world and both the earliest legal texts and the emergence of professional jurists may date from as early as the thirteenth century. They in turn may have borrowed from substantially older Mon writings and were ultimately inspired by early Buddhist ideas on ethics and society.[18] Much of this legal tradition may already have been quite developed by the beginning of the early modern period. But the writing, reading and use of legal texts more likely expanded in the early modern era even if basic principles had remained fairly unchanged since the Pagan era.

Burmese law was ordinarily divided into two spheres: that of *lawka-wut* or, loosely, civil law, concerning all manner of disputes between private parties; and *raza-wut* or criminal law, meaning acts against the king or state and including failure to perform customary obligations, pay taxes or obey royal orders. *Lawka-wut* disputes were settled with reference to the *dhammathat*, a huge body of legal writings which included detailed expositions on the proper ordering of society and ways of dealing with transgressions, including writing in both prose and verse in Pali and Burmese.

---

[17] Maung Maung, *Law and Custom in Burma and the Burmese Family*, The Hague, 1963; Htin Aung, *Burmese Law Tales*, London, 1962, introduction.

[18] Unpublished manuscripts by Andrew Huxley, 'How Buddhist is Theravada Buddhist Law?', pp. 2–19; and 'Sanction in the Buddhist Southeast Asian Kingdoms'; Htin Aung, *Burmese Law Tales*, introduction.

They were written by Buddhist monks, government officials, professional jurists and others, the study of law being seen as a very suitable pastime for the aristocracy.[19] In general, arbitration resulting in compensation for the plaintiff rather than other types of redress was the aim of much of the legal process, and ordinary people, particularly if they were not literate, were represented by a *shay-nay*, or legal repre-sentative.[20] *Raza-wut* cases, by contrast, were dealt with through penal sanctions imposed by government officials, including imprisonment, corporal punishment, tattooing (to mark a person for life as a felon) and execution.[21]

Thus, by the late eighteenth century, a common language, a common religion, a common set of legal and political ideas and institutions, and even a shared written history existed throughout the core area of the Ava kingdom. But to what extent was this related to a notion of a common Myanma identity? The Myanma identity, like all identities, was (and is) a partial identity. People would likely have also seen themselves as Buddhists or Muslims, members of a particular descent group or lineage, members of a crown service division or social class. They may also have identified strongly with their *zati*, their 'home place', as people of Pegu, Alon, Prome or Salin, all before seeing themselves as Myanma. But certainly there was a sense of a Myanma identity in opposition to other 'ethnic' identities, one based on an idea of shared culture and ancestry, of the Myanma as a 'race' or *lu-myo*.

To the early modern people of Ava, the world was divided into a number of different *lu-myo*. As mentioned already, *myo* means 'seed' and was used commonly to mean a descent group or kinship. The Myanma *lu-myo* was thus an expanded descent group, an identity perhaps also tied to language, religion, political institutions and a common historical experience, but perceived to be tied by blood (or semen in the local metaphor) as well. As early as the early seventeenth century, court records list the 'one hundred and one *lu-myo* of the world'.[22] By the early nineteenth century, these were classed into five overarching categories: Myanma, Tayok, Shan, Mon and Kala.[23] Language appears to be at least one import-

---

[19] See Richardson, *The Damathat*, for earliest translation of the principal *dhammathats*.
[20] Than Tun, 'Administration under King Thalun (1629–1648)', *JBRS*, 51(1968), 125–7.
[21] See Gouger, *Narrative*, p. 161, for graphic descriptions of Burmese torture.
[22] *ROB*, 22 November 1628, 2 June 1679.
[23] *MMOS*, vol. II, pp. 24–31. 'Chin' was an occasional extra category, and 'Shan' and 'Tayok' were sometimes merged.

ant component in the thinking behind these divisions. The Arakanese, for example, who spoke a near identical language but who were as similar or distinct from the people of the Irrawaddy valley in other ways as the Mon, were lumped together under the 'Myanma' heading. Similarly, all the various Tai-speaking peoples, from the people of the Hukawng valley in the Himalayan foothills to the people of Bangkok, were all seen as 'Shan'. The idea of language, orthography and translation were all subjects of considerable study at Ava, being related in different ways to Buddhism and the search for 'authentic' texts. Discovering which languages were related to which others was perhaps a topic of interest as well.

But language was not the only component in a still somewhat hazy classification schema. The Khmer or *Gywan* as well as the Jingpaw or *Kachin* were also placed within the 'Shan' category. The third category after Myanma and Shan was the Tayok, alternatively spelled 'Tarup' or 'Taruk', a word apparently derived from 'Turk'. This category was applied to the Han Chinese, and more generally to all the people across the immediate eastern highlands. The fourth and broadest category included the many and varied Kalas. *Kala* in early-nineteenth-century Burma roughly meant an 'overseas person', a person from south Asia, west Asia or Europe and probably insular south-east Asia as well. It included the English, the French, the Armenians, the Jews, and all the various people of the sub-continent with whom the Burmese were familiar. It included the Bengalis but not the Arakanese. The Kalas were seen as a people with certain cultural and perhaps physical similarities, though the latter is not spelled out. For example, for the Burmese, a 'Kala seat' (*kala-htaing*) is the word for a chair as opposed to a stool and a Kala temporary dwelling (*kala-tè*) is the word for a 'cloth tent'. The Kala religion was Islam.

Kala was an ethnic category, a division of *lu-myo*, before the first European contact with Burma. Thus, the Europeans were fitted into an existing category. They were viewed as 'Indians', different from say Gujaratis and Tamils, but no more different from either of those people than they were from each other. The Europeans were a sub-group of Kalas and were initially labelled *bayingyi*, a Burmese corruption of the Arabic *feringhi*. The word was applied mainly to the Portuguese, the European people with whom the Burmese had by far the most contact until the late eighteenth century. Then, as other Europeans appeared on the scene, *bayingyi* came to mean 'Roman Catholic', and the newly arrived English were simply termed the English Kala (*Ingaleit kala*). The English were more commonly referred to as the *thosaung kala*, the 'sheep-wearing kala', a reference to their woollen clothes and hats. The British were well aware that they were being lumped together with their Indian subjects into a single ethnic category. They also realised that the Burmese often regarded them as somewhat low in the hierarchy of Kalas.

But while these scholarly divisions of the early nineteenth century seem to be very clear and precise, what is unclear is the actual usage of these categories in other aspects of political and social thought, and political or social organisation. The Irrawaddy valley was and has always been a receptacle for immigrants from near and far. How and in what way did, say, Maru people from the northern hills, royal captives from Bangkok or mercenaries from Brittany 'become Burmese'? Were emergent ethnic identities embedded in local class relations? Were, for example, crown service descendants of Lao captives seen as 'Lao' long after their cousins at court were viewed as Myanma? Given the paucity of the material at hand, these are very difficult questions to answer. But what we know is that the late eighteenth and early nineteenth centuries witnessed considerable political turmoil, dislocations and demographic shifts, foreign invasion followed by great conquests and then renewed threat; and that at the middle of the nineteenth century, we see a valley-wide Myanma identity which included nearly all the local population and which in turn gave rise to a new and militant patriotism.

War and identity

The mid-eighteenth century witnessed a series of devastating external attacks into the Ava heartland. The Manipuri raids of the 1740s and the invasion from Pegu in the 1750s created a long period of fighting and instability. What emerged was a new dynasty firmly rooted in the countryside, one which proclaimed a notion of Myanma identity, and which would go on to create the substantial empire based around a 'Burmese' core. During the height of campaigns against the Mon-speaking Pegu regime, Alaungpaya appealed to a fellow gentry leader, Letya Pyanchi, the chief of Hkin-U, for support. He wrote: 'although you are of the Burmese race (*myanma lu-myo*) and a brave man, in planning to remain a subject of the Mon, you are acting contrary to your lineage and descent (*amyo-anwè*) and your abilities'.[24]

We can only imagine that a long period of external invasion of the rural Ava hinterland, from Manipur and Pegu and later from China, would only have hardened a local sense of common identity. Invasion and devastation by foreigners – Hindu Manipuris under their proselytising Raja, Gharib Newaz, people from Pegu with their distinct hairstyles, dress and different language, Manchu cavalry and Chinese foot soldiers – all came within the space of a generation, a generation which then produced Alaungpaya from the depths of the Myanma countryside. Invasion was then followed by expansion, economic growth, immigration and the forced importation of tens of thousands more foreigners. Foreigners worked the mills, foreigners cleaned the streets, foreigners dug new irrigation ditches, while the Myanma generals claimed new lands for their king. In 1824 this came to an end, and a long period of encroaching British Indian power began. Exactly how all this relates to a growing patriotism based on a Myanma identity is impossible to know in any detail. But surely we can see how these events may have helped to further mould local notions of belonging and nurture a sense of patriotism. New histories and poems celebrated distant victories. In part, these were celebrations of dynastic achievements of kings and princes. But they were also in part a celebration of the accomplishment of the Burmese people. When a grandee of the Court of Ava told a visiting Englishman in 1826, 'you see, we have never met a people who can withstand us', he was revealing more than a pride in his royal family.

Was Myanma just a people or was there a Myanma place as well? A number of different words may be seen as approximate equivalents of the English words 'country', 'kingdom', 'empire' or 'land'. As we have seen, *pyi* could refer to both the capital city and to the king's dominions as a whole. The Myanma *pyi* was both Ava and the Ava kingdom, and was set against the Mon *pyi* or the Shan *pyi*, for example. *Naing-ngan* during the Pagan period meant the peripheral parts of the polity which had been conquered but were not quite under full royal administration. By the early 1800s, *naing-ngan* took on the modern connotation of 'kingdom' and the *Myanma Naing-ngan* was the 'Kingdom of Burma'. This is how the Eng-

---

[24] Victor Lieberman, 'Ethnic Politics in Eighteenth-Century Burma', *MAS* 12 (1978), 455–83.

lish phrase was translated in the 1826 Treaty of Yandabo and later texts. *Detha*, from the Sanskrit-Pali *desa* or *desh*, and other words denoting a spatial realm were also used.

There was a blurry but not entirely vague notion of what this 'Kingdom of Burma' was. As early as 1578, for example, a royal order defined the limits of the kingdom as being more or less the entire Irrawaddy valley, together with the Shan hills 'to the iron bridge in the east and the lands of the Big Ears, the Kadu and the Kathé in the north'.[25] Much later, in 1822, instructions to a royal embassy to the Vietnamese court at Hué carefully surveyed the geography of the kingdom, listing important towns, landmarks and sacred places.[26] Poems sung at palace celebrated the landscape of the realm.[27]

One might ask to what extent these ideas related to identity and place were confined to the scholarly world of the court and to what extent there existed a diffusion of knowledge and a shared emergent patriotism. Whilst conclusive evidence is lacking, we may point to two important vehicles of intra-valley information: itinerant monks and itinerant entertainers.

Buddhist monks were among the most important vehicles through which knowledge circulated, was challenged, interpreted and changed throughout the kingdom, bridging the world of the aristocracy and the countryside. This they did in part through their role in monastic education. A large proportion of boys attended monastic schools in their home communities, studying not only Buddhist Pali texts but also Burmese, law, history and other secular subjects. Many of the brighter students then went on to higher learning at one of the several monastic colleges at Ava or elsewhere. Some then stayed on to teach, while others re-entered lay society. The overall proportion of monks and novices in the late nineteenth century was around 2 per cent of the male population. The tens of thousands of men who wore the saffron robes at any given time, drawn from a cross-section of society and memorising the same Theravada canon, must have exercised a powerful homogenising force throughout the country. Monks were also great travellers. Through public sermons, their ideas were spread to the whole of society.

The second important vehicle was the rise of popular theatre. The emergence of Burmese drama and from it the more popular theatre of the

[25] *ROB*, 5 November 1578.
[26] *Ibid.*, 9 February 1822, 25 April 1822, 5 September 1824, 22 November 1824.
[27] *Ibid.*, 25 April 1822.

nineteenth century was a direct result of the Burmese occupation (and destruction) of the Siamese capital Ayuthaya in 1767. The sack of Ayuthaya had been accompanied by the forced relocation of thousands of Siamese captives, including the royal family, officials, actors, dancers, playwrights and many or most of that country's intellectual class. The resulting contact between the Burmese court and these Siamese captives produced what one Burmese historian has called a 'renaissance of Burmese culture'.[28] The immediate effect was on aristocratic society at the capital, as Siamese plays were translated and transformed by Burmese writers and performed at the palace under the patronage of the king and royal family. Theatre very quickly became the favourite entertainment of the palace and dramatic performances took on the role of a regular state function, with the king and royal family and many senior officials and their guests in attendance.

It was only in the early nineteenth century that court drama travelled into the countryside. Soon, however, country-wide interest in this new art form was so great that a new ministry, that of theatre, was created. Puppet shows, inspired from Siam, also became popular with the encouragement of the first 'minister for theatre' under King Bodawpaya. In part, the spread took place through local officials imitating court life and holding smaller dramatic performances of their own. Court patronage of the theatre had lifted the status of travelling entertainment companies and some now styled themselves as a 'royal company' or as having performed for a particular senior official or on a state occasion. Though the various plays presented at court were performed in some other towns, it was the Ramayana plays which reached the entire countryside. These performances reproduced many aspects of court life – in dress, manners and speech, for example – and thus while the form of the original Indian play was preserved to some extent, aesthetic representations became those of the contemporary Burmese palace circles. The Ramayana became a vehicle through which elite culture from the capital was directly displayed for a huge audience of common people, providing an image of royal life which remains largely unchanged to this day.[29]

Because of these two vehicles, itinerant monks and itinerant entertainers, the two worlds of city and countryside would not have remained

---

[28] Htin Aung, *History of Burma*.

[29] Htin Aung, *Burmese Drama: A Study With Translations of Burmese Plays*, Oxford, 1937, pp. 49–52.

completely isolated from one another in culture and ideas. While early entertainers brought court styles and thinking to the towns and villages, later innovations may have found much of their inspiration from beyond Ava's walls. The Buddhist establishment was even more of a vehicle for cross-country intellectual exchanges, as many leading *sayadaw*, after making their name in their provincial seat, moved on to the capital to preach their comments on the Theravada recension. These two vehicles in turn may have been linked, in still unexplored ways, with a growing intolerance of social deviancy. We have seen that as early as the fifteenth century, Ava's monarchs, in their self-proclaimed role of Buddhist ruler, attempted to enforce stricter adherence to perceived Theravada ethical precepts. Through the early Konbaung period, these trends gained pace. In 1782, for example, the consumption of alcohol, opium and opium derivatives, and gambling and hunting were banned.[30] In 1785, prostitution was similarly proscribed.[31] A generation later, in 1811, royal authorities were even dictating hairstyles and prohibited the wearing of short hair, the mark of the Mon, by men.[32]

Within the next decade or so, a new element would be thrown into this changing mix of ideas: the western campaigns and Ava's dreams of conquest in India.

Expansion and information

By the turn of the nineteenth century, the Court of Ava could claim a series of spectacular successes on the battlefield. Burmese armies had defeated not only Ayuthaya but also China itself, an unheard-of feat in the royal chronicles. Captive Siamese had brought about a renaissance in local music, theatre and cuisine. But it was the kingdom's western conquests which would most excite the thinking of the court. Though these were ultimately limited to Arakan and the Brahmaputra basin, they did, for a while, hold out the possibility of an Indian empire and the restoration of Buddhism to the Buddha's own homeland, perhaps the greatest meritmaking exercise the Konbaung rulers could imagine.

The areas occupied by the Burmese through their western campaigns were themselves experiencing considerable social and cultural change. In Manipur, the spread of Bengali Vaishnavism had continued into the

[30] *ROB*, 20 February 1782.   [31] *Ibid.*, 12 February 1785.
[32] *Ibid.*, 26 January 1811.

nineteenth century and the influence of court Brahmins was very strong.[33] Vaishnavite influence had also become powerful in Assam, having gradually spread from Bengal to the Brahmaputra valley since at least the sixteenth century.[34] The educated among the new captives were integrated into a long-established structure of secular and religious scholarship.

The erudite men of the Court of Ava were known as *pyinnya-shi*, a Burmese-Pali word meaning 'possessors of learning', and a synonym of the Pali *pandit*. This was a formal title, the gaining of which involved some sort of examination (*sa-pyan-pwè*) in divers branches of sacred and profane knowledge.[35] These men, who often also held other unrelated offices, officiated at court rituals and determined the most auspicious time for all kingly actions. Buddhist monks could be *pyinnya-shi*, as could laymen. Many, if not most, however, were neither monks nor ordinary laymen but members of the small *ponna* community. The word *ponna* itself may be a corruption of the Sanskrit word for Brahmin, but if so it is an old corruption which has taken on special local meanings. The *ponna* of Ava may be seen in a variety of ways. Firstly, they were a collection of descent groups in a special relationship to the crown, providing service on a hereditary basis in a way not very different from other crown service divisions. Secondly, they, the *ponna-myo*, were one of the four main social divisions into which all people were theoretically classed. Thirdly, they were seen as an 'ethnic' group, with their own community leader, much like resident Chinese or Manipuris. And finally, they were seen as possessing their own 'religion', separate from Buddhism. But to say that they were 'Indian' or 'Hindu' or 'Brahmins' would be an oversimplification and largely incorrect. There were, for example, Myanma *ponna*, and *ponna* who were categorised as *Ksatriya*, *Vaishya* or *Sudra* as well as *Brahmin*.[36]

The conquests of Manipur and Arakan led to a significant influx of foreign ritualists, astronomers and other learned men into the Ava court. Many were classed as *ponna* and integrated into the *ponna* establishment.[37] In 1785, one of these *ponna* was appointed *Ponna Thathanabaing* or 'Primate of the *Ponna* Religion'. The style 'Thathanabaing' had until then been reserved for the Buddhist primate. The Arakanese, who had

---

[33] Kabui, *History of Manipur*, vol. I, pp. 270–92.

[34] Baruah, *History of Assam*, pp. 295–6.

[35] Chan Mya, 'Shay Hkit Pyinnashi Yway Pwe', in *Myanma-sa Pyinnya Padetha Sasaung*, 1 (1966), 250–85.   [36] See, for example, *KBZ*, vol. I, pp. 169–70.

[37] *ROB*, 31 January 1822.

been in much closer contact with centres of knowledge in India and the wider Islamic world, brought with them religious as well as secular texts on science, medicine and astrology. They also brought with them small-pox inoculation which helped to reduce the very high infant mortality rates which were reflected in the loss of almost half the royal children.

Brahmins from Arakan were soon joined by Brahmins from Benares. The city of Benares occupied a special place in the minds of learned early modern Burmans, being closely associated with the Buddha. Such was the high status accorded to the new Brahmins from Benares that they were exempted by royal order from prostrating themselves in the presence of princes and ministers, a status formerly reserved only for members of the Sangha. With the aid, and probably the encouragement, of the Indians, court rituals were carefully reviewed and amended. The leader of the first large delegation of Brahmans, named Govinda, was granted the title 'Govinda Maha Rajendra Agga Maha Dhamma Rajadhiraja Guru'. While he later returned to India, he left behind two of his nephews, Bhisunnath and Gajanath and a disciple, Vasita. Altogether by 1810, twenty-seven Brahmans were said to have arrived from Benares. Acting as ritual consul-tants, the newly arrived team went quickly to work in criticising existing practices and suggesting alterations. For example, the worship of the Maha Pinnai *nat*, identified explicitly with Ganesh, had been long-stand-ing, and Burmese Brahman *ponna* from Sagaing were in charge of regular *puja* ceremonies in his honour. Under a royal order, Bodawpaya accepted the suggestion of Govinda and his team to replace the worship of Ganesh with the worship of Skanda, the god of war.[38]

A wide range of Sanskrit and Indian vernacular texts were imported, adding to the growing library at Amarapura, and in 1812 a mission returned with a statue of 'Kapilamuni the Risi', the king duly making the appropriate offerings and building a special shrine.[39] Such was the influ-ence of these new Brahmins that, in 1813, a royal order insisted on reviewing and confirming the *varna* position of each resident of the capital area, expressing the hope that this review could then be extended throughout the kingdom.[40]

The *Myanma Min Okchokpon Sadan*, the near contemporary text which includes a detailed discussion about *ponna*, states that there were three different internal divisions of this community. The first was their

[38] *Ibid.*, 21 January 1811, 2 September 1811, 8 November 1811.
[39] *Ibid.*, 30 April 1810, 21 June 1812, 2 July 1812.   [40] *Ibid.*, 8 March 1813.

division by the Court of Ava into four classes: a superior class (*myat-tan*), a middle class (*alè-tan*), a lower class (*auk-tan*) and an inferior class (*anyant-tan*). Those of the superior class were entitled to wear a nine- to twelve-stranded *salway*, signifying that they were of approximately the same rank as a senior official. The middle-class *ponna* wore a six-stranded salway, the lower class wore a three-stranded *salway* and those of the inferior class were not entitled to one at all. The second division was by their 'origin', whether Burmese, Arakanese, Manipuri or from Benares. The oldest of the *ponna* lineages in the kingdom was believed to be those of 'Myanma' *ponna* who could trace their ancestry back in unbroken descent to the *ponna* of Pyu, capital of Sri Ksetra in the mid-first millennium AD. Manipuri *ponna* were said to have been present at the royal court since at least the mid-sixteenth century. The third division was between *Brahmin, Ksatriya, Vaishya* and *Sudra.*

Thus, a particular *ponna* could be classed as a 'three-*salway* Manipuri Vaishya *ponna*' or a 'twelve-*salway* Arakanese Brahmin *ponna*'. The Benares *ponna* were said to almost always be from the upper three ranks of *ponna* (that is to say, not Sudras), but otherwise communities of *ponna* from various descent groups could be of any classification. Only *ponna* of the very highest status, that is Brahmin *ponna* who had been granted twelve *salway*, were permitted to preside over royal consecration ceremonies as the 'Eight Ponna of the Right' and the 'Eight Ponna of the Left' of the reigning king.

Royal ceremonies officiated by the *ponna* included the thrice annual *puja* of images of deceased kings and queens. Other responsibilities of the *ponna* and other *pyinnya-shi* included time-keeping and the setting of the calendar, and special *puja* (or *puzaw*) ceremonies for various deities related to the sun, the moon and individual planets. The *Myanma Min Okchokpon Sadan* alleged that in the setting of the annual calendar, if there were any disputes between Burmese pandits and *ponna* pandits, Buddhist monk pandits would be called in to make a final decision. *Ponna* and other *pyinnya-shi* also played key roles in the all-important royal consecration ceremonies, the *abhiseka*, held at various times throughout a king's reign.[41]

Despite the centuries-long association between successive Burmese courts and all manner of Indian knowledge, religious and secular, there

---

[41] See, for example, *KBZ*, vol. III, pp. 395–7.

was, in the early nineteenth century, a curiosity of a sort one normally associates with the discovery of something completely new. After the invasion and occupation of Assam in 1817, an Assamese princess was brought back to the capital with a small retinue of officials. Bodawpaya's own Benares and Manipuri Brahmins were sent to meet with the Brahmins of the princess and one of the king's private secretaries was also ordered along with instructions to see if the various Brahmins were able to communicate with one another.[42] While the court drew a distinction between Buddhism and the Hindu beliefs and rituals of the western immigrants, there appears to have also been a strong sense of compatibility, at least among the official classes, if not among the Buddhist monks and Indian Brahmins themselves.

The relationship between a strengthening conservative Buddhism, emergent local patriotism and the new ideas deriving from these western campaigns is impossible to know without a much more detailed examination of the many extant plays, poems and scholarly texts from the period, many written in Pali. But we may say, however tentatively, that a growing patriotism, tied to the Court of Ava and the Konbaung dynasty, but also to the Irrawaddy valley as a place and the Burmese as a people, found new forms of expression and new sources of inspiration from the court's contact with the kingdoms to the west. India was the homeland of the religion, the place of authenticity from which learning and culture could be imported. But Buddhism and Buddhist kings survived only at Ava, and Ava was a conquering power, the true heir to the great tradition of Maghada and the 'sixteen kingdoms of the middle land'.[43]

At least some at the court, confident in their strength at arms, became excited by the possibilities. In 1813 a royal order declared that India was to be invaded, Benares occupied by the king in person, and Buddhism restored to its place of birth.[44]

Thinking about *Wilayat*

As ambitions in India grew, so did suspicions about the English, known to live in an island somewhere to the west. The Mughal term for a province is *wilayat*. The word came later to apply only to the provinces of the north-

---

[42] *ROB*, 5 September 1817.
[43] See *ROB*, 10 July 1810 for a reference to the Maghada script as the 'authentic' script for the writing of Buddhist texts.   [44] *Ibid*., 11 April 1813.

west, in modern-day Afghanistan. The Burmese adopted the word and *Wilayat*, corrupted into Bilat, came to mean all the countries of the 'far west' and specifically Britain.

Little was known about the new *Bilat Kala*, the English, only that they were traders and were rapidly expanding their power throughout India. Spies had been sent west by Bodawpaya. One who returned in 1815 had spent three years in eastern and southern India as well as Ceylon, and reported to the king that only the English flag now flew all along the Coromandel coast. He also reported that Ceylon had passed from the hands of the Dutch to the East India Company and that the kingdom of Kandy had also fallen to the English.[45] Spying was followed by more active attempts at diplomacy. By the late 1810s, the Burmese were sending an increasing number of missions to India, including one to the Mughal court, apparently to suggest an anti-British alliance. Contacts had also been made with Nepal, the Marathas and Ranjit Singh in the Punjab, but none of these missions seems to have produced any real results.

In one intelligence extract, a former palace steward, Maha Minhla Thagathu, sent around India at the turn of century, warns his king of the untrustworthiness of their new rivals.[46] Drawing on recent events in Mysore and in Maharastra, as well as older events in Siam, the writer compares the British to a banyan tree which leans on others at first, but then drains the life from all around. Interestingly, this comparison of the British Raj in India to a banyan tree was apparently not confined to the Burmese. In 1836, after the Court of Ava had allowed a British officer to accompany a government party to its northernmost post of Mogaung, a protest was received from the Manchurian Viceroy of Yunnan, who also made the same comparison.

Attempts at a grand coalition against the British may always have been partly fanciful. What was not, however, were increasingly belligerent designs on adjacent territory close to or within the British Bengal frontier. As we have seen, probing movements by Thado Maha Bandula from Assam into the Jaintia and Cachar hills had ignited the First Anglo-Burmese War. But the principal Burmese aim seems to have been the annexation of the area just to the north of Arakan. Two court documents from 1817 reasoned that the eastern Bengal had belonged to the kings of Arakan. As the Burmese king was now sovereign over Arakan, eastern

---

[45] Cox, *Journal*, pp. 53–4.   [46] *MMOS*, vol. III, pp. 70–1; *ROB*, 21 January 1823.

Bengal should also come under his authority. One order argued that while the 'English may have a right of possession over all the British Isles they cannot possibly have a legitimate claim over the territory just to the west of Arakan'. The same order demanded that the English, 'who are now in occupation of Benares and Lucknow', must return Mushidabad, Chittagong and Dacca to the Burmese Myowun of Mrohaung.[47] A letter to the East India Company was sent at the same time demanding an end to tax collection in the area.[48]

The Burmese went into the first war with at least some optimism. The defeat was difficult to accept as were the terms of the Treaty of Yandabo. But while some in the Court of Ava had long harboured resentment against the English, and while this resentment only intensified as a result of the war, many others in the palace took an active interest in learning more about the 'lands of Wilayat'. Two leading intellectuals during this period were the Myoza of Myawaddy and the Prince of Mekkaya.[49]

We have already met the Myoza of Myawaddy, born Maung Sa. He had commanded troops at Ramu at the start of the First Anglo-Burmese War. He was also a great scholar and composer and was among the first to foray into the new areas of knowledge made available by greater contact with Europe. By the late 1820s English-language newspapers were being brought across the hills from British Akyab to Ava and these were translated by the Spaniard Lanciego under Myawaddy's direction for the king and court. Burney noted that the old minister was himself able to read the Devanagari script of north India and spoke 'a little Hindustani'. He also sang for the British envoy a few lines of a Latin hymn he had apparently learned from resident missionaries.[50] Burney had tried to persuade the Ava grandees to send young Burmese noblemen to school in Calcutta. To this, however, the Myoza of Myawaddy replied: 'Burmese parents are not like English parents. We cannot part with our children and let them, when young, go away to such a distance and for such a long time, as you appear to do.'[51]

Another pioneer of European learning was the Prince of Mekkaya. The prince, whose personal name was Maung Myo and whose princely style

---

[47] *ROB*, 16 September 1817, 22 December 1817.   [48] *Ibid.*, 18 February 1817.

[49] For short biographies of these two men, see Maung Tin (ed.), *Yaw Mingyi U Po Hlaing Attuppattihnin Raza Dhamma Thingaha Kyan*, Rangoon, 1992, pp. 15–18. On Mekkaya, see also Maung Maung Tin, *Ahmat-saya Pokko-mya*, pp. 195–200; Hmawbi Saya Thein, *Pyinnyashi Gyi Mya Akyaung*, Rangoon, 1966.

[50] Burney, 'Population of the Burman Empire', 75.   [51] *Ibid.*, 155.

was Minyé Kyawswa, was born in 1792, and was a younger son of Bodaw-paya. Judson described him as 'a great metaphysician, theologian and meddler in ecclesiastical affairs'. He had been taught to read and understand English by a British merchant resident at Amarapura and had obtained a copy of *Rees' Cyclopaedia*, published in Calcutta. He translated portions of the cyclopaedia, especially articles on *lawka-dat*, or the 'elements of the world', in which he was keenly interested. Later, he worked together with Charles Lane to put together the very first English–Burmese dictionary.

The British Resident Henry Burney developed a close relationship with the prince. In their numerous meetings, Mekkaya questioned him on 'the latitude and longitude of London, Calcutta, Ava and Bangkok, the cause of the polarity of the needle, the re-appearance of the last comet, the properties of the Barometer and Thermometer . . . and the nature of Algebra'. Burney noted that the prince had both a barometer and thermometer hanging in his apartment and that his personal library included *Rees' Cyclopaedia*, Johnson's *Dictionary*, the Holy Bible and recently translated papers on the calculation of eclipses and the formation of hailstones. Burney concluded that he had 'never met an individual with as great a thirst for knowledge as this Prince'.[52]

This new learning, pioneered by these two men and followed by many others through the 1830s and 1840s, led to a renaissance in local scholarship which affected many and divers fields of knowledge, including geography, astronomy, history and the natural sciences. The arrival of European learning also displaced India as the ultimate and natural source for outside information, and marked the beginnings of a long relationship between modern science and Theravada Buddhism. The *ponna* appear to have been early losers in this development, their influence at court falling rapidly after the 1820s. The new geography, a source of great interest, may also be linked back to local patriotic sentiments. Ava had always had a fairly clear grasp of internal spatial boundaries, but only after 1826 were the kingdom's external limits marked out on a modern map. The Burmese kingdom's tenuous position next to an expanding British India was, for the first time, plain to see.

Anti-British sentiment rose even further in the years after the first war. Burney reported that the king and his ministers were 'inclined to give credence to rumours which tended to place the British in India or Europe in difficulties' and that Ranjit Singh in the Punjab was said to have figured prominently in Burmese imagination.[53] Among those spreading somewhat skewed information about the British position in India were two court Muslims, Ali Khan and Agha Hussein, the latter being the king's physician. Embellishing stories about Afghanistan in the press, they told Tharrawaddy that Calcutta was deserted, 'as all English, with the exception of some clerks had proceeded north to assist in the defense of Delhi'.[54]

News of British reverses on other imperial frontiers were always welcomed by the court. In an interview with visiting Muslim traders, Tharrawaddy stated his intention to retake the Tennasserim and even make a grab for Calcutta through Arakan. Though this may have been mere bravado, he was apparently buoyed by the news of the imminent British defeat in Afghanistan, and told his visitors he understood British forces had been surrounded at Kandahar by Dost Mohammed.[55]

But the Court of Ava was not entirely uncritical in receiving news from abroad. In the 1830s, an Indian 'fakir' told the Prince of Prome that the English had been 'routed and cut to pieces' by the people of 'Rom'. He was then introduced to several ministers of the Hluttaw, who refused to believe him. They had discovered that he knew little about who the people of 'Rom', or Constantinople, really were, and enjoyed 'a hearty laugh' at his ignorance over the difference between the Turks and the Russians.[56]

But Burney noticed that the attitude even of ordinary Burmese was hostile to him and others at the Residency. He wrote:

> from my first arrival I have always observed that the feelings of the common people of the country are very rancorous and sore against us ... We never meet with a drunken man who does not try to provoke us; and many disreputable characters among the lower orders often take an opportunity, when they can do with impunity, of throwing out abuse against the Kalas as we pass in the streets.[57]

Popular hostility was not confined to the official British delegation and seemed to extend to all the western Kalas. In April 1831, a boat belonging to an old Armenian merchant was attacked by river pirates near Pagan in broad daylight. The bandits, when boarding the vessel, were reported as

---

[53] *Ibid.*, 182.   [54] *Ibid.*, 403–4.   [55] *Ibid.*, 441.

[56] Secret Correspondence with India. India Secret Consultations, vol. 22, McLeod's Journal, p. 14.   [57] Burney, 'Population of the Burman Empire', 182.

having cried out: 'You Kalas have forced us to pay plenty of money, we will now retake some of it.'[58] Even natural disasters were blamed on the English. In 1839, a major flood devastated parts of the countryside near the capital. Many people called the flood *Kala-yay*, the 'Kala waters'.

Centuries-long processes of linguistic and religious homogenisation, followed by a turbulent era of war and defeat, had produced a strong sense of Myanma patriotism, tied to the Irrawaddy valley and to the Burmese as a people, a patriotism which now hardened under the threatening shadow of imperial Britain.

[58] *Ibid.*, 147.

5 | The grand reforms of King Mindon

The Second Anglo-Burmese War had shattered conservative forces at the Court of Ava and ushered in the forward-looking and modernising reign of King Mindon. The new ruler had come to power after defeating his elder half-brother Pagan in a bloody struggle for the throne, a palace revolution fought in the shadow of even bloodier battlefield losses against the British Indian army. By the late summer of 1852, Martaban, Rangoon and Bassein had all been lost to the British Indian offensive. Burmese forces, led in part by the eldest son of the great general Thado Maha Bandula, had been decimated and thousands of hastily mustered conscripts had died in futile attempts to hold the king's southern forts.

In Calcutta, the Governor-General, Lord Dalhousie, having entered the war without clear objectives, proposed annexing the new territories now under occupation. British Tennasserim and Arakan could thereby be united and the rump Ava kingdom would be deprived of its outlet to the sea. But as fighting continued in heavy monsoon rains along a broad west to east front, from Prome to the Shan hills, Dalhousie was unsure as to how to bring the war to a speedy conclusion. But news soon arrived of the revolt in Ava, and the new king quickly sent a message agreeing to a comprehensive ceasefire.

Mindon's seizure of the throne had occurred in the wake of growing animosity between him and the more conservative and militant wing surrounding Pagan. Mindon was already in a position of considerable power when the war began as President of the Council of State. But he apparently opposed a continued prosecution of the war and his policy of appeasement angered a number of influential court grandees, as well as the king himself. His closest ally was his full-brother the Kanaung Prince, a senior military commander who had first-hand experience of British superiority in arms and who also counselled for peace.

In November, the Myowun of Amarapura was ordered by the king to investigate a series of violent robberies in the Danun quarter of the city which had taken place in recent weeks. The *myowun*, or governor, was a man of the war party and conspired with others to implicate Mindon and Kanaung. Members of their personal staff were arrested, while evidence was collected against the two princes. As the investigation came closer, Mindon became convinced that the *myowun*'s actions were part of a plot to discredit him in the eyes of the king. He and Kanaung fled, together with their immediate families and over 300 private retainers, retreating to the Konbaung heartland along the Mu valley. There the princes mustered an army to attack Shwébo, overwhelming the 3,000-strong garrison. The Shwébo governor was said to have been a very unpopular man and Mindon may have been assisted by supporters from within the town.

Now ensconced in the home of his great-great-grandfather Alaungpaya, Mindon was in open revolt, and his actions split the Amarapura court and paralysed government for weeks. The regular army was now fighting on two fronts, against the British and against Mindon, and within weeks, Pagan's grip both on the battlefield and over the governing establishment began to slip. After a decisive defeat along the banks of the Irrawaddy, and as the rebels approached Ava, loyalist resolve crumbled. The nobility switched sides. Two of the most influential grandees, the Myoza of Kyaukmaw and the Myoza of Yénangyaung, persuaded royal guardsmen to stand down and allow Mindon and Kanaung to enter the city unopposed. Pagan was placed under house arrest. The new monarch assumed the regal title Thiri Thudhamma Tilawka Pawara Maha Dhamma Razadiraza. He was thirty-nine years old. His personal name was Maung Lwin, and he had been born on a Friday.[1]

Pressures for change

Mindon was the first ruler in the nineteenth century to reform political institutions and processes in an attempt to make the Ava kingdom more internationally viable in the face of British expansion. Many of the reforms begun by Mindon were never followed through to completion. A changing international environment worked with more local influences to prevent their successful implementation. Nevertheless, the new policies and practices which he placed in motion did critically affect the ways in which Irrawaddy valley society developed during this formative time and created the all-important context within which the colonial state was established.

The sudden burst of reformist policies which sprang forth from the Court of Ava in the 1850s was the product of a generation of quiet

[1] *KBZ*, vol. III, pp. 145–6.

education. By the time of the 1852–3 war, the old men of the former empire had finally left the stage of government. These included men such as the accomplished general Mingyi Maha Minhla Minkaung, who had begun life as a hereditary retainer to the royal family and had originally served as a pageboy in Bodawpaya's royal suite. He later rose through the cavalry ranks to become commander of the main cavalry regiments and had led the army in Manipur and Assam in the 1810s and early 1820s. In a way, his death, at the very beginning of Mindon's reign in 1853 when he was 76, signalled the end of an era.[2] Mindon and Kanaung represented a new generation who had grown up in the shadow of British power and at a time of rapidly increasing access to knowledge about the outside world. Their great-uncle, the Mekkaya Prince, and others since had made available a growing body of translated works. A desire to reform and to adapt to a Western-dominated modern world was at the very centre of new government policies.

The kingdom of 1853 was a very different place from the kingdom of 1824. Most obviously, the core area of the Irrawaddy valley had been shorn of all its imperial possessions with the exception of the nearest Shan-speaking principalities. The importation of captive workers from peripheral areas had ended as had the whole notion of Ava being at the centre of an imperial polity. But while the British annexations of Arakan and the Himalayan kingdoms had sapped the strength and the pride of the Burmese court, the new annexation, of the entire Irrawaddy delta, was to be far more devastating.

The most critical result of the annexation of what was to be called 'Lower Burma' was that rice surpluses from that region now could no longer be procured through state-controlled channels of redistribution. Instead they would have to be bought in cash at international prices. Overnight, the economy and, indirectly, the politics of the Burmese kingdom would become intimately tied to the global market. Lord Amherst, in 1824 had stated:

> As any active and successful hostilities in which we may engage with that proud, arrogant and irascible people, will necessarily make them for ever our fixed and deadly enemies, every maxim of sound policy suggests that, when once this Government has embarked on measures for coercing them, it should require such concessions as must materially circumscribe their means of doing future injury to the British Power.[3]

[2] Hmawbi Saya Thein, *Wungyi Hmugyi*, p. 151.
[3] India Secret Consultation, 24 February 1824.

The annexation of the delta, Ava's 'frontier', was to be the most important element in 'circumscribing' the capacity of the Burmese state to reform and adapt to the unfolding modern world. Beyond the tightening of the food supply, the loss of the south diminished the revenue base for both the treasury and an aristocracy of no smaller size. *Appanages* in the delta were lost and the need to compensate nobles and a still growing royal family would only increase income and labour demands on the core population remaining under Ava's rule.

Furthermore, the loss of the delta was taking place at a time when it was becoming an important frontier for colonisation and immigration. Large numbers of people from the upper valley had already been migrating south to newly reclaimed land and this trend was to intensify greatly over the next half-century. By 1881, more than 300,000 people living in Lower Burma were recorded as having been born outside of the region, the vast majority being cultivators from the Ava kingdom.[4] If the delta had remained under royal authority this might have been a welcome development. But now, crown service families as well as others were leaving their labour and revenue obligations as well as their ancestral homes for areas under foreign occupation. The governing structures of old village communities would gradually weaken under the effects of this enormous demographic shift and the tax base of the Court of Ava would slide into further and further decline.[5]

Mindon and his government

It was in the face of these unprecedented challenges that Mindon came to power in 1853. He would shape the course of the nineteenth century in Burma more than any other individual. His ideas on the reform of Burmese institutions, on the strategy shaping Burmese foreign policy, and on the roles of Buddhism and of the king at this difficult time, all firmly influenced the emergence of a modern Burmese society. Born in 1814 he was a younger son of Tharrawaddy by a junior queen, and a great-great-grandson of Alaungpaya. He had spent all his youth until aged 23 as a student at the Maha Zawtika monastic college at Amarapura; he was a deeply religious man who displayed a constant passion

[4] *Census of India*, 1891, 1901; Michael Adas, *The Burma Delta: Economic Development and Social Change on an Asian Rice Frontier, 1852–1941*, Madison, 1974, pp. 41–57; Aung Tun Thet, *Burmese Entrepreneurship: Creative Responses in the Colonial Economy*, Stuttgart, 1989, pp. 126–45.   [5] *Census of India*, 1881.

for Buddhist learning throughout his secular career. His respect for tradi-tional Pali and Burmese scholarship and political ideals was combined with a genuinely reformist zeal. Mindon wanted a modern Burma in which the key symbiotic institutions of monarchy and the Buddhist order would remain and be strengthened alongside imported technologies, science, industry and new structures of bureaucratic government. He also wanted a modern Burma which would remain independent and be a friend of Britain.

The king was interested in every detail of government, personally overseeing many of his crown agencies. He arranged for direct popular petitions to be sent and these occasionally led him to overturn decisions of the Hluttaw.[6] British observers in the 1850s were all full of praise for the new king. Thomas Spears, the informal British agent at the time, noted his 'wisdom and cunning' and his 'infinite superiority' over others in his court in *'the art of managing people'*.[7] Sir Henry Yule, a visitor to the court in the 1850s, wrote of Mindon:

> the Sovereign of Burma is just and mild in temper, easy of access, hears or seeks to hear everything for himself, is heartily desirous that his subjects shall not be oppressed, and strives to secure their happiness. He is, in fact, as far as we can judge, a man of conscience and principle... And if there is any extravagance in his expenditure, it shows itself rather in the liberality of his gifts than in selfish indulgences.[8]

The early years of Mindon's reign were very much a joint government between him and the Kanaung Prince. The two brothers appeared to enjoy a very close relationship. Kanaung was designated heir apparent and was allowed to maintain a very large personal court, much greater than an ordinary prince, and rivalling that of the king himself. He was given responsibility for new technologies, military modernisation and the arts, while Mindon reserved for himself diplomacy, administrative reform, economic affairs and the traditional role of the king as patron and de-fender of Buddhism.[9] Styled Thiri Pawara Maha Thudhamma Raza and granted the towns of Dabayin, Taungdwingyi, Pyinsala and Salay as his *appanages*, Kanaung was also given considerable landed estates close to the royal city.[10]

6 *DPC*, 30 April 1854.   7 *Ibid.*, 26 May 1855, emphasis in original.
8 Yule, *Mission*, p. 193.   9 Pollack, *Empires in Collision*, p. 114.
10 *KBZ*, vol. III, p. 160.

Another critical influence over Mindon was that of his chief queen. A daughter of Bagyidaw and full-sister of Pagan, she was Mindon's first cousin, and closer to the senior lineage within the Alaungpaya house. She was well known for her interest in modern science and for her dominance over the dozens of other royal women. Renowned as a skilled astrologer, she came to use an English nautical almanac for her calculations. British visitors regarded her in high esteem and brought her various gifts, telescopes and barometers, related to her scientific interests.[11] She too maintained a large privy court, complete with her own minister of state and a chief secretary.

After these three leading figures of the Konbaung family, nearly all the important members of the new court were men of the nobility. Alaungpaya had come to power with the aid of key gentry allies. Mindon had come to power with the backing of important Ava grandees. Those who had assisted him most directly in his coup against Pagan were rewarded with the highest offices. The Myoza of Magwé (formerly Kyaukmaw), Thalun and Myèdaung had been Privy Councillors before throwing their support behind Mindon. They were now made senior ministers with Magwé as *de facto* president of the Council of State. A large number of other more junior officials also stayed in place. But in appointing a fourth senior minister, Mindon reached beyond officialdom and called his former tutor to the royal service: Maung Yan Way, formerly of the Bagaya monastery. Now created the Myoza of Pahkangyi, he would keep a steady grip on day-to-day administration until his death in 1875. He had left the Sangha several years before and had been serving as private advisor to Mindon. Quick to set up a loyal following of his own within the court, he appointed a number of his protégés to key positions. Minhla Sithu was made a deputy senior minister. Maha Minhla Thiri was made commander of the main cavalry regiments. Mingyi Maha Tarabya was made commander of the Left Household Brigade. All had been secretaries under the Myoza of Pahkangyi in Mindon's princely court.

Once the government was formed, the Shan princes were quick to offer their oaths of allegiance. The Sawbwa of Taungpeng arrived personally at Shwébo with his family and a small army of retainers, bringing gifts of gold, silver and horses. Mindon, in return, gave presents of precious stones

---

[11] *DPC*, 3 July 1855; Myo Myint, 'The Politics of Survival in Burma: Diplomacy and Statecraft in the Reign of King Mindon, 1853–1878', Ph.D. dissertation, Cornell University, 1987, p. 82.

and cloth.[12] The Chinese also responded promptly to the change of regime and an embassy arrived in early 1853 with gifts and seals of recognition from the Manchu court.

Gifts were also conferred on crown servants and representative groups of his majesty's subjects. At the foot of the Shwetansa Pagoda at Shwébo, Mindon made donations to groups of 'monks, nuns, *ponna*, Indians, Chinese, Manipuris, Siamese, old people, beggars and others'. Gifts were also made to members of the military, court officials and palace retainers.[13] Ministers and princes were awarded new titles and Mindon's sons were arranged into an appropriate hierarchy. The gentry were also not forgotten. Over a thousand members were granted new titles, including 12 cavalry chiefs, 11 cavalry officers, 98 village and town heads, and 890 mounted gentlemen.[14] At the same time, the royal women were reorganised. Queens were appointed from members of the House of Alaungpaya and married to Mindon; appropriate titles and *appanages* were conferred and the Chief Queen was now styled Thiri Tilawka Maha Ratana Dewi. Strategic marriages with daughters of tributary chiefs and ministers of state were also speedily arranged.

A cessation of hostilities against the English did not mean an immediate peace on all fronts. At home, a local rising at Kanpyin had accompanied the more important fighting around the capital and a force under the Myoza of Mohnyin had to be organised to quell the unrest.[15] Farther to the east, Siam had viewed the new Anglo-Burmese war as an opportunity for further expansion in their far north. A large infantry and elephant force had marched from Chiang Mai and attacked the trans-Salween area around Keng Tung. In reply, Mindon dispatched an army of several thousand regular troops under the command of the new commander of the Mong Nai garrison, Mingyi Maha Minhla Minkaung. This army, together with assistance from the Sawbwa of Keng Tung, managed to push back the Siamese attack by late 1853, but only after heavy loss of life. Another invasion soon followed. In 1854, with the British front quiet, Ava was able to send a much larger force of over 3,000 cavalry, backed by artillery, and placed under the command of the Prince of Chundaung, Thiri Maha Dhammaraza. The threat from Siam was held in check.[16]

While securing Ava's position in the east, the new government also began work aimed at repairing and expanding the irrigation system and

[12] *KBZ*, vol. III, p. 149.   [13] *Ibid.*, p. 170.   [14] *Ibid.*, p. 167.   [15] *Ibid.*, pp. 164–5.
[16] *Ibid.*, p. 196.

improving road infrastructure in and around the Ava area. Building work was undertaken to expand several reservoirs and the Kyaukse governor was charged with overseeing repairs to the entire Kyaukse water system. An aristocrat of the old school, the governor was a direct descendent of Shin Saw Bu, the fifteenth-century queen of Pegu and builder of the Shwédagon Pagoda. He is remembered for his harsh rule, but also for the extensive reconstruction which he and the king oversaw. Mindon himself attended several ceremonies marking new work, including one at the beginning of expansion efforts at the Shwébo lake.[17]

All these early events of Mindon's reign are not very different from those of his predecessors. The re-organisation of court grandees and of the Western Court, the acceptance of tribute, the repairing of irrigation works and the launching of campaigns against neighbouring powers, these had all been the stuff of early rule for many Konbaung kings. Auspiciously, a white elephant was caught by the Sawbwa of Thaungthut in the north-west and another near Thonzè and both were appropriately welcomed with great ceremony.[18] In late 1853, a formal consecration ceremony was held to mark the king's assumption of power. By all accounts, Mindon was off to a good start.

Once the fighting was finally over on the many and varied fronts, the remainder of the 1850s and early 1860s was a time of considerable hope in the Burmese court, with the threat of renewed war receding and an expanding trade bringing increased income to some individuals and to the royal coffers.[19] Contemporary British reports stressed the optimistic mood and often mentioned the absence of crime and general peace in the countryside.[20] Many of the key reforms discussed below were set in motion during this period of renewed confidence and relative prosperity, reforms which would only be reinforced over the years despite the political and economic troubles which were to come.

Mindon's reign was also a time of great expansion in popular theatre as well as many notable achievements in literature and the arts in Mandalay. One of the most famous playwrights of the nineteenth century was Salay Maung Ponnya who had risen to fame as a poet in the court of the

---

[17] *Ibid.*, pp. 211–12.

[18] The Kanimyo Sitkè, *Mandalay Yadanapon Mahayazawindawgyi* (History of Mandalay), Rangoon, 1969, pp. 103–4; *GUBSS*, vol. II, p. 45; *KBZ*, vol. III, p. 195.

[19] See, for example, *DPC*, 9 February 1855 for favourable British reports of the situation at this time.   [20] See, for example, *ibid.*, 7 March 1854.

Kanaung Prince in the early 1850s.[21] He had been born in 1812 into the Ponnya Thaman family, one of the two chiefly families of Salay. His father had been called into the king's service during Tharrawaddy's early years in power and the young Ponnya had spent his formative years at the Bhamo monastic college at Amarapura. He left the monastery to join the Kanaung Prince's establishment and soon became widely known for his singular literary skills, skills which he often employed in the service of local patriotism. In 1852, on the eve of the Second Anglo-Burmese War, he had written a poem celebrating Ava's military victories over Ayuthaya and Chiang Mai. In a later play, *Wizaya*, he subtly emphasises the importance of devotion to one's country above all else, including even the monarchy. He was conferred the title Minhla Thinhkaya and granted the village of Ywasi as his *appanage*.[22]

Mindon's modernisations

The better known of Mindon's reforms are his attempts to modernise the military, develop manufacturing industries, import new technologies, especially in transportation and communications, and broaden access to Western learning. In the early 1860s the size of the army was estimated as approximately 50,000.[23] Modernising the military meant in part the incorporation of up-to-date technology and included the development of a domestic weapons industry. Factories under the Kanaung Prince's control soon began producing rifles and ammunition to replace the antiquated muskets still in use. Artillery, however, still had to be imported and several large guns were procured with the permission of Rangoon, as were a total of ten steamers, which would play an increasingly important role in maintaining internal security.[24] The army was also reorganised along professional lines. This meant creating a standing army to replace the old rotating crown service system of the past. Much more will be said below on the effects of dismantling hereditary service arrangements. A few army officers received training in Europe and by the late 1870s a number of

---

[21] Htin Aung, *Burmese Drama*, pp. 76–108.

[22] Sosodaw Mya Attuppatti (Biographies of Royal Poets), Hmawbi Saya Thein, pp. 390–4.

[23] Pollack, *Empires in Collision*, p. 119.

[24] Grattan Geary, *Burma, After the Conquest, Viewed in its Political, Social and Commercial Aspects from Mandalay*, London, 1886, pp. 39–40.

Europeans, mainly Frenchmen and Italians, were brought to Mandalay as advisors for the construction of new forts along the Irrawaddy. A team of Italian consultants helped map out a general defence plan. Mindon's government clearly hoped not only to be able to meet any internal threat, but also to be able to offer at least some resistance against an invading European force.

Attempts were also made to improve transportation and communications.[25] In 1870 a telegraph line was completed linking Mandalay with Rangoon as well as a few regional towns and a Burmese system of Morse code was developed. Steamers, as mentioned, were also imported from overseas, but though these were useful for internal security, they were never developed into a proper transport service. They were apparently not well maintained and could not compete commercially with the Irrawaddy Flotilla Company which ran up and down the Irrawaddy and eventually part of the Chindwin as well.[26] The government's desire to extend the railway line through the upper valley to the Chinese border, however, never came to fruition. In 1864 the government granted a railway concession to a British firm but the proposed route turned out to be impractical and subsequent negotiations with British entreprenuers proved unsuccessful.

The government also attempted to encourage manufacturing industries by establishing state-owned factories, with European machinery and in some cases under European management, for the manufacture of lac,[27] cutch,[28] sugar,[29] and of cotton[30] and silk goods.[31] These ventures were very expensive, costing approximately £400,000 in the late 1850s and early 1860s, and were of questionable value. They were showpiece projects, intended to demonstrate the kingdom's ability to develop its own manufacturing base, and certainly excited local pride.

Part of the modernisation drive also involved attempts to introduce Western secular education. Until British rule, education for the vast majority would remain firmly male and monastic, but an English-language

---

[25] On Mindon's enthusiasm for new technologies, see 'Mandalay Diary', India Foreign Proceedings (hereafter IFP), 9 November 1872.

[26] Alistar McCrae and Alan Prentice, *Irrawaddy Flotilla*, London, 1978, p. 65.

[27] *Annual Report of Maritime Trade and Customs* (hereafter *RTC*), 1874/5, p. 24.

[28] *Report on the Administration of Burma* (hereafter *RAB*), 1877/8, p. 54.

[29] *Ibid.*, 1879/80, p. 68.

[30] 'Mandalay Diary', IFP, 16 November 1872; *RAB*, 1877/8, p. 51; 1879/80, p. 66.

[31] *RAB*, 1877/8, p. 51.

school was established just outside the royal city in 1870 on Mindon's initiative. It was funded by the government and run by Dr John Marks of the Society for the Propagation of the Gospels.[32] The school's pupils were primarily the sons of noblemen, though a number of princes, Mindon's own sons, also attended for a while, including the future King Thibaw. Though royal interest and the number of princes enrolled declined over the years, the school continued to operate until the flight of foreigners from Mandalay in 1879.[33] A much more concerted attempt was made to send students abroad. Overturning the Myoza of Myawaddy's views in the 1820s that Burmese parents could never part with their children 'as the English appear to do', a sizeable group of children and young adults were sent abroad in the 1850s and 1860s, to India and Europe. One group of six whose backgrounds can be clearly identified all belonged to noble families, and it is reasonable to assume that this was true of most others. The six were sent to St Xavier's School in Calcutta in 1872. They were aged 15–17 and were the sons, grandsons or nephews of the *myaung wun* (the irrigation minister); the *hledaw ttaukké* (an officer of the Royal Boats); the *naukwin min* (a Household Guards officer); a *nahkandaw* (a court reporter); the *pantin wun* (the master of the coppersmiths); and a *sayédawgyi* (a chief secretary).[34]

The first state scholars were sent to France in 1859, to St Cyr and the Ecole Polytechnique. They were followed by others throughout Mindon's reign. A total of at least seventy were sent abroad during the period 1859–75, most to France, England and India. At least one, the son of the senior diplomat, the Myoza of Myaunghla, was sent to school in Turin and a few others might also have been sent to Italy. The returned students all seem to have followed official careers. The St Cyr student became a cavalry commander; at least three other returners had reached cabinet-level positions with the rank of *wundauk* or *atwinwun* by 1885.[35] Men such as the Myoza of Kyaukmyaung, who was educated at the Sorbonne, would play an important role in the final drama before the occupation.

New rifles and cannon, steamships and telegraphs, smoke-billowing mills, the first students to the West: these were all the better known reforms, and, in many ways, they may be said to have failed. The military

---

[32] E. Marks, *Forty Years in Burma*, London, 1917.
[33] See Paul J. Bennett, *Conference under the Tamarind Tree: Three Essays in Burmese History*, New Haven, 1971.
[34] Maung Maung Tin, *Sadanmya*, Rangoon, 1975, pp. 87–92.   [35] *Ibid.*

was never improved sufficiently to meet the British challenge. Efforts to develop an industrial base cost huge amounts of money with little or no return. Their effects would pale besides the much greater changes in technology and learning which would accompany colonial rule. But the king and his ministers also embarked on a whole other area of modernisation, one much less appreciated but much more important. This venture, an attempt completely to refashion state authority, to place existing institutions within the framework of a new type of political authority, would be of great consequence and would set the stage for the colonial state and society to follow.

Refashioning the state

There does not exist, and probably never existed, a document or an old palm-leaf manuscript outlining plans for a thorough overhaul of the Court of Ava. No royal order details a coherent plan to revolutionise state authority or to fundamentally reform the government of the Irrawaddy plain. Nevertheless, between 1853 and 1878, and especially in the late 1850s and early 1860s, Mindon and his ministers set in motion a series of policies which, taken together, amounted to a vast change in the working of political power. Administration was centralised, royal agencies were bureaucratised, and a completely new system of taxation was constructed. Underlying these reforms were efforts to rationalise government, to do away with vagueness, haphazardness and local variation, to construct clear lines of authority and more definite boundaries of jurisdiction.

Centralisation of administration meant increasing the power of appointed provincial officials over the many and varied chiefs of the rural office-holding class and, in turn, of increasing the power of Mandalay over these appointed provincial officials. The first area targeted was Mandalay's supervision of judicial courts. These courts or *yon* , presided over by the appointed *myowun*, had increased their influence at the expense of the gentry throughout the early modern era. With little or no local background and no claim to the throne, they were unlikely to rebel and were thus traditionally given considerable leeway in exercising their duties. But while a certain degree of autonomy on their part had perhaps not been problematic in the past, Mindon and his ministers now clearly saw a need to supervise their work more effectively. Several of Mindon's early edicts were orders to review and revise the judicial system, attempting to divide responsibility clearly between provincial and high courts as well as between the different high courts over various types of cases.[36]

Over the next twenty years numerous orders would reinforce these attempts to bureaucratise the judiciary and rein in provincial offices.[37] In this effort Mindon's government was only at best partially successful, and Burmese records note the unwillingness of provincial *yon* to pass on to Mandalay cases which were theoretically under Hluttaw jurisdiction.[38] This problem lasted until the very end of the monarchy, with *myowun* in 1884 still promising to send cases for central decision.[39] Corruption was seen to be a major problem in establishing a functioning centrally controlled judicial bureaucracy. Immediately after assuming power, Mindon fixed judicial fees, that is the fees which were to be given to the local or high court judges for various types of cases.[40] The failure of this policy is evidenced by the series of royal orders condemning the acceptance of 'extra fees',[41] the passage of an anti-bribery act listing harsh punishments,[42] and the ordering of all cases to be heard only in the provincial or high court and not in the residence of the adjudicating magistrate.[43]

There were complementary efforts to rein in the gentry and place them more fully under crown authority. There were also attempts to rationalise their position *vis-à-vis* Mandalay and to establish a single category of local hereditary officer in place of the enormously confusing and varied patchwork of local magnates which still existed. In the wake of the 1853 palace revolution, Mindon, having just become king and perhaps being in a still tenuous position, temporarily confirmed all incumbent chiefs in their positions, but this soon gave way to a more interventionist approach.[44]

In Salin, the government tried to find a single hereditary chief to replace the local oligarchy. A network of inter-related families had ruled the area for 500 years and the complexity of their elite organisation had begun to trouble Mandalay. Several times orders were given to restrict government to the rule of a single chiefly line, including one to appoint the head of the Zeyya Battara Maha family as the sole lord of Salin.[45] But this rich and distant gentry elite was able to an extent to thwart Mandalay's plans and the Zeyya Battara Maha family never ruled alone. But in many other localities, the Court of Ava was much more successful in arbitrating

---

[36] *ROB*, 24 April 1853.   [37] *Ibid.*, 26 April 1866.   [38] *Ibid.*, 10 March 1859.
[39] *Ibid.*, 27 February 1884.   [40] *Ibid.*, 24 April 1853.
[41] *Ibid.*, 23 April 1854, 10 March 1859, 24 February 1866, 9 December 1878, 17 March 1882.   [42] *Ibid.*, 10 February 1869.   [43] *Ibid.*, 10 September 1873.
[44] *Ibid.*, 3 March 1853.   [45] Ohn Kyi, 'Salin Thugaung Thamaing', pp. 55–84.

succession questions, aggressively confirming new chiefs and dismissing others.

Gentry office-holders were dismissed for various reasons: for alleged 'repressive practices' such as over-taxation, causing a flight of villagers and the 'ruin of the village';[46] for being involved in criminal activity, such as running a distillery or operating a gambling centre;[47] for 'incompetence';[48] for 'unpopularity';[49] and for misappropriation of funds. In at least a couple of cases, chiefs were dismissed for 'not being of the chiefly family' as listed in the 1783 and 1802 inquests,[50] evidence not only that the crown still supported traditional local elites but also that more outsiders were penetrating local communities. Mindon's government also apparently experimented with the establishment of *myo-ok*, or township officers, as royal agents who would work together with or replace hereditary chiefs. The *myo-ok* was a British Burma invention and the adoption of this institution by Mandalay represented a further attempt to centralise political authority. They were appointed mainly in places close to the capital, such as in Kyauksè where hereditary office-holders were quickly losing power to Mindon's ministers.

But while the state was able to dominate the countryside to a great degree in much of the valley, in more peripheral areas, such as in the areas north of Shwébo or down towards the British Burma border, hereditary elites continued to resist Mandalay's interventions. Several royal orders directed at townships in outlying areas vigorously condemned the practice of deciding on local succession without royal sanction.[51] In at least one case, the royal appointment, when finally made, was accompanied by an explanation that the selection was based on the advice of the traditional leading family.[52] In other cases dismissals and new appointments were made explicitly on the advice of provincial governors and army officers who often claimed that their choice was based on a 'local consensus'.[53] Important monks from the area also began to have a say by the mid-1870s.[54]

[46] *ROB*, 15 November 1853, 5 June 1858.
[47] *Ibid.*, 6 October 1858, 31 July 1871, 11 September 1872, 30 January 1874, 8 January 1879, 20 June 1873.   [48] *Ibid.*, 6 October 1858, 16 October 1858.
[49] *Ibid.*, 31 August 1872.
[50] *Ibid.*, 28 October 1858 (and, continuing on under Thibaw, 20 June 1883).
[51] *Ibid.*, January 1855, 9 January 1875.   [52] *Ibid.*, 12 July 1858.
[53] For selection by the provincial governor (*myowun*), see *ibid.*, 6 October 1858, 31 July 1871, 31 August 1872, 29 October 1872, 27 May 1874. For selection by army officers or *thwéthaukgyi* under their charge, see *ibid.*, 20 August 1873 and 28 December 1878.

The government also attempted to improve its ability to collect better and more up-to-date information. Mindon, apparently in line with his predecessors, maintained a personal intelligence system with a network of secret informants around the capital.[55] Some attempts were made to circumvent local elites and obtain information more directly, in particular through the Sangha. Improved transportation and communication would certainly have aided the centre in obtaining news, though in general it seems problems in collecting reliable information from local government continued to plague Mandalay until the very end of the monarchy.[56]

A fiscal revolution

Overarching these attempts to reform administration were attempts to implement new financial policies. Among the more important policy problems facing Mindon was that of finding a way to improve the poor state of the royal treasury. On coming to power, the king, in a somewhat tenuous position, made the politically astute and familiar promise of no new taxes, stating that his government would levy only customary fees. This was in part related to the growing concerns of officials over the state of indebtedness in the countryside. There appears to have been a substantial increase in the extent of rural indebtedness in the years since the First Anglo-Burmese War, though the evidence is sketchy.[57] A palace memorandum of 20 April 1855 summarises its view of the 'debt problem':

> In instances where the creditor is a notable or powerful person, unjust methods have at times been employed to pressure debtors to pay back their loans. In other cases, the debtor has gained office or status since initially incurring the debt and has then tried to evade repayment. Cumulative debt has, for some become an enormous burden as a result of compounded interest charges. It is not the case that all debt repayments should stop or that all debts should be paid off. [The government] shall decide on a case-by-case basis.[58]

Mindon himself felt strongly that money-lending at interest rates which

[54] *Ibid.*, 23 April 1873, 27 May 1874.
[55] *MMOS*, vol. III, pp. 81–4; *ROB*, 6 April 1853.   [56] *ROB*, 4 May 1854.
[57] Part of the evidence on debt and its effects could be found in the existing *thetkhayits* or commercial contracts. See 'List of Microfilms Deposited in the Centre for East Asian Cultural Studies, Toyo Bunko, Part Eight, Burma', Tokyo, 1976. See also Toe Hla, 'Moneylending and Contractual Thet-kayits'.   [58] *ROB*, 20 April 1855.

caused distress was contrary to justice and caused the lender to forfeit merit in both his or her present and future existences. Though nothing suggests that attempts to reform the situation made much difference, the royal court was, by the 1850s, reluctant to place new revenue burdens on the countryside.[59]

Contemporary British observers generally believed that direct taxation by Mindon on agriculture in his early years was lower than that of previous reigns.[60] But this meant that the treasury desperately needed to find alternative sources of income. Despite now ruling over a smaller territory, the revenue requirements of the state remained very high. This was partly a result of Mindon's modernisation programme and expensive diplomatic missions abroad. It was also a result of his extensive patronage of the Sangha, the construction of Mandalay in the late 1850s as the new Konbaung seat, and other projects designed in part to demonstrate that his court was still the 'exemplary centre' of the entire country.

Mindon first turned to trade, first and foremost trade in cotton. From 1853 to 1857 Mindon effectively taxed the export of cotton to China by acting as middleman between cultivators and Chinese firms operating out of Amarapura.[61] These dozen or so firms represented commercial houses in Yunnan and elsewhere in China and dominated both the export of cotton and the import of Chinese goods. The king's agents collected the cotton on site, paying approximately twenty kyat of silver per hundred viss for cleaned cotton. This was then delivered to Chinese merchants at Amarapura or at various points along the Irrawaddy and sold at fifty kyat per hundred viss. Reports from the informal British agent at Amarapura stated that in 1855 four million viss was sold to China in this way. To a much lesser extent, Mindon also traded in timber cutch, wheat and gram. Timber and cutch were sold to firms in Rangoon[62] and wheat and gram were sold directly to British authorities for use as food for Indian troops stationed in Lower Burma.[63] Mindon also traded in rubies, which were brought in from crown-controlled mines in Sayin and Mogok, then sold wholesale to Chinese and other purchasers. In 1855, Sir Henry Yule estimated Mindon's profits as totalling nearly £230,000 sterling a year.[64]

As both the sale of forest and other natural resources claimed by the crown and the crown's intervention in the export market became critical

---

[59] *Ibid.*, 10 April 1853.   [60] Yule, *Mission*, p. 256.
[61] *DPC*, 22 April 1854, 17 March 1855.   [62] *Ibid.*, 13 January 1855, 15 May 1855.
[63] *Ibid.*, 18 February 1854, 7 March 1854.   [64] Yule, *Mission*, pp. 256–7.

sources of income, royal agents undertook numerous attempts to discover new sources of mineral wealth. The government funded several explorations, including partially successful ones for lead, coal, copper, rubies, petroleum oil, amber, iron ore and gold.[65] Similarly, explorations were undertaken to search for new forest areas which could be commercially exploited.[66]

Thus, even in the early years of his reign, Mindon, though not imposing new direct taxes, did significantly tax the commercial sector of the economy through interventions in growing markets. The effects of this taxation were thus not uniform; it affected mainly areas growing cash crops, areas from which natural resources were extracted, and the Burmese *thuhtay*. Mindon's policy virtually removed Burmese merchants from the profits of the China trade and established a direct business relationship between large Chinese firms and royal agents. The initial impact on cotton and other cash crop cultivators, however, might not have been particularly negative and Mindon himself explained that his intervention, through the provision of cash advances, provided in effect interest-free loans and a secure market. Mindon apparently did absorb losses when they occurred and his monopoly on foreign sales would have increased the price which Chinese and Rangoon buyers were obliged to pay. The difference in price may then have been passed on to the producers.

The government's policy of 'monopolies', of playing the role of the 'chief trader' in Upper Burma quickly drew British criticism. Said Yule: '[there is] little doubt that the amount drawn from the country by direct taxation is very much less than has been extracted in previous reigns, yet it must be most injurious to the interests of the great body of the people to be obliged to sell their staple articles of produce at a fixed price to the Sovereign'.[67] However, throughout the 1850s and early 1860s, Mindon and his government were still strong enough to resist demands for greater free trade and foreign access to local markets.

They did run into problems early on, however, as a consequence of the sudden disruption of the China trade due to the outbreak of the Panthay Rebellion in 1857. The Panthay Rebellion involved the secession of western Yunnan from China under a Muslim leadership based in Dali and lasted from 1857 to 1873.[68] The rebellion placed the Burmese government

[65] Pollack, *Empires in Collision*, p. 124.   [66] *Ibid.*, p. 125.   [67] Yule, *Mission*, p. 257.
[68] Denis Twitchett and John K. Fairbank (eds.), *The Cambridge History of China*, vol. II: *Late Ch'ing, 1800–1911*, part 2, Cambridge, 1980, pp. 211–14.

in the awkward position of either banning trade with Yunnan or risking incurring the anger of the Qing government in Peking. Official policy was not to trade or to recognise Yunnan's independence, and though some private trade did continue, crown revenues from the old caravan routes dropped precipitously through the late 1850s and 1860s.[69]

Mindon was thus compelled to rely ever more on trade with Lower Burma and, through Rangoon, with international markets. Demand for cotton was increasing and would continue to increase through the years of the American Civil War and the related 'cotton famine' in Britain. But, as we shall see, successful British pressure in the 1860s to open up Burmese markets and end competition from the Burmese state meant that the state could not turn to intervention in trade to solve its financial difficulties and that new sources of revenue still needed to be found. Therefore, as a result of British free-trade imperialism a much more direct tax had to be devised, and this in turn required a complete overhaul of the early modern system of state revenue. As we have seen, the system of taxation up until that time was one divided between the granting of *appanages*, collecting rent on crown lands and receiving a portion of the various gentry-controlled customary fees and obligations, as much in kind or specialised manpower as in cash.

An early decision was made to end the *appanage* system and instead provide cash salaries to all officials and members of the military. This was initially unanimously opposed by Mindon's ministers but finally adopted by the early 1860s.[70] *Myoza*, whether members of the royal family or nobility holding *appanages*, now simply drew the allotted cash income from their *appanage*'s contribution to the royal treasury.[71] Links between individual members of the aristocracy and local communities were thus severed and remuneration for equivalent positions in the official hierarchy was made (at least in theory) uniform. Members of the military or other crown service groups faced even greater change as their new salaried status meant an end to land which their families had held for generations in return for their labour obligations. The land theoretically now reverted back to the state which demanded an effective rent; needless to

[69] 'Memorandum on the Panthays or Mohommedan Population of Yunnan', in Albert Fytche, *Burma Past and Present with Personal Reminiscences of the Country in Two Volumes*, London, 1878.

[70] Arthur Phayre, 'Private Journal of Sir Arthur Phayre', in Yule, *Mission*, p. xxxiv.

[71] *MMOS*, vol. III, p. 207.

say, this rent was less than forthcoming and much of this land began to fall into private hands.[72]

Also by the early 1860s the government decided to introduce, after consultation with the Buddhist Sangha, the new *thathameda* tax, effectively abolishing (though over many years) the entire early modern system of revenue and elite income upon which the state had rested.[73] The *thathameda* tax was theoretically an income tax, amounting to exactly one-tenth the income of all citizens, and was intended to replace *all* other existing and customary taxes and fees.[74] It was, in fact, much more a property tax with collection left largely in the hands of rural magnates who were expected to report to the treasury an assessed sum based on the number of households they reported to be under their charge.[75] They then collected the revenue (in kind or in cash) within their villages, based mainly on the property wealth of the particular household, and then handed over the sum to the provincial *myoyon* in cash. Destitute households or individuals (*dukkhita*) were listed and were not expected to pay any tax.

For the purpose of assessing the *thathameda* each *myo* was classified according to its perceived wealth or prosperity.[76] Within each area, however, it seems townspeople and the more commercialised cultivators often bore the brunt of uneven assessment. Financiers, traders, artisans and craftsmen were carefully scrutinised and assessed and then the balance was distributed over the rest of the population. Given limits on the mobility of royal officials (compared with colonial officers) and the absence of any tradition of 'touring' the countryside, it is perhaps not surprising that agricultural holdings were assessed somewhat indiscriminately and inadequately. British reports state that those cultivators who were taxed very highly were those who produced mainly for the market and who had become 'conspicuous' for money-lending and acquiring mortgaged land.[77]

This new fiscal system could obviously not be imposed overnight. One major problem was the difficulty faced by the king's men in gaining

---

[72] *Ibid.*, vol. IV, pp. 207–9.   [73] *KBZ*, vol. III, p. 251.

[74] *ROB*, 10 March 1859, 22 March 1869, 5 February 1869, 17 April 1882.

[75] *Ibid.*, 30 April 1868, 22 May 1868, 15 May 1881, 30 July 1881, 30 November 1883 all make reference to the role of headmen.

[76] *GUBSS*, vol. II, pp. 414–15. See also *MMOS*, vol. IV, pp. 306–12.

[77] *GUBSS*, vol. II, p. 417.

accurate information on the number of households in a particular locality and on local economic conditions to the extent that a 'fair' assessment could be made. A few hereditary office-holders were punished for misinformation, under-reporting the number of households and over-reporting the number of destitute families. Officials were also reprimanded for not collecting enough necessary information.[78] But in general, the crown seemed resigned to not being able to administer the revenue system properly and as late as the 1880s the discovery of under-taxation usually resulted only in a request to the local authorities to collect arrears as soon as possible.[79]

In addition, it seems small *de facto appanages* continued to be granted to members of the royal family. In at least one case (in 1872), the widow of a senior official was granted the right to continue to receive personally all revenue from a particular market.[80] Finally, whatever the system was in theory, in practice as with all aspects of Burmese government, exceptions were made when they came into conflict with patronage obligations, including the obligations of the king to rule in the interests of his people. Many exemptions to payment of the *thathameda* tax were made, including perpetual exemptions for members of selected aristocratic families,[81] *ponna*,[82] important gentry families,[83] and also, as a general policy, cultivators reclaiming waste land.[84]

More importantly, it seems that many Mandalay aristocrats were not at all content to give up their links with their erstwhile *appanages* or other places where they might have some claim or connection. Dozens of royal orders from the late 1850s until the end of the monarchy dealt specifically with petitions from crown servicemen and chiefs to be 'allowed to work undisturbed' by a member of the court aristocracy.[85] As only accepted petitions were recorded, one might assume that many local communities continued to be harassed by influential outsiders. The crown also continued to allow members of the royal family to recruit personal dependants from among the general population, and specifically from among crown servants. Several hundred cavalrymen were transferred from the

---

[78] *ROB*, 13 August 1854.   [79] *Ibid.*, 30 November 1883.   [80] *Ibid.*, 26 October 1872.
[81] *Ibid.*, 26 February 1859.   [82] Such as court Brahmins. *Ibid.*, 23 May 1871.
[83] Such as the very important and very old families of the *mintha* of Pagan. *Ibid.*, 31 July 1871.   [84] *Ibid.*, 29 August 1873.
[85] For petitions from crown servicemen, see *ibid.*, 5 June 1858, 1 October 1858, 4 October 1858, 8 February 1859, 6 March 1859. For petitions from headmen, see *ibid.*, 12 July 1858, 27 October 1858.

charge of their officer to the chief queen shortly after Mindon's coming to power.[86] Another royal order confirmed the status of her personal slaves and their exemption from taxation and other state obligations.[87] New groups of slaves were also recruited for other members of the royal family[88] and their exemption from any other service was noted.[89] Thus, while salaries were instituted, the members of the aristocracy fought a rearguard action to preserve the lucrative aspects of their relationship with the countryside in the past.

Though some writers early in the colonial period described the attempt to impose the *thathameda* tax as unsuccessful, this establishment of an entirely new system of taxation carried with it wide repercussions which critically influenced the course of social change in the Irrawaddy plain in the years prior to British annexation. First, if we assume that in some areas the *thathameda* did work as conceived and did replace older taxes and fees, then the effect would have been to lighten the tax burden on some people, especially crown servicemen and those classified as 'destitute'. But it would have increased taxation on the commercial class which was expanding with the growth of foreign trade and a more export-oriented agriculture. In this way, the *thathameda* and Mindon's interventions in trade, a *de facto* taxation of foreign trade, would have combined to curtail severely the development of a 'private sector' in the most dynamic part of the economy. The state might have thus stood in opposition to the interests of the indigenous commercial class and certainly this is how contemporary British 'free traders' accessed the situation.

Second, and with the same assumption, the entire revenue position of hereditary local office-holders, would have been completely undermined. Rural chiefs and others commissioned to take part in *thathameda* assessment and collection were compensated, but this would have been only a fraction of their previous income. Certainly the extent to which the assumption (that older taxes were abolished) was true varied from place to place and stronger gentry leaders would have perhaps been able to satisfy or ignore central demands while still collecting customary taxes for themselves. But as attempts to centralise political authority increased, and with the country becoming smaller as a result of improvements in transportation, the position of some local chiefs, forced to accept a much smaller part in the revenue system, would have been dramatically altered.

[86] *Ibid.*, 15 September 1853.   [87] *Ibid.*, 6 April 1853.   [88] *Ibid.*, 4 March 1859.
[89] *Ibid.*, 17 July 1878.

Third, to the extent that the *thathameda* was imposed in addition to existing taxes, the tax burden of the population generally would have increased. It seems unlikely that all (or even most) rural chiefs would have stopped collection of their long-standing dues and all evidence suggests that many *ad hoc* exactions such as for festivals and religious celebrations continued much as before.[90] As will be discussed in the next part, the *thathameda* tax was one of the key complaints of groups which turned to armed rebellion in the early 1880s.

A final effect of the new *thathameda* tax was its role in furthering the monetisation of the economy. The *thathameda* may have been collected in kind at the source, but was deposited in cash at provincial *myoyon* offices and certainly was received in cash at the royal treasury. Labour and even rice and other food supplies were no longer received by royal agencies. While direct evidence is lacking, taxation would thus have produced an increasing demand for money. Local office-holders as well as common cultivators began to fall into debt, in turn strengthening the position of money-lending outsiders and fuelling the social instability of the last years of the Konbaung dynasty.[91]

Mandalay and Calcutta

The establishment of a British 'informal empire' over what remained of the Burmese kingdom occurred during the course of Mindon's quarter-century reign. The local economy, once jealously guarded by mercantilist kings, was cracked open to almost unbridled British commercial expansion, and British political influence came to be felt in all corners of the country, from distant Shan principalities to the very centres of palace intrigue. The Burmese kingdom under Mindon, however, did maintain its nominal sovereignty. The overriding aim of the Burmese government's foreign policy during these years was the preservation of the kingdom's independence through the cultivation of good relations with Britain on the one hand, and the establishment of diplomatic and commercial relations with rival powers on the other. Mindon and his ministers apparently believed that they could court the friendship of Britain's European competitors, France in particular, while avoiding renewed confrontation with Calcutta. Under his son and successor Thibaw this tightrope act was to

---

[90] *Ibid.*, 15 August 1864.   [91] *MMOS*, vol. II, 155–6.

prove impossible, leading to annexation in 1885. But in the 1853–78 period Mandalay was still able to stave off demands for British control over Burma's foreign affairs, though paying a heavy price in allowing free trade and its attendant social effects.

This history of Anglo-Burmese relations over the thirty or so years between the second and third wars might be best seen as a failed attempt to reach some sort of mutual accommodation. On the one side were Burmese desires to preserve at least some measure of national sovereignty and pride. On the other were British desires to achieve a suitable local framework within which commercial and, to a lesser extent, strategic interests might be promoted and protected. Mindon had come to power during the Second Anglo-Burmese War largely as the head of a palace faction opposed to continued fighting. As a result he needed to be very careful about seeming excessively conciliatory towards the British, at least in the early part of his reign. The king and his government appeared to believe that a clear demonstration of future peaceful intentions would lead to the return of Pegu, which was obviously the overriding political concern at the time. But Lord Dalhousie, the Indian governor-general had already decided to annex Pegu to his existing Burmese possessions and unilaterally create the new province of British Burma.

Mindon's initial attempts at using diplomacy to gain back the lost territory, for example the dispatch of his senior minister, the Myoza of Magwé, in 1854 to Calcutta, were thus fated to be complete failures, weakening Mindon's position internally. The formal annexation of Lower Burma had also led to a series of revolts in British territory including quite serious ones headed by local Burmese acting with the tacit encouragement of some in Mandalay.[92] Rumours spread of renewed war in both Rangoon and Amarapura, but Mindon and Sir Arthur Phayre, the Chief Commissioner of British Burma, were both committed to maintain peace, and their communications, through the informal British agent, Thomas Spears, a Scottish businessman in Amarapura, gradually eased tensions. Phayre even arranged for 250 durians, the foul-smelling 'king of fruits', to be delivered to Ava. Durians were a favourite of Mindon and were native to parts of British Burma but not to the dry upper valley.[93]

The first attempt to achieve a long-term mutually agreeable framework

---

[92] For example, Maung Bo, Myowun of Malun, led a guerilla resistance against the new colonial authorities but was soon afterwards replaced by Mindon with an official of Armenian descent. *DPC*, 12 November 1855.   [93] *KBZ*, vol. III, p. 209.

for bilateral relations took place from August through October 1855 with the mission of Phayre as representative of the Governor-General of India to the Court of Ava. Phayre was accompanied by several experts including geographers and scientists, and a detailed account of the mission was subsequently written by Sir Henry Yule. Phayre's mission, which travelled in two steamers, included no less than 440 soldiers and a personal escort of cavalry. He was met at the border by the deputy senior minister Maha Minhtin Kyaw, the chief secretary to the chief queen, and a large flotilla of over a thousand war-boats and royal barges.

The primary goal of the mission for the British was to induce Mindon to sign a peace treaty acknowledging Burma's cession of the province of Pegu, which, together with Arakan and the Tennasserim, now formed 'British Burma'. Mindon was very keen to extend every hospitality to the visiting delegation. They were quite free to travel around as they wished, and trips were conducted to Bhamo as well as places closer to Amarapura. What Mindon was careful not to do, however, was to appear in any way a subject ruler and great care was taken to play the part of a sovereign head of state hosting a mission from an equal foreign power. In several areas of protocol, differences appeared between the two sides which remained until annexation.

The most well known was the so-called 'shoe question'.[94] It was the custom that shoes were taken off when entering a building as a mark of respect similar to the removal of one's hat in Europe. The British, however, felt that the Burmese were insisting on their taking off their shoes, at royal audiences or even on the approach to the audience hall, in an attempt to humiliate them. They were never quite sure where custom ended and a deliberate slight began. There are many other similar examples of this sort of passive protest by the Burmese, as well as related attempts by Mindon and officials not to give in to British displays of their superior position. Phayre's steamer was not allowed all the way up to Amarapura,[95] for example, and Mindon insisted on financing himself the cost of their stay.

The decision not to sign an accord, as proposed by Phayre, was made by Mindon against the advice of his ministers who were apparently united in favouring a treaty.[96] His stated reason, which he repeated many times, was his fear of how he would be portrayed in future chronicles as the king who

[94] Yule, *Mission*, p. 79.   [95] *DPC*, 21 August 1855.   [96] Yule, *Mission*, p. 109.

signed away half his country. He said to Phayre: 'If I were to sanction a treaty discreditable to me, I should lose my reputation in history just as a thousand years hence your name would be stained, if you did anything to the damage of your country. Ponder upon this.'[97] But he was also apparently hoping that his position *vis-à-vis* the British might soon change; specifically, that a British loss in the Crimean War or the costs of the Santal insurrection, both of which were occurring at the time, might increase his bargaining position. His reading of the London papers suggested that he would receive a more favourable hearing in England than in India and so increased his desire for direct representation. In any case, he thought it prudent to wait for the coming change in viceroy.[98]

Thus, the failure of the mission to achieve its primary aim reflected one key difficulty preventing the Burmese government from becoming the sort of local collaborator desired by British interests: the unwillingness of Mindon and his officials to see themselves as anything less than a sovereign state. Everything else was possible, and, over the next thirty years, many concessions would be made to British demands on trade, extraterritorial rights and protection for the Residency. The hope of reasserting Burma's complete independence, however, was never lost. Efforts were continually made to formalise direct representation with London and to enmesh Burma in a web of international contacts which would make further British expansion as diplomatically costly as possible.

By 1862, Mindon apparently felt in a strong enough position internally to finally sign not a formal peace treaty ceding Lower Burma but a commercial treaty proposed by Calcutta. The early 1860s were a time of a certain degree of optimism, with the economy benefiting from increased trade, particularly the export of cotton, and the government's own policies perhaps winning, if not 'popular' support, at least the confidence of the Mandalay elite. The treaty itself, the effects of which will be discussed in detail below, was designed to protect and promote trade between Upper Burma and the British Empire. Tariffs on trade between Lower and Upper Burma were reduced, goods travelling between Lower Burma and China were exempted from Burmese taxation and British merchants were given special protection and privileges including the right to proceed up the Irrawaddy 'in such manner as they please without hindrance'.[99] Not included in the treaty but subsequently agreed by Mindon was a joint

[97] *Ibid.*, pp. 96–8.   [98] *Ibid.*, p. 195.

[99] B.R. Pearn, 'The Commercial Treaty of 1862', *JBRS*, 27 (1937), 33–53.

survey mission which was to be allowed to explore the trade route from Bhamo to Yunnan. The 1862 treaty heralded the beginning of vigorous attempts by the growing British commercial community at Rangoon to secure greater and greater access to Burmese markets, largely undoing in the process the very financial basis of Mindon's reformed state. It also marked the beginning of sustained commercial interest in the China market and a desire to prevent other Western countries from accessing this market through Upper Burma.[100]

The immediate effect of the 1862 treaty was a considerable expansion of bilateral trade. Despite this, the foreign business community at Rangoon began to criticise the Burmese government's upholding of the agreement's provisions. In particular, foreign firms, supported by most British officials, felt that the Burmese government, though no longer working through official monopolies, nevertheless remained unfairly involved in trade. In addition, the Burmese government, though it was bound to abolish specific frontier duties within a reasonable amount of time did not do so until five years later. The reason was clearly the state's financial situation, already damaged by the relaxation on tariffs which had taken place. According to the Resident, Col. Edward Sladen, the Myoza of Pakhangyi, a senior minister, told him that the Burmese government 'never intended at the time the treaty was made to abolish the duties, but [that] the Article was inserted for mere form's sake'. Sladen went on that the minister 'pleaded almost pitifully' that the 'very low state of the country's finances' – due to the expenditure incurred in the construction of Mandalay and the 'extraordinary demands of the priesthood on the State purse' and the reduction in the size of the kingdom – made it practically impossible for them to give up even a single item of the current revenue.[101]

By the mid-1860s, as the government's financial worries continued, a new crisis would threaten to derail Mindon's entire reform process: a great rebellion which shook the kingdom to its very foundations.

[100] Dorothy Woodman, *The Making of Burma*, London, 1962, pp. 171–204; Ralph Charles Croziet, 'Antecedents of the Burma Road: Nineteenth Century British Interest in Trans-Burma Trade Routes to China', M.A. dissertation, University of Washington, Seattle, 1960.   [101] IFP, Sept. 1865, no. 23.

6 | Revolt and the coming of British rule

The first dozen years of Mindon's reign had been marked by an increasing pace of reform. They had also been marked by increasing stresses and strains, as Burmese society entered an unprecedented period of social change. By the mid-1860s another problem, much more traditional in nature, reared its head. The failure of the House of Alaungpaya to regularise succession to the monarchy yet again threatened to divide the court. All sons of a king by a senior queen remained at least theoretically eligible. Among the fourth and fifth generations of descent from the founder were dozens of men with some claim to the throne. Mindon had clearly marked Kanaung as his successor and had appointed him Prince of the Eastern Palace, or crown prince. But now, many of Mindon's own numerous sons were reaching maturity and resented their uncle's position. Mindon had used Kanaung on at least one occasion to discipline some of the royal princes for bad behaviour. Two of the eldest, the Princes of Myingun and Myinhkondaing were among those who had been disciplined. Their personal ambitions would soon combine with the volatile atmosphere of the countryside to produce the worst fighting in the Irrawaddy valley in nearly a generation.

Princes and rebels

At noon on 2 August 1866, the Myingun and Myinhkondaing princes set fire to several buildings within the royal city to signal the start of their rebellion.[1] Kanaung had been chairing a high-level meeting to review fiscal policies at a small pavilion near the palace. Halfway through the proceedings, the two princes, assisted by several dozen followers, entered the building, drew their swords and killed Kanaung, as well as six other senior officials. Among those killed were the army commander, the Myoza of Myadaung, the senior minister, the Myoza of Laungshay, and the Captain of the Letway Guards, the Myoza of Myèdu. Ten others attending the meeting escaped. The author's own great-great-great-grandfather,

---

[1] *KBZ*, vol. III, pp. 333–50.

Maha Mindin Thinkaya, the Myoza of Dabessway, escaped assassination as he had stayed at home that day owing to a bad cold. Kanaung, though, was decapitated and his head was paraded about the nearby passage by Myinhkondaing. Soon afterwards, the Princes of Malun, Pyinsi and Sagu were also assassinated, all after having received bogus messages purporting to be from the king.

General fighting within the palace walls then broke out between the rival sides and a number of high-ranking military officers were killed in the ensuing confrontation over the next several hours. Mindon at the time was at a temporary summer residence at the foot of Mandalay Hill, where he had been supervising the construction of a pagoda complex. Together with the Mekkaya Prince, other family and the Royal Bodyguard, he managed to re-enter the city in the confusion. Two of the king's senior ministers were now dead, one was captured, and only one, his old tutor, the Myoza of Pahkangyi remained with him. Only after fierce fighting through the afternoon, did loyalist forces manage to reorganise and throw the two princes and their followers on the defensive, the rebels realising they would not be able to reach the king, and retreating through the Red Gate. They commandeered the king's ship the *Yenan Setkya* and headed downriver.

The Myingun and Myinhkondaing princes regrouped their army at Malun, near the British Burma border and began to march north once again, capturing several towns in the area. They were assisted by the local Karen people of the area, though other Karen, under their own chiefs, aided the loyalist side. The king sent a column under the command of the experienced general the Myoza of Yénangyaung, who established a forward base at Pagan and slowly moved downriver. By September, heavy rains hampered all military action, but the rebel side was facing greater hardship, having run out of supplies and being faced by sky-rocketing local food prices. The British then allowed Mandalay to send a small force across the border and escort two of Mindon's steamers which had been docked in Rangoon. A huge force comprising of the steamships, 200 boats and over 10,000 soldiers then began a final assault on rebel positions. On 6 October, Myingun and Minhkondaing fled to British territory and surrendered.

But by this time another, even more serious rebellion had threatened the monarchy. The Prince of Padein, a son of Kanaung, had left Mandalay soon after his father was killed, fearing that he would be the next to be assassinated. Others in Kanaung's family had followed his example, including his younger brothers the Princes of Kyemyint, Taingda, Taungsin and Ywatha. They decamped to Madaya and then marched on Shwébo, which they took by force with the aid of local people. Mindon requested Padein to return, offering complete amnesty and protection. But encouraged by a growing crowd of advisors and hangers-on, he refused and instead raised the standard of rebellion. The governor of Tabayin had joined him, and he was appointed his army commander. A new rebel force was mustered and soon began to march on Mandalay.

At one point, in the third week of August, the government's position seemed extremely precarious. The British Resident, Col. Sladen, was certain Mindon would be dethroned and refused appeals for use of the Residency steamer. Padein's forces approached the royal city from the north, east and west, while provincial officials to the south rallied to the rebel prince's standard and raised another force of 10,000 anti-government troops. Mindon considered surrender to avoid further bloodshed. But his chief queen consulted her astrological charts and predicted victory, if he persevered.

Finally, by late September, when the Myingun rebellion had been crushed, the tide began to turn against Padein as well. A new force of 12,000 men backed by three steamers was divided into twelve separate commands, including one Shan division under the Sawbwa of Yawnghwe. A delegation of monks was then sent to make a last attempt at reconciliation. When this failed, an auspicious time for the counter-offensive was chosen and the lead companies of the royal army, lead by the Prince of Nyaungyan, crossed the Irrawaddy with 16 elephants, 18 cannon and 600 hand-picked cavalry. Padein's forces were routed in a series of engagements and the prince himself finally took refuge in a monastery. On 2 November he was arrested and led back to Mandalay, where he was first placed in detention at the Privy Treasury, and then executed for treason.

Days later, the Kanaung Prince was cremated in a grand funeral, attended by Mindon as well as an assortment of Kanaung's 144 children and grandchildren. He had been married to ten women, all daughters of noblemen, Shan chiefs and gentry leaders. His considerable family would remain a force in Burmese politics to the end of the monarchy and beyond.[2]

---

[2] *Ibid.*, pp. 355–61.

The rebellion was a political turning point for the Mindon regime, ending the fourteen-year partnership between the king and his brother. Mindon himself gradually withdrew from the day-to-day business of government, concentrating on projects of religious merit. A number of steps were undertaken to prevent a similar occurrence from happening again. In November, an attempt was made to collect arms throughout the country and to redistribute them to the local *myowun* and other provincial officials who were made directly responsible for their safekeeping.[3] Most importantly, Mindon decided not to appoint a new heir-apparent, apparently for fear that the selected prince would become a new target of assassination. This decision was to be of great consequence a little more than a decade later as we shall see in chapter 7.

Despite these political changes, however, the reform process itself not only continued but was strengthened. A whole new generation of reform-minded officials came into prominence in the late 1860s. These included several young men who had recently been sent to study abroad and who now returned to take up official positions. Among the returners was the future Myoza of Kyaukmyaung, who was rushed back from the Ecole Central des Arts et Manufactures in Paris to fill one of the new upper-level vacancies. He had also been educated at Doveton College in Calcutta and at the Panthéon, having gone to Paris after a chance meeting with a Frenchman, the Comte de Sacy on a steamer voyage across the Bay of Bengal. He was of partial European, perhaps Portuguese, descent, and is better remembered as the *pangyet wun* or 'Master of the Glass Factories', a reference to his critical role in setting up local industries.[4]

The most conservative of the old senior ministers, the Myoza of Magwé, had been implicated in the rebellion and was subsequently jailed. The much more forward-looking Myoza of Pahkangyi, Mindon's old tutor, was thereafter able to consolidate his position as the most important member of the new government. A new title of *wun-shindaw* or 'Chief Minister' was created and the Myoza of Laungshay and Hkampat were promoted to that role, in addition to Pahkangyi himself. The British henceforth referred to the Myoza of Pahkangyi as 'Prime Minister', and one report described him approvingly as 'an experienced and highly respected official [who] on all occasions conducted the communications

---

[3] *GUBSS*, vol. II, p. 59.
[4] On Kyaukmyaung's ancestry, I am indebted to a personal communication from Saya U Than Htut of Rangoon University.

between the two governments in an intelligent and friendly manner'.[5]

The fourth most important member of the government was the up-and-coming Myoza of Lègaing, better known to history as the Kinwun Mingyi. Born in 1822 near Alon to an old army family, he had studied under the Myoza of Pahkangyi at the Bagaya monastic college until 1849. A great classical scholar and poet and the author of numerous works on jurisprudence, he was given overall charge of foreign relations. He was later promoted to Chief Minister and would succeed his mentor as the President of the Council of State on the latter's death in 1873.

A final member of the Court of Ava at this time who should be mentioned was the young Myoza of Yaw. Born Maung Hlaing in 1829, he was from an old aristocratic clan which had served the Konbaung dynasty for four generations. His father, the Myoza of Yindaw, was a senior minister to Tharrawaddy who was executed for alleged complicity in the abortive *coup d'état* of 1844. Maung Hlaing was entrusted to Prince Mindon as guardian and completed his studies at the prestigious Bagaya monastic college. A great intellectual in the tradition of the old Mekkaya Prince (not Mindon's son of the same title), he eventually authored twenty books, including a famous medical manual and a book on chemistry. He also developed a Burmese version of the Morse Code and built, near Mandalay Hill, a beautiful brick monastery in imitation of an hotel he had seen while travelling in the south of Italy. He was always very close to the king, who now made him Privy Councillor, except during a brief period in the early 1870s when he fell from royal favour. This was over alcohol consumption: Mindon, as a good Buddhist, was opposed to all intoxicants, while the Myoza of Yaw was an enthusiastic drinker of imported beer. A supporter of the Kinwun Mingyi, he constantly pressed for rapid administrative reform and the importation of Western science and technology.[6] He was also married to the daughter of the conservative Magwé Mingyi, the king-maker who had been succeeded by the Myoza of Pakhangyi as Mindon's leading minister.

Of the remaining princes, the Prince of Mekkaya was now the most senior. He had proved himself staunchly loyal to his father during the revolt and Mindon rewarded him with an increasing role in government. He was placed in overall charge of industrial policy and supervised the many factories being built outside the city walls. He also handled many of

---

[5] *RAB*, 1873/4, p. 4.   [6] Maung Tin (ed.), *Yaw Mingyi Attuppatti*.

his father's business dealings with foreign firms.[7] But the king, though he hinted at times that he would prefer Mekkaya to succeed him, never took the final step of naming him his heir and, within a few years, relying on even this favourite son proved troublesome. In 1871, following a murky affair in which Mekkaya seemed to have been engaged in some sort of conspiracy, he was deprived of most of his official duties. The Council of State then imposed strict rules to prevent any informal contact between royal princes and ministers. No powerful prince remained at Mandalay, leaving the way clear for the grandees of the court to dominate the succession.[8]

Establishing an informal empire

As the Irrawaddy valley's economy was opening up to British trade, British trade began to set its sights on a much greater prize: a backdoor access to China. By the 1860s, China had come to dominate British thinking on the future of Burma and this was noted in a letter written in 1867 from the Secretary of State, Lord Cranbourne, to the Governor-General, Sir John Lawrence:

> it is of primary importance to allow no other European power to insert itself between British Burmah and China. Our influence in that country ought to be paramount. The country itself is of no great importance. But an easy communication with the multitudes who inhabit Western China is an object of national importance.

Lawrence replied:

> All our merchants and traders long for a *bouleversement* and would probably do what they could to bring one on. The annexation of Burmah proper will no doubt come sooner or later, but the longer it can be staved off the better.[9]

Here we see a number of factors at work which would later combine to shape the course of events leading to annexation. First was the idea, in London, that Upper Burma was strategically important because of its position next to China. Second was the idea, in Calcutta, that annexation was not wanted and, thus, that a successful 'informal empire' in Upper Burma was preferred. And third was the idea, in Rangoon, among the

---

[7] *KBZ*, vol. III, p. 390. See also 'Mandalay Diary', IFP, 2 August 1872, 28 October 1872, 21 December 1872, 16 January 1873.   [8] *GUBSS*, vol. II, p. 73.

[9] Quoted in Woodman, *The Making of Burma*, p. 184.

business community, that outright annexation or at least the establishment of a protectorate would very much help the further expansion and profitability of British trade.

A few months later, in October 1867, Sir Albert Fytche, the Chief Commissioner, headed a new mission to Mandalay. The Court of Ava, then still reeling from the effects of the Myingun rebellion, could offer little resistance to Fytche's demands for all sorts of new commercial concessions. The Burmese agreed to stronger terms barring state involvement in trade including the surrender of all royal monopolies save those on timber, oil and precious stones. Frontier duties were further lowered from 10 per cent to 5 per cent *ad valorem* on imports and to 5–6 per cent on exports. They also agreed to the stationing of an Assistant Resident at Bhamo; permission for the Irrawaddy Flotilla Company to sail up to Bhamo and the granting of extrajudicial rights for British subjects in Burmese territory. Nevertheless, Fytche did not see it as appropriate to go as far as his brief allowed: his instructions from the Governor-General had instructed him to include, if possible, the following stipulation: 'The Burmese ruler engages not to enter into negotiations or communication of any kind with any foreign power, except with the consent, previously obtained, of the British ruler.'[10] Fytche apparently realised that the Burmese were still not ready to make this final concession to informal empire and did not press the issue. In exchange for the concessions which were made, the Burmese government were given Article 8, which read: 'The Burmese Government shall further be allowed permission to purchase arms and ammunition and war materials generally in British territory subject to the consent and approval in each case, of the Chief Commissioner of British Burma.' Very importantly, in an attached annex to the treaty, it was stated that such consent and approval would 'ordinarily be given'. The Burmese government also received from Fytche a separate agreement allowing the procurement of arms through British territory.[11]

In 1868, funded by commercial interests in Rangoon and not the government, Col. Sladen, then Resident at Ava, received permission from Mandalay to head an exploration team into China. His team included

---

[10] Pearn, 'Commercial Treaty'.

[11] *Papers Relating to British Burma. Correspondence Relative to the Treaty of the 26th October 1867*, London, 1868.

both a scientist and a commercial agent.[12] Sladen was clearly intent on expanding British trade with China through Bhamo and on weakening the government's control over the border area in the process. He thought about paying Shan and Kachin chiefs annual subsidies and later arranged for small shipments of arms and ammunition. G.A. Stover of the Madras Staff Corps was assigned in 1869 to be the Assistant Resident in Bhamo, and Sladen organised the sending of several other officers, including engineers, to consider preparations for 'a highway (road, tramway, or railway) which must eventually and at no great distance in time connect the Irrawaddy with Yunnan, or Bhamo with Momein'.[13] Sladen also persuaded the Irrawaddy Flotilla Company to make a monthly run to Bhamo with a monthly government subsidy of 5,000 rupees.

By this time British commercial interests were becoming increasingly intent on removing competition from the Burmese government. In 1871, Mindon had appointed a Mr Edmund Jones as the 'Mercantile Agent of the King of Burma' at Rangoon. This capable man defended the king's involvement in trade by explaining that he was not buying up 'all the produce of the country' for the sake of profit, and saying that 'people were poor and unable to meet expenses of cultivation and of maintaining themselves till the harvesting of crops and [thus] had to borrow money at exorbitant rates of interest'. 'To mitigate this evil', he argued, the king advanced money to those who could not afford to borrow money elsewhere, and at the time of repayment, the produce was delivered to one of his agents. Others, he said, were perfectly free to sell their produce to anyone.[14] Despite these explanations, Mindon, under continued pressure from Rangoon, in 1871 finally gave up trading in cotton completely, thus removing all remaining official barriers between Burmese cultivators and international markets.

The imposition of an informal British empire over Upper Burma was thus secured through the commercial treaties of 1862 and 1867. These, together with other arrangements made to facilitate British trade, largely ended any real control on the part of the Burmese government over the economy, an economy already firmly tied to foreign markets. A principal

---

[12] *Official Narrative of the Expedition to Explore the Trade Routes to China via Bhamo under the Guidance of Major E.B. Sladen, Political Agent, Mandalay, with Connected Papers*, 1871.   [13] Quoted in Woodman, *The Making of Burma*, p. 189.
[14] IFP, October 1871, no. 409. See also 'Mandalay Diary', IFP, 31 December 1872.

concern of British Indian officials from the beginning of Mindon's reign was commercial expansion and this might be divided into several areas. The first was an interest on the part of British officials to see a continuation of normal trade between British Lower Burma and Upper Burma as a way of ensuring economic stability for their new possession. The second was an interest in securing products from Upper Burma directly needed by the colonial regime, such as wheat for its army which otherwise had to be imported from India. The third was the sale of British goods and services, including cotton textiles and river transport. The fourth, by the late 1850s, was the purchase of an increasing array of Upper Burma products for re-export to Britain or other foreign markets, with the most valuable commodities being raw cotton and teak. The last area of concern, from the 1860s onwards, was in some way the most important: the already-mentioned desire to establish direct overland access to the China market, thereby beating off the Americans and the French.

Opening of trade routes with China acquired greater significance in 1872 when the Panthay rebellion in Yunnan was ruthlessly crushed and Chinese authority was re-established up to Momein. The Chinese themselves were anxious to revive trade and the governor of Yunnan informed Mindon that he hoped routes would at once be reopened. By the end of that year, a few large Chinese caravans began to reappear along the road to Bhamo. The Irrawaddy Flotilla Company first placed more steamers on its monthly service from Mandalay to Bhamo and eventually made a fortnightly run.[15] Certainly there were great hopes among European businessmen in Rangoon for access to western China through Upper Burma and Mindon himself was said to have eagerly awaited possible new revenues from the resumption of trade.[16] One problem in further encouraging trade, however, was the still unsettled nature of the border areas despite the collapse of the Panthay rebellion. Chinese policy during the rebellion, when Peking was tied down elsewhere by the much larger Taiping rebellion was to arm local freebooters and warlords, mostly ethnic Chinese, along the Burmese border to harass the Muslim army from the rear. This problem was then compounded by British moves to win friends in the area by supplying arms as well.[17] Thus, even after 1873, the chronic unrest in

---

[15] 'Mandalay Diary', IFP, 23 January 1873; Woodman, *The Making of Burma*, pp. 196–7.

[16] 'Mandalay Diary', IFP, 20 November 1872, 9 December 1872; *RTC*, 1867/8, p. 2.

[17] On British policy towards the Panthay rebels, see Brian L. Evans, 'The Panthay Mission of 1872 and its Legacies', *JSEAS*, 16 (1985), 117–29.

the hills beyond Bhamo remained unconducive to a major expansion of commerce.

In Upper Burma itself, by the 1870s, several large British firms had established themselves at Rangoon and were engaged in business all around the country. These included the Irrawaddy Flotilla Company; Gillanders Ogilvy & Co.; the Bombay Burma Trading Corporation, which in 1863 obtained its first logging concession around Pyinmina; and the Rangoon Oil Company which in 1876 became Burmah Oil. Nearly all the 'British' firms in Rangoon were actually Scottish, and some, such as Burmah Oil had their main offices in Glasgow.[18] In 1877 the Rangoon Chamber of Commerce was reorganised under the very effective Alexander Watson, Agent of the Chartered Bank of India, Australia and China. The largely Scottish Chamber was to become the most strident advocate of British intervention in the years between Mindon's death and the annexation.[19]

In 1871, a Burmese embassy headed by the Kinwun Mingyi was sent on a visit lasting several months to Europe. He was now promoted to Chief Minister and was bestowed the highest noble title of *thado* just prior to his departure. His brief was to attempt to persuade London to establish direct ties with Mandalay and to secure European friends if this failed.[20] The Burmese thus began playing for much higher stakes and realised the risks involved in courting British rivals. The embassy stopped in both Italy and France on the way to London, successfully negotiating treaties of friendship and commerce. This was the beginning of a renewed relationship with France, and came at a time when Paris, emerging from defeat in the Franco-Prussian War, had embarked on a new round of expansion in what was to become French Indochina.

In Britain itself, the Kinwun Mingyi and his associates were, by all accounts, accorded a very hospitable reception, touring Ireland, Scotland and England, attending the Eton and Harrow cricket match and watching the races at Ascot. Queen Victoria herself was recorded by the Kinwun Mingyi as having been particularly gracious, and though the Burmese at

18 Alistar McCrae, *Scots in Burma*, Edinburgh, 1990, pp. 19–48.
19 D.R. SarDesai, *British Trade and Expansion in Southeast Asia, 1830–1914*, New Delhi, 1977, p. 202.
20 *Kinwun Mingyi London Myo Thwa Nezinhmat Sadan* (London Diary of the Kinwun Mingyi), reprint, Rangoon, 1953; Maung Maung, *Burma in the Family of Nations*, Djambatan, 1956, p. 51.

first hoped that this meeting would pave the way for direct representation in London, they understood the implications of their presentation to the Queen not by the Foreign Secretary but by the Secretary of State for India. The Kinwun Mingyi was deeply angered at the British government's insistence on maintaining only indirect ties with Mandalay via Calcutta, especially given Siam's recognition in 1855 through the Bowring treaty as an equal power with an ambassador in London. When they stopped in Paris again on their return to complete their negotiations, the British ambassador, apparently to underscore London's position, offered to present them to the French foreign minister, an offer firmly if diplomatically refused.

Calcutta and Rangoon also refused to sanction, as they had pledged under the 1867 accords, the importation of arms through British territory to Upper Burma. Mindon had on many occasions requested permission to purchase current military hardware, only to be consistently refused.[21] The kingdom's increasing ties with European governments were worrying London, but this embargo on arms, arms which Mandalay believed were needed for internal security, only served to push the Burmese towards closer relations with the French and the Italians in particular.

By the mid-1870s, British officials were also becoming increasingly involved in internal Burmese politics in a way which further weakened Mindon's authority and set the stage for the collapse of state control, especially in outlying areas shortly after the king's death. One area of interference was directly into the affairs of the palace, with the British Residency becoming a magnet for would-be conspirators and various rival factions. There is no evidence of British complicity in the Myingun rebellion, but certainly by 1878 the Residency had become deeply involved in the intrigues which surrounded Thibaw's succession. Asylum was granted to several Burmese princes and British territory became the staging-ground for more than one failed attempt to overthrow the government at Mandalay.

The second area of interference was, as mentioned, along the Yunnan border, where certain officials such as G.A. Strover (the Assistant Resident) and Edward Sladen (the Resident) believed that a replacement of crown authority with that of local chiefs friendly to Rangoon would better serve expanding British interests.[22] From the time of Sladen's trip to the

---

[21] 'Mandalay Diary', IFP, 12 January 1874.   [22] McCrae, *Scots in Burma*, p. 74.

border in 1868 and especially following the establishment of a consulate at Bhamo in 1871, the British maintained contact with various local Kachin and Chinese 'warlords'. In the Shan states as well, some attempt were made to encourage the *sawbwa* to look to British Burma for support. Also by the 1870s, the British, through the Irrawaddy Flotilla Company, had come to dominate internal transportation, with no Burmese controls on the movement of ships. This was demonstrated by the flight of the Nyaungyan Prince on a steamer to Rangoon in 1878 against Mandalay's wishes. This control of transportation along the rivers also meant that in many ways Bhamo and the Chinese border were more accessible to the British in Rangoon than to the Burmese government at Mandalay. It was in the Karenni states further south, however, where Rangoon not only established direct contact with local chiefs but then forced the Burmese government to withdraw completely.[23]

The Karenni area was ruled by a few hereditary chiefs in a tributary relationship to Mandalay not unlike that of the more important Shan *sawbwa*. The area had not been very important in the past but was now becoming an object of dispute between Mandalay and Rangoon mainly because of its vast teak forests. British attempts to send officials to negotiate directly with the chiefs was met with Burmese condemnation and in March 1875 a mission from the Governor-General of India headed by Sir Douglas Forsythe was sent to Mandalay to discuss the matter. Forsythe was given explicit instructions to inform the Burmese government that any further interference on their part into the affairs of the western Karenni would be deemed an act of war. Mindon felt compelled to back down and, within four days of the mission's arrival, had his government sign a treaty under which both sides agreed to recognise the independence of the state. But though Burmese officials were all subsequently pulled out, British officers remained, a clear diplomatic humiliation which cost Mindon considerable prestige at home in the remaining years of his life.

British policy-makers then decided to increase pressure further, in an apparent hope that confrontation would precipitate the establishment of a full protectorate over the kingdom. Forsythe had complained bitterly on his return from Mandalay, as had all earlier missions, of having to remove his shoes during his audience with the king. The British Indian government then decided that at all future royal meetings, British

---

[23] Woodman, *The Making of Burma*, pp. 205–21.

representatives, including the Resident, would remain fully shod. This, Mindon felt, would be an impossible concession as it would destroy in the eyes of Mandalay his legitimacy as a Burmese ruler. From then on, until the arrival of General Prendergast's army in 1885, all direct communications were ended between the British and both Mindon and, later, Thibaw. Calcutta had pushed itself closer to intervention.

The changing structure of foreign trade

The structure of the Burmese kingdom's foreign trade changed dramatically over the quarter-century of Mindon's rule. In general, trade expanded rapidly, while the country's terms of trade first improved and then precipitously declined in the 1870s.

The Irrawaddy valley, as a result of long-term demographic growth, was suffering a deficit in rice production by the early nineteenth century. A key aspect of internal trade was thus the redistribution from the delta to the drier northern regions. Some of this was in the form of state taxation, some in the form of private sales. In return, various manufactured goods, including textiles as well as oil and foodstuffs grown only in Upper Burma, such as sesame, were sent to markets in Rangoon and elsewhere. International trade through Rangoon and other ports provided a wide array of products from throughout the Indian Ocean region and the West, and provided markets for Burmese timber and other goods, creating significant income for local elites as well as for temporarily assigned senior officials. The trade here was at best at balance, and it seems that the valley may have experienced a significant trade deficit paid for in silver, despite government attempts to prevent an outflow of precious metals. It was with China, however, that a significant surplus was maintained, through the development of a large trade in Burmese cotton, in return for Chinese silk. Chinese gold and silver provided cash for an expanding economy as well as the royal treasury and silk was at the centre of an important manufacturing industry. It was this structure of foreign trade which was so suddenly changed in the mid-nineteenth century.

The annexation of the delta affected the valley's rice supply in two ways. First, rice redistribution through state taxation was obviously no longer possible, forcing the royal treasury to procure rice more locally and placing increased pressure on cultivators around the capital and the Kyauksè. Second, all rice which needed to be imported from the delta now had to be bought in cash, whether by the royal treasury or by private traders. As a result the rump kingdom became quite quickly dependent on finding new sources of gold and silver, and here there were two options. The first was literally to find new sources of gold and silver through new mining operations; Mindon's government funded numerous expeditions to the Shan states but these expeditions met with at best only marginal success.[24] The second possibility was to divert cash surpluses from the China trade to buy rice from British Burma. This might have been possible had it not been for a second 'shock' to the kingdom's economy – the Panthay rebellion in Yunnan from 1857 to 1871, which effectively suspended all major trading. The valley's cotton needed new markets: Chinese silk went from being an affordable good to being very much a luxury good, and the economy, with government encouragement, turned to selling raw cotton and other cash crops to new global markets.

Mindon's government clearly saw a strong role for the state in trying to provide an adequate supply of rice for the general population. Mindon, in 1853–4, when rice production in Upper Burma was particularly good and when Lower Burma was witnessing food problems as a result of the unrest which accompanied formal annexation, shipped rice south. This might have been partly a tactic to score points with British officials as he was then still trying to negotiate the return of Pegu, but it was also probably a result of his self-image as ruler of all the Burmese, and his ideas about the role of the state in ensuring proper supplies of food. But this was certainly the last time rice would be delivered in bulk in that direction. The mid-1850s witnessed several consecutive years of poor rainfall, and from then on there were many desperate government interventions in the rice market to stabilise wildly fluctuating, but generally rising, rice prices.[25] Prior to state intervention in 1856 the price of rice in Amarapura on average had risen to approximately three times that at Prome on the British Burma border.[26] Imports of rice from Lower Burma varied considerably from year to year throughout Mindon's reign, depending on the local harvest, from as little as 20,000 tons to close to 100,000 tons a year.

Under official encouragement and with significant foreign investment the Irrawaddy delta, in the late nineteenth century, witnessed a phenomenal expansion in rice production and in the export of rice to foreign markets.[27] Increased demand for rice, both within the region and in

[24] *ROB*, 7 April 1856, 3 April 1857.   [25] Pollack, *Empires in Collision*, p. 124.
[26] *Ibid.*, p. 123.

Europe, meant that prices continued to rise gradually throughout this period, despite the growing supply from Siam as well as Lower Burma. For Upper Burma, that meant not only having to pay for rice imports with cash, but having to pay for them at prices driven by international demand, the Rangoon price of rice increasing from 8 rupees per hundred baskets in 1845 to 45 rupees ten years later following the annexation of Pegu. Prices increased steadily from then on, to 50 rupees in 1865, 65 rupees in 1875 and 95 rupees in 1885. During the American Civil War, the price of rice was temporarily inflated to around 75 rupees but fell back soon after. As the staple of the Burmese diet, rising rice prices would have caused general inflationary pressures throughout the economy. While the volume of imports fluctuated considerably from year to year, the total value of rice imports increased steadily, from only 6.22 lakh rupees in 1872/3 to over 30 lakh rupees five years later.[28]

Other goods were imported from Lower Burma, the most important being *ngapi*, or fermented fish, the main dietary staple in addition to rice. *Ngapi* was produced only in the south and thus the volume of imports remained fairly stable. But aside from these two products, together with betel nut and salt, the extent to which other goods were bought depended from year to year on the extent to which disposable income was available. In years of good harvests in Upper Burma, when only a small amount of delta rice needed to be bought, money was spent on buying the many different products now becoming available, especially cotton cloth from Britain and India. Raw silk, which had been manufactured into cloth in Amarapura and then Mandalay, now had to be shipped through Rangoon from China, and the value of this trade rose to 1.6 million rupees by the late 1870s.[29]

This balance of trade was redressed to an extent in the 1850s and 1860s through the export of primary goods from Upper Burma, mainly raw cotton, wheat, oil and timber. The rising price of cotton on international markets, particularly during the American Civil War was of significant benefit to crown finances. The government often paid large advances to cultivators and sold in bulk to European firms in Rangoon and Calcutta. With the exception of 1855, good rainfall had led to good cotton harvests from 1854 to 1858. Prices rose 100 per cent in the year 1854/5 alone and

[27] Adas, *The Burma Delta*, pp. 58–60.
[28] All trade statistics in this chapter are compiled by the author from *RAB*, 1871/2 to 1877/8.   [29] *RAB*, 1865/6, pp. 18–19.

the enormous drop in the world's cotton supply resulting from Washington's blockade of her southern ports meant higher prices still. Cultivators were paid 5 rupees per 100 viss, commercial buyers were paid 35–40 rupees and the cotton was then exported at 150–200 rupees per 100 viss to Rangoon. These early 1860s prices represented a 600–800 per cent increase over the 1854 export price of just 25 rupees per 100 viss. By 1865, however, the American Civil War had ended, and there began a downward spiral in cotton prices. A few years of heavy rain and drought in the late 1860s and early 1870s compounded the fall in income for large groups of cultivators.[30] Despite the fall in prices, however, the total volume of cotton exported and the total value of exports continued to rise, from 710,000 rupees in 1868/9 to 2,500,000 rupees in 1872/3, reflecting increases in the total area of cultivation.[31]

Timber, mainly teak, was the other major export commodity for the Burmese government and teak became increasingly important from the mid-1860s onwards as profits from cotton fell. The Bombay Burma Trading Corporation as well as smaller Burmese firms had been granted several concessions, mainly in the Yamèthin region across the British Burma border from Toungoo and in the large swathe of forest north of Prome.[32] Teak exported for international markets through Rangoon was almost entirely of Upper Burma origin. Total exports rose from 24,000 tons (of 50 cubic feet) in the five years 1856–60, to 44,000 tons in 1861–5, 56,000 tons in 1866–70, 71,000 tons in 1871–5 and 73,000 tons in 1876–80.[33] Mindon's government also traded in wheat and chickpeas. These were staple foods for British troops in Lower Burma which had to be imported from India but which were, by the mid-1860s, grown under crown encouragement in Upper Burma. As with cotton, royal agents bought large advances from cultivators and then sold them to official agents in Rangoon.[34]

Total trade between Upper and Lower Burma in the late 1850s averaged around 4 million rupees with imports slightly higher than exports.[35] Over the next twenty years bilateral trade increased steadily with almost

[30] Pollack, *Empires in Collision*, pp. 126–7.

[31] *Annual Statement of the Trade and Navigation of the Province of British Burma Having a Seaborne Trade*, 1868/9–1872/3.

[32] For an official history of the company, see A.C. Pointon, *The Bombay Burma Trading Corporation Limited 1863–1963*, Southampton, 1964.

[33] *Ibid*. Also see Aye Hlaing, 'Trends of Economic Growth and Income Distribution in Burma, 1870–1940', *JBRS*, 47 (1964), 57–108.

[34] Pollack, *Empires in Collision*, p. 126.   [35] *RAB*, 1858/9, p. 5.

no interruption, the only significant exception being the disruption of trade caused by the political unrest surrounding the Myingun rebellion in 1867–8. The commercial treaties of 1862 and 1867 both resulted in a further rise in the volume of trade. The second treaty, coming at the same time as the official reopening of the China border led to a near doubling of trade between 1868/9 and 1877/8; it grew in value from approximately 20 million rupees to over 35 million rupees.[36] The chief exports were timber and cotton with some lacquer, cutch, cotton cloth and jaggery also being exported. The main import of Upper Burma at this time, other than rice and *ngapi*, was cloth, the main non-food personal expenditure. While the value of silk imports rose steadily throughout this period (from about 1 million to 1.6 million rupees), the value of woollens remained fairly constant (at between 3 and 4 million rupees) and the value of cotton cloth imports fell in the late 1870s (from 2.8 million rupees in 1872/3 to 1.8 million in 1878/9).

These trade figures are not entirely accurate in that some illicit exports by private traders not holding royal licences for the export of precious stones and some other commodities were not registered.[37] Nevertheless, we may conclude that there was certainly a huge growth in trade between Upper and Lower Burma. Many of Upper Burma's exports reached international markets through Rangoon and the vast majority of these exports were destined for the United Kingdom, India and the Straits Settlements. This growth of bilateral trade has often been used to demonstrate that, contrary to contemporary British observations stating that economic conditions in Upper Burma were worsening, there was at least no real decline, and perhaps even an improvement, in conditions under Mindon.

What the statistics for the growth and volume of trade miss entirely, however, are the structure and terms of trade. The export of raw cotton increased dramatically in the 1860s and 1870s, from only approximately 23,000 rupees a year in the mid-1860s to approximately 400,000 rupees a year in the early 1870s and then to 1,500,000 rupees at the end of the decade. During the same period, however, the price of raw cotton declined from 11 rupees per pound to 8 rupees per pound (around 30 per cent). The prices of some other important export commodities also declined, including those for oil (30 per cent decline) and tea (40 per cent), though prices for timber remained stable. Timber was, however, the one

[36] Compiled from the *RAB*s of that period.   [37] *RAB*, 1865/6, pp. 18–19.

commodity which did not involve ordinary cultivators and the benefits from its export went almost exclusively to the government and the Bombay Burma Trading Corporation. At the same time, the volume and total value of imports, especially manufactured goods from the United Kingdom, increased significantly.

Examining the cloth trade in isolation also gives some indication of the effects of economic change at this time on popular consumption and relative incomes. What we see from the statistics is first that the import of silk increased and, since silk was a luxury item within existing sumptuary laws prohibiting general wear, consumption of silk by the elite probably increased or remained the same. Second, the import of cotton cloth also increased for a time and then declined while the export of cotton cloth first declined and then increased. This inverse relationship between the export of locally made cotton cloth and the import of foreign cotton cloth suggests strongly that in the years 1868–73 a relatively large amount of cloth was being consumed locally, while in subsequent years, this amount declined. As cotton cloth was a fairly commercialised, generally consumed commodity, we might infer that popular incomes also rose and then declined in the 1870s.

These figures though do not include overland trade with China. Overland trade virtually stopped during the Panthay rebellion in part because of the actual fighting and in part because the Burmese government was afraid of incurring Peking's anger. Mindon was apparently sympathetic to the rebels, whom he considered the 'natives', as opposed to the Manchu 'foreigners', and the embargo on trade meant that what trade occurred was not officially taxed. Once the Panthay rebellion ended in 1873, the Mindon government became very interested in furthering trade between Upper Burma and Yunnan as well as between British Burma and Yunnan. His ministers tried unsuccessfully to raise funds for the construction of a railway line through Mandalay partly for this purpose. But it does not seem that trade ever reached pre-rebellion levels, mainly the result of continued unrest and a breaking down of Mandalay's control along border areas. Possibly, some cotton was now exported again to China and this may have provided some relief to a depressed market.

But it seems that China itself had begun to import British cotton textiles not only through coastal ports but through Rangoon and Upper Burma as well. However much trade revived, it almost certainly dropped from 1880 onwards as a result of the economic crisis in China which caused a large contraction in economic activity. One contemporary source states that before annexation and for a few years after, Yunnan paid for all its imports through Bhamo with opium.[38] This was not mentioned in any earlier sources. If true, the development of a market for Chinese opium in Upper Burma would have meant that the resumption of the China trade did not lead to a renewed source of cash for the economy, even if there was, through exports of cotton and other goods, otherwise a trade surplus.

Thus generally, we can say that Upper Burma's foreign trade from the early 1850s to the late 1870s changed in three major ways: a large increase in foreign trade; a dependence on imported rice and other staple food; and a changed direction of trade, away from China and towards overseas markets, particularly Britain. Because of this state of affairs disruptions to trade quickly and severely affected local living standards. The global depression[39] of the 1870s which lowered primary commodities' prices and which reached Upper Burma in the late 1870s would thus have a considerable impact, something we shall consider in chapter 7.

An exemplary centre

The decline in royal prestige resulting from the second defeat at the hands of the British and the loss of Pegu impressed upon Mindon the need to meet or even exceed what was perceived as the 'traditional' ceremonial and religious obligations of a Burmese monarch. This is not to say that Mindon was not following genuinely felt religious motivations. His personal correspondence with Buddhist figures in Siam and Ceylon reveal clearly his own deep devotion to Theravada Buddhism. Nevertheless, Mindon must have seen the usefulness, at a time of increasing threats to royal authority, of strengthening religious institutions through lavish patronage, and to associate the state, especially the monarchy, as closely as possible with a reinvigorated and centralised Buddhist Sangha.

One of his first projects was, literally, the building of a new 'exemplary centre', the new royal city of Mandalay.[40] Problems related to health and sanitation, or overcrowding may have been part of the reasons for the move. The move may also have been related to defence considerations,

---

[38] Nisbit, *Burma*, vol. II, p. 448.

[39] Rondo Cameron, *A Concise Economic History of the World*, New York, 1993, p. 281.

[40] *KBZ*, vol. III, pp. 240–51. See also Maung Maung Tin and Thomas Owen Morris, 'Mindon Min's Development Plan for the Mandalay Area', *JBRS*, 44 (1966), 29–34.

Amarapura being within range of steamer guns, while Mandalay was built a few miles inland on a large plain at the foot of the Shan Plateau. Though the government of Mindon was not a 'theatre state' in the sense that state power existed centrally to produce royal ceremony,[41] royal ceremonies were certainly still a very important part of what government was all about, setting an aesthetic, religious and political example for local elites and others in whose hands remained much day-to-day administration. Of the surviving royal edicts from Mindon's reign, close to half deal with royal ceremonies or with royal grants to individuals, mainly princes and nobles, to conduct ceremonies of their own.[42] Mindon as king presided over at least one major religious ceremony each month and often many more, as well as attending weddings, funerals, monastic initiations, ceremonies marking the construction of new monasteries or pagodas and naming ceremonies for the royal children.

Another area of exemplary rule was the protection of animals. From the very beginning of his reign, Mindon had followed the initiatives of many of his predecessors and sought to improve animal welfare, in line with Buddhist teachings. In 1853, when he ordered irrigation repairs to be undertaken around Shwébo, he also ordered that no fish were to be harmed as a result.[43] Soon afterwards, a special wildlife sanctuary was established just outside of Sagaing and others were later established at Maungdaung, near Alon, and around the Meiktila lake.[44] In 1854, all hunting and trapping of animals in the Lower Chindwin was banned. Others followed Mindon's example. The Mekkaya Prince established a wildlife sanctuary of his own as did the Myoza of Myothit, a deputy senior minster, who created a protected place for animals in his new *appanage*.[45]

The late nineteenth century saw a strengthening of earlier trends towards greater state-sponsored Sangha centralisation. Movement towards increasing 'fundamentalism', a strict interpretation of the Theravada canon coupled with rigorous observance of codified rules of self-discipline, also continued. Strong state intervention under Bodawpaya before the First Anglo-Burmese War had lead to the unification of the Sangha under the state-patronised Thudhamma sect.[46] But soon afterwards, numerous challenges to the orthodoxy reappeared, both from within and

---

[41] Clifford Geertz, *Negara: The Theatre State in Nineteenth-Century Bali*, Princeton, 1980, pp. 123–36.   [42] See also *KBZ*, vol. III, pp. 162–465 *passim*.

[43] *Ibid.*, p. 162.   [44] *Ibid.*, pp. 174–5, 203, 213, 221.   [45] *Ibid.*, p. 216.

[46] *MMOS*, vol. II, pp. 2, 128–40.

without the Sangha and Mindon's government again felt the need for intervention. The annexation of Pegu had led to a large migration of monks from British territory and was followed by a noticeable decline in religious activity and patronage as well as a growing autonomy and lax observance of disciplinary rules on the part of monks who remained behind. Mindon attempted to encourage monks from Upper Burma to return, at least temporarily, to Lower Burma, but with only some success.

In 1871, he held a Buddhist synod for monks from all over the country, as well as a few from Ceylon, Siam and elsewhere. This was also in part an attempt to maintain some sort of country-wide organisation despite the British occupation of the delta.[47] At around the same time, he funded a project to review the Tripitika canon and to inscribe an authoritative copy in stone at the foot of Mandalay Hill. The project was placed under the charge of three leading *sayadaw*: the Taungsaung Sayadaw, who was the queen's tutor, the tutor of the Captain of the Musketeers, the Myoza of Myadaung, and the tutor of the Master of the King's Horses. Mindon's Privy Councillors were also involved.[48] In a more political vein, Mindon also donated a *hti* (a jewelled spire) for the Shwedagon pagoda in Rangoon. After some official debate, the British decided not to allow the king to travel to Rangoon for the actual donation ceremony.[49] Extensive preparations for the new *hti* were made between royal courtiers and the new Rangoon Burmese elite, and the *hti* was accompanied along its entire route by the Myoza of Poppa, a deputy senior minister, with considerable pomp and huge crowds lining the way.[50]

The other main challenge facing Burmese Buddhism was the emergence of several extreme 'fundamentalist' sects which advocated a further 'reformation' of religious practices. During Mindon's reign thousands of monks and lay followers moved from Mandalay to the Sagaing Hills on the other side of the Irrawaddy, believing that the capital's monasteries had encouraged lavish lifestyles. Sagaing was transformed in the 1860s into a new city of monasteries, preaching halls and rest houses.[51] As part of the same popular movement, the Hngettwin Sayadaw established a new faction within the Sangha, preaching that religious practices needed to be radically altered, and insisting that meditation was necessary for all Buddhists and that mere charity and an observance of Buddhist ethics was not

---

[47] *Ibid.*, vol. III, pp. 141–2.   [48] *KBZ*, vol. II, pp. 388–90.   [49] *RAB*, 1871/2, p. 24.
[50] *KBZ*, pp. 375–6, 387.
[51] Htin Aung, *Burmese Monks' Tales*, New York, 1966, pp. 20–6.

enough. He attacked the offering of flowers and candles to Buddha images as useless and called for stricter adherence to *vinaya* discipline for his monks, adding new requirements. On the one hand, his sect might be seen as a reaction to the increased institutionalisation of the Sangha and the emphasis on textual learning. On the other hand, his teachings were very much in line with the historical tendency towards increased discipline and intolerance of social deviancy.

In the delta meanwhile, the Okpo Sayadaw similarly challenged existing practices and stated that the Sangha, so long as it observed the *vinaya* strictly, did not need intervention from the state. He also argued that mental attitude or motivation behind an action was more important than the actual act, a thesis which then created considerable debate not only within religious discourses but also on contemporary issues in language and civil law. A third main religious figure of the time was the Shwegyin Sayadaw,[52] who was much more part of the Mandalay-based religious establishment but who nevertheless agreed that monks needed to improve their self-discipline and give up remaining luxuries. In particular he called for two new rules of conduct, the banning of betel nut and tobacco consumption after noon (no food is generally eaten by monks after noon). His was an attempt to steer a middle way between the more extreme fundamentalists and the Ecclesiastical Council, controlled by the moderate Thudhamma sect, under the Thathanabaing, or Primate. Mindon's attempts to reunify the Sangha, perhaps under Shwegyin leadership, however, failed. His synod of 1871 did admit to some of the criticisms of the Sangha by the Okpo Sayadaw and others, but saw its main task as the further refinement of religious texts.

Despite these challenges to the state-sponsored Sangha leadership, by the late 1860s the government increasingly turned to Buddhist monks through their central structures for assistance, primarily in the area of information. Monks were asked to convey information to the villages on government revenue policy,[53] and were asked to report to the royal agencies on any repressive practices being committed by local officials,

---

52 Than Tun, 'History of the Shwegyin Sect of Burma', in Than Tun, *Essays on the History and Buddhism of Burma*. See also John Ferguson, 'The Quest for Legitimation by Burmese Monks and Kings: The Case of the Shwegyin Sect (19th and 20th Centuries)', in B.L. Smith (ed.), *Religion and the Legitimation of Power in Thailand, Laos and Burma*, Philadelphia, 1978.
53 *ROB*, 15 May 1867.

including headmen.[54] Monks were also being asked at this time to assist in the repatriation of persons displaced by the 1866 Myingun rebellion and the government accepted their advice on tax and debt relief for these people.[55] Monks were even asked to assist directly in the collection of the *thathameda* tax in 1868.

With increasing popular and intra-Sangha criticism of monks for lax observance of monastic vows, information was sought on the monks by local officials as well. A series of royal orders and orders from the head of the Sangha condemned infringement of discipline and reiterated the rules all monks were expected to follow.[56] Popular patronage of 'corrupt' monks was condemned and rural chiefs were requested to report on such monks to provincial authorities.[57] Mindon may have viewed his support for a strong centralised Sangha as politically beneficial, both in underscoring his legitimacy at a time when secular institutions were coming under increasing pressure, but also in providing the state with an allied structure which could assist in shoring up Mandalay's influence over the countryside. Mindon made large daily donations to the Sangha, according to one account supporting 217 monasteries, mainly in the capital, or a total of 15,366 monks and novices. The same Burmese source estimates a total expenditure by Mindon over his twenty-six years as king at 226 million rupees or an average of nearly 9 million rupees a year.[58]

But Mandalay by the 1870s was not simply the cultural capital of a remote Buddhist kingdom, but also part and parcel of a fast-changing and ever-shrinking world. The mid-nineteenth century nearly everywhere was a time of momentous technological change. From the first photographic portraits of Burmese aristocrats to the electrification of parts of the Mandalay palace, the Court of Ava was far from isolated from new inventions and new ideas. Through the popular plays and other literary works from this period, we see clearly that the people of the Irrawaddy valley, as well, were increasingly aware of the great transformations taking place around them.

The first Burmese-language printing presses, however, appeared in the late 1860s, and by about 1870, Burmese presses, in Rangoon, became very active.[59] The appeal was to a public which had a great demand for theatre

---

[54] *Ibid.*, 14 March 1872, 21 April 1873.   [55] *Ibid.*, 19 January 1868.

[56] *Ibid.*, 15 February 1856, 25 March 1856, 25 May 1867.   [57] *Ibid.*, 15 February 1856.

[58] *MMOS*, vol. III, p. 143. See also India Foreign (Political) Proceedings, Sept. 1865, p. 23.

but perhaps only too few occasions to actually attend performances. The published plays were written at nearly full-length in the authentic stage idiom, complete with songs and stage directions. The plots were taken from the Buddha's birth stories, or *Jataka*, from mythology and history, or were original – and the supernatural often played an important part in the story. The scene was set, however, in nineteenth-century Burma, as both the writers and the readers seemed most interested in contemporary events.

The printed plays which survive are full of descriptions of new technologies, information about distant places and, most of all, a world dominated by economic forces beyond the control of the ordinary individual. In the middle of the traditional Jataka-based stories with *naga*, *garuda* and *yogi*, there are also references to trains, steamships, telegrams, newspapers, cameras, thermometers, brandy and champagne.[60] In one play, *Luwun Maung Hnama*, the people of a small village in Lower Burma borrow a large sum of money from Indian money-lenders during a period of high rice prices but then squander the money on new houses, buffaloes and gifts for their daughters. Soon, the economic situation turns and the money-lenders call in their loans and the families, summoned to court for non-payment, are forced to flee. In another, *Shan Min*, the guardian spirit of a banyan tree refuses permission for the burial of a corpse under his tree on the pretext that the tree does not legally belong to him anymore, having had to mortgage the tree in order to pay barrister fees in the original suit through which he had gained possession. These plays were written almost entirely by a new generation of playwrights from Lower Burma and printed in Rangoon but they were read and performed in Upper Burma as well.[61]

It was within this context of often confusing economic, intellectual and cultural changes, that the final Konbaung succession took place, with an ambitious essay at sweeping political reforms, one which would lead directly to the fall of the kingdom in 1885.

[59] Hla Pe, 'The Beginnings of Modern Popular Burmese Literature', in Hla Pe, *Burma*, pp. 20–31.

[60] Hla Pe, 'Social Conditions as Reflected in the Popular Drama', in his introduction to *Konmara Pya Zat: An Example of Popular Burmese Drama in the Nineteenth Century by Pok Ni*, London, 1952, pp. 22–30.   [61] See Allott, Herbert and Okell, 'Burma'.

7 | Reformists and royalists at the court of King Thibaw

In October 1877, King Mindon became ill with dysentery and his condition rapidly deteriorated.[1] His German physician, Dr Marfels, declared His Majesty's condition to be critical and Mindon was soon confined to the gilded *thalun* bed in his private apartments. His wives and daughters were in constant attendance and he was visited by a number of his sons and ministers.

A few hundred yards away, in the lacquered teak pavilion of the Council of State, the most senior grandees of the Court gathered to discuss the royal succession. Ever since the assassination of the Kanaung Prince in 1866, Mindon had steadfastly refused to appoint a new heir apparent, for fear that the chosen prince would become, in turn, a target for murder.[2] The prime movers of the 1866 rebellion, the Myingun and Myinhkondaing Princes, were the eldest princes of their generation with excellent claims to the throne. But they had been living in exile since their failed coup and no attempt at reconciliation between father and sons had been made. The obvious candidates for the throne were the three senior princes who had remained loyal to Mindon: the Princes of Mekkaya, Nyaungyan and Thonzè. The Mekkaya Prince, who had been by his father's side during the worst days of the 1866 rebellion, was thought to be Mindon's favourite. He had substantial experience in government and was for a while in charge of the new factories being built outside the city. But a choice of any one over the other would almost certainly have resulted in a long period of infighting among this fifth generation in descent from Alaungpaya.

Instability was the last thing the old court grandees wanted when they assembled to choose the next king. As no heir apparent had been selected by the incumbent, the choice, by tradition, fell to the senior ministers of

---

[1] *KBZ*, vol. III, pp. 436–64. See also Bennett, *Conference under the Tamarind Tree*, pp. 70–84.

[2] The problem of succession during the Konbaung dynasty was a recurrent one. See Koenig, *Burmese Polity*, pp. 165–87.

the Hluttaw. None wanted any of the three elder sons. Instead, their desire was for a young pliant prince, someone they could control. Their aim was to establish a government of the senior nobility, with as weak a king as possible. The royal family, some thought, had caused nothing but trouble with their constant in-fighting and intrigues. All were of course devoted monarchists, but a limited monarchy, on European lines, seems to have been the ambition of at least the majority.

The Myoza of Yénangyaung was one of the chief ministers, perhaps the most powerful of the four. He was allied by marriage with a number of important ministerial and military office holding families. He was also a member of the hereditary Twinzayo gentry of Yénangyaung, the rich oil-producing region south of Pagan. A tough-talking old man, he had fought in the 1853 war and enjoyed showing off his battle-scars. He also enjoyed showing off his twenty-something wife and boasted of his in-numerable children. One of his daughters, the Kyèmyint Queen, had become one of Mindon's also numerous wives and her son, the Pyinmina Prince, was his natural choice for king. Only eight, Pyinmina would have well suited the Council's desire for a pliant figurehead. A regency would undoubtedly have been established, along the lines of the contemporary Chuan Bunnag regency in Siam, and ministers would have had ample time to consolidate their hold on power. Other noblemen, however, had other ideas. The Thonzè Prince was the nephew of the Myoza of Bhamo, then a Privy Councillor. The Nyaungyan Prince, now in British territory, was the nephew of a retired, but still influential cavalry commander. Both men wanted one of these elder and popular princes to be elected.

The deciding influence was to come from the Kinwun Mingyi, the second most important official in the land, and the leader of the reformist wing at Court. He had travelled extensively through Asia and Europe during his diplomatic missions in 1871 and had been clearly impressed with the magnitude of the challenges facing his small kingdom. He gathered around him a circle of young, Western-educated scholar offi-cials. This group, the product of the state scholarship programme of the 1860s, now dominated a number of key middle-ranking offices. Their aim was more than just a limited monarchy, more than just a tilt in the balance of power towards the nobility. They wanted nothing less than a complete overhaul of the existing system. As a former holder of high military office, he enjoyed a certain backing within the army, in particular the regular infantry. He had also served as governor of Alon, the principal recruiting ground for the Household Guards, and had married into the family of the hereditary *myothugyi* of that province.

For the Kinwun Mingyi and his followers, the implementation of their reform plans required not only a weak prince, but also the removal of the old establishment as represented by the Myoza of Yénangyaung. The election of the Pyinmina Prince would have meant government by the nobility, but a nobility led by the Myoza of Yénangyaung and his some-what backward-looking clients. They turned therefore to the third power-ful faction at court, the faction of the Middle Palace Queen.

The Middle Palace Queen was, at the time of Mindon's death, his most senior queen, his chief queen having died a few years before. The Middle Palace Queen had no sons, but was ambitious, and her main ambition was to have one, or all, of her three young daughters married to whoever became the next king. She too wanted a pliant prince, but for completely different reasons. Her choice was the Thibaw Prince, a younger son of Mindon by the Laungshay Queen.

The Thibaw Prince was twenty years old, a shy, somewhat unknown figure at the court. He had spent part of his youth at Dr Marks' Anglican school, just across the street from the southern city wall, where he studied English as well as other subjects and was known to have been a fairly keen batsman. He was also remembered for having used 'unprincely language' when bowled. On leaving the Anglican school he entered the Bagaya monastic college, becoming an accomplished Pali scholar. In 1877 he had passed the highest *Patamabyan* monastic examination, and had been feted by his father in a grand ceremony at court. Most importantly, he was in love with his half-sister, the Princess of Myadaung, also known as Supayalat, the strong-willed second daughter of the Middle Palace Queen.[3] With the backing of the Kinwun Mingyi and the dying king's most senior wife, the Council of State, on 15 September, elected Thibaw as heir apparent and their nominee soon received the guarded approval of Mindon himself.

The coup d'état of 1878

The election of Thibaw was only the initial phase of the Kinwun Mingyi's designs. He and the Middle Palace Queen first managed to secure control

[3]   On Thibaw's background, see Kanimyo Sitkè, *Mandalay Yadanapon Mahayazawindawgyi*, reprint, Rangoon, 1969, pp. 175–6.

of the palace environs with support from the Household Guards and then ordered the arrest of many prominent members of the royal family, including all the elder princes. When Mindon, during a brief recovery, heard of these developments, he ordered the imprisoned royals released, appointing his three eldest sons, the Nyaungyan, Mekkaya and Thonzè Princes as joint heirs and ordering them to be sent off immediately as 'viceroys' to three different parts of the country. This he most probably did for their own safety, hoping that they would be able to flee the city immediately. But as the king's condition worsened, these orders were ignored and all the elder princes and their families were rearrested. Only the Nyaungyan Prince, disguised as a coolie, managed to escape to the British Residency and from there, with British aid, onto a waiting steamer. On 15 September, Thibaw was officially proclaimed as crown prince with Supayalat and her older sister as his future queens.[4]

The king himself passed away on 1 October knowing that Thibaw would ascend the throne but believing in all likelihood that his other children were safe from harm. His funeral, which followed seven days of mourning, was to be the last state funeral of a Burmese monarch and was a strange affair. By now, so many princes and princesses were in detention that the cortege was led by the former king Pagan, who survived his half-brother, and by male members of the extended royal family. The men were followed by the Middle Palace Queen and her daughters, already trying to assert themselves as the powers behind the throne. All were dressed in a brilliant white, the colour of death as well as the colour of sovereignty.

What happened in the final few days of Mindon's reign and the first few weeks of Thibaw can only be described as a palace coup. On 11 November, during the *thadingyut* festival which marks the end of the Buddhist Lent, the Kinwun Mingyi and other government leaders met in the Southern Royal Gardens to set in motion the series of sweeping reforms which they believed were critical for preserving the country's independence.[5] First, the Kinwun Mingyi and his allies reshuffled the top ranks of the administration. The Myoza of Yénangyaung and Magwé, the Kinwun Mingyi's only near rivals, were summarily dismissed together with dozens of others. At the same time, those ministers and army officers who had supported the coup were then rewarded with key positions and new

[4] *KBZ*, vol. III, pp. 564–70.   [5] *MMOS*, vol. II, pp. 241–6.

titles.[6] The Kinwun Mingyi himself not only retained his position of Chief Minister, but had conferred on him the special style of Mingyi Thet-tawshé.[7] This granted him immunity from prosecution. He retained his military rank as commander of all infantry regiments. Thibaw himself later said that for most of his first year as king he was a virtual prisoner of his own government[8] and British reports of that time also state that he was 'more or less a puppet of his Ministers', with the oaths taken by the sixty ministers of the new government being made not to the 'king' but to the 'king-in-council'.[9]

The Kinwun Mingyi's plan was to establish a proper system of ministries along Western lines. Though Burmese official positions and offices had become increasingly specialised over the previous twenty years, they were still extremely disorganised, with *ad hoc* responsibilities being given to various officials with antiquated titles such as 'Master of the Ironworks' or 'Captain of the Musketeers'. Within a few weeks of Thibaw's accession fourteen ministries covering the entire government, each with approximately forty officials, were established.[10] The various functional titles of the early modern state, such as *thandawzin* or *wundauk*, became bureaucratic ranks within the revamped structure. The old system whereby the Hluttaw and the Byèdaik met separately each day and then together with the king in an afternoon audience, or *nyilagan*, was abolished and replaced by meetings of the full cabinet and several subordinate committees.[11] All policy matters were to be discussed and decided by the full cabinet and only the cabinet as a whole, rather than individual ministers, was allowed to meet with the king. Importantly, the treasury was ordered not to pay out any funds to the king or queen, or anyone else, without the approval of the Myoza of Yaw, the new minister for finance.[12] According to one former official writing after annexation, these reforms were enacted in clear emulation of Western governments.[13]

---

[6] *KBZ*, vol. III, pp. 464–6.   [7] *Ibid.*, pp. 492–504.

[8] Interview with Thibaw by E.K. Moylan, *The Times*, 5 December 1885.

[9] Shaw to the Foreign Secretary, in *Correspondence Relating to the Affairs of Burmah Since the Death of the Late King*, 13 November 1878; Kanimyo Sitkè, *Mandalay*, pp. 189–90; *KBZ*, vol. III, p. 473.

[10] Agriculture, Public Works, War, Finance, Religion and Educational Affairs, Legislation, Mandalay, Justice, Marine, Foreign Affairs, Telecommunications, Resident Foreigners, Home, and Industries. *KBZ*, vol. III, pp. 485–8. See also *MMOS*, vol. III, p. 210.   [11] *MMOS*, vol. III, p. 209.

[12] *KBZ*, vol. III, pp. 570–9; *MMOS*, vol. II, pp. 241–6; Bennett, *Conference under the Tamarind Tree*, pp. 76–7.

[13] Shaw to the Foreign Secretary, in *Correspondence Relating to the Affairs of Burmah*

In order that this new government might consolidate its position and policies without royal interference, the Kinwun Mingyi further suggested that Thibaw undertake a long trip abroad, to Britain and Europe. The Kinwun Mingyi perhaps hoped that through this trip Thibaw would also become firmly convinced of the need for accelerated reforms, and he was probably influenced by the successful trip around the world of Chulalongkorn several years earlier during the regency of Chuan Bunnag.[14] The Myoza of Yaw wrote a large collection of essays for the young king, brought together as the *Raza Dhamma Thingaha Kyan*, or 'Treatise on the Compassionate Disposition of Righteous Government'. Deriving his ideas from classical Pali sources, the minister argued in favour of limits on royal authority and in favour of constitutional government. It was an exhortation to Thibaw to rule through the cabinet and in the interest of all subjects and to consider even wider-ranging political reforms. The Myoza of Yaw, now with the rank of *wungyi*, had emerged as the most radical of all the new government ministers. The treatise was to be among the last of the great scholar and statesman's twenty wide-ranging books.

The ministerial government quickly went to work. A tentative agreement was reached with a British firm for the construction of a railway through Upper Burma, trade restrictions were relaxed, and, as a friendly gesture, an armed guard was permitted to be stationed around the British Residency. Clearly, the government's new policies were directed towards increased accommodation with British demands, a more liberal trade regime and intensified administrative and infrastructure modernisation. Furthermore, in line with Mindon's policies towards the Sangha, the old king's *sayadaw*, or senior monks, were confirmed in their position and other prominent monks brought into the state-sponsored hierarchy. Perhaps seeing a relationship between a standardisation of the vernacular language and the development of a 'modern nation-state', the government convened a meeting of nearly all senior officials and other scholars to begin preparation of a definitive treatise on Burmese orthography. Thirty-six works on orthography were subsequently presented to the king.[15]

Alongside this reorganisation was another, inner reorganisation whose

---

Since the Death of the Late King, 13 November 1878.   [14] *MMOS*, vol. II, p. 252.

[15] *ROB*, 19 December 1878; Bennett, *Conference under the Tamarind Tree*, p. 79. See Benedict Anderson, *Imagined Communities: Reflections on the Origin and Spread of Nationalism*, London, 1983, pp. 67–82, on the relationship between the rising importance of vernacular languages in Europe and the spread of nationalism.

significance would soon become apparent. In a thorough reshuffling of the Household Division and the Royal Suite, a number of childhood friends and hangers-on of Thibaw rose to powerful positions.[16] The most important of this circle around the king was the Myoza of Yanaung, raised to the status of prince (*mintha*) by Thibaw even though he was not of royal blood. He was from an old military family and his father was still a top-ranking serving officer. Yanaung was appointed colonel of the Northern Tavoy Guards.

The royalist reaction was not long in coming. It was the young Supayalat who most visibly emerged to undermine the Kinwun Mingyi's plans. She was certainly a critical influence over the new king and early on had pushed aside her sister to have herself proclaimed sole queen.[17] While not known to have been against any of the modernisations proposed by the Kinwun Mingyi and his ministers, Supayalat as well as many of the retainers around the new king resented the unprecedented constraints placed on royal power, particularly those on royal spending. As a result of their counselling, Thibaw decided not to take a long foreign trip despite his earlier enthusiasm.[18] Then, on 13 February 1879, several ministers of the new government were dismissed and imprisoned by the units of the Household Guards, under Yanaung's direction.[19] Those arrested included the Myoza of Yaw, who died not long afterwards.

The Yanaung Prince was, as mentioned, the most important of the royalist circle, other than Supayalat herself and her mother, the Middle Palace Queen. Others included the Myoza of Taingda, an enigmatic figure who was to be villainised in the British press as the dark influence over the Thibaw government in its final years. He was descended from a long line of officials, most of whom had held office in Arakan during the period of Burmese occupation. With little formal schooling himself, he seemed typical of the army officers who stood in opposition to the scholar-bureaucrats around the Kinwun Mingyi. But for whatever reason, he had married his daughter, or at least allowed his daughter to be married, to the young Myoza of Kyaukmyaung, the Sorbonne-educated minister and leading light of the reformist wing.

Both the reformist-dominated government, the new household establishment and the military had seen common purpose in a further crack-

[16] *KBZ*, vol. III, pp. 475–6.   [17] *MMOS*, vol. II, p. 251.
[18] *Ibid.*, p. 252.   [19] *KBZ*, vol. III, pp. 500–5.

down on potentially troublesome members of the Alaungpaya family. A son of the Padein Prince, the leader of one of the 1866 rebellions, was arrested soon after Mindon's funeral, and later all royal women were prohibited from leaving the immediate palace area.[20] The Kinwun Mingyi himself had justified the earlier arrests. But what is unclear is the extent of tacit approval, throughout governing circles, for what happened next: the execution of all imprisoned princes and princesses in the period 14–16 February.

A number of elite military units participated in the executions. The condemned wives and children of Mindon were taken away in groups through the western gates to a burial ground outside the royal city. The killings themselves, which took two days to complete, were almost certainly supervised by the Yanaung Prince. He was directly supported by his own Northern Tavoy regiment as well as by the men of the Southern Tavoy regiment commanded by his friend the Myoza of Kyauksauk. Those killed included thirty-one of Mindon's forty-eight sons and nine of his sixty-two daughters.[21]

Thibaw's own complicity in the murder of his siblings is not known. Most Burmese sources insist Thibaw's innocence[22] and it is possible that the military faction acted with only Supayalat and Yanaung's active support. British intelligence reports at the time believed that most officials and military were against the killings, which only had the support of the Household Guards.[23] Whatever the truth, the massacre shifted power in Mandalay back towards the royal couple and their allies in the military and this was reflected in the distribution of new titles and positions to officers involved. An important beneficiary was the Taingda Mingyi, who rose in rank and brought to high office a number of his clients.[24] Thibaw was finally formally installed as king with the title Thiri Pawara Wizaya Nanda Yatha Tilawkadipati Pandita Maha Dhammayazadhiyaza. Spending restraints on the royal family were removed and Thibaw's retainer friends were given a fairly free hand to interfere as they pleased. The Kinwun Mingyi's government was thus critically weakened.[25]

The British reacted strongly to the massacre. The Rangoon commercial

---

[20] *Ibid.*, vol. III, pp. 470, 477.   [21] *Ibid.*, p. 500; *MMOS*, vol. II, p. 229.

[22] *KBZ*, vol. III, pp. 505–10.

[23] Shaw to Government of India, *Correspondence Relating to the Affairs of Burmah Since the Death of the Late King*, 20 March 1879.   [24] *RAB*, 1878/9, p. 3.

[25] *KBZ*, vol. III, p. 571; *MMOS*, vol. II, pp. 241–6.

community had already been calling for intervention and the massacre was seized upon by British firms as a reason to resolve the 'Burma problem' once and for all. Calcutta's thinking was not far removed from this and the British Indian Army began preparations for war. Reinforcements arrived from India and were quickly dispatched to posts along the Upper Burma frontier. The plan was for the dethronement of Thibaw and his replacement by the Nyaungyan Prince, who was now safely in India.[26] Before an offensive could be launched, however, British policy-makers abandoned their scheme, not because of the situation in Mandalay, but because of developments in Afghanistan and to a lesser extent South Africa which had overstretched resources. The massacre of the British Resident at Kabul and his entire staff had led to a momentary panic in Calcutta and to a sudden decision to withdraw the Residency in Mandalay, though the Thibaw government had done nothing, despite the killings, to actual threaten either the Resident, Horace Browne, or any of the European community in Mandalay.[27]

The Burmese government after 1879 may be seen as a sort of coalition of two factions. One faction was composed of reformist ministers loyal mainly to the Kinwun Mingyi. Of increasing importance were several Indian- or European-educated officials such as the Myoza of Kyaukmyaung. The other was the royalist faction, represented by Supayalat and friends of Thibaw as well as the conservative Taingda Mingyi and his allies, especially in the military.[28] But this latter faction underwent its own internal divisions and in 1882 these divisions would lead to the execution of Thibaw's erstwhile closest confidante, the Myoza of Yanaung. He had apparently advised his childhood friend to take further wives, additional to Supayalat, in the custom of Burmese kingship. Yanaung probably saw an increased number of wives as a way of diluting Supayalat's influence, Thibaw's lack of wives being an incredible departure from the norm and preventing him from cementing ties with important noble families, and more importantly with Shan courts, many of which were now in rebellion. His scheme was for Thibaw to take Mi Hkin-gyi as his minor wife. She was the daughter of the Myoza of Kanni, the granddaughter of the Myoza of Kampat, and the niece of the Myoza of Pagan, all serving cabinet ministers. Supayalat, perhaps a selective modernist, was determined to see this

[26] *KBZ*, vol. III, p. 532.
[27] *Ibid.*, p. 523; see also Horace Browne, *Reminiscences of the Court of Mandalay*, London, 1907.   [28] *MMOS*, vol. II, pp. 241–6.

one custom not followed and conflict between the two soon erupted. Yanaung lost the power struggle and was killed on the queen's orders. Mi Hkin-gyi, seventeen years old, was also executed.[29]

Though the reformist-designed administration still existed in form, this 'Fourteen Department' government was never able to fully function as intended. The number of departments constantly changed over the next six years, with various departments merging or being reconstituted.[30] While some of the departments, namely Civil Justice, Education, Religious Affairs and Legislation, were able to operate under autonomous minister-ial direction, the others came under continual interference. Two of the most important ministries – War and Revenue – as well as the appoint-ments office, were effectively under royal or palace control.[31]

Policies and practices of the Thibaw government

The seven-year reign of Thibaw is usually contrasted negatively with that of his father. While Mindon is portrayed as 'realistic' in his dealings with the British, Thibaw is seen as ignorant of the outside world and unwilling to appreciate the weakness of his position and accommodate British interests accordingly. Whereas Mindon is seen as 'progressive' in his attitudes towards government, Thibaw, or at least his government, is seen as reactionary, the nature of the new government seemingly exemplified by the political executions of 1878. From this perspective, Thibaw is viewed as responsible for a period of administrative decline, and the emergence of the 'chaotic' conditions throughout the country which seemed to warrant, and were used to help justify, British intervention in 1885.

But despite the sense of insecurity in Mandalay caused by the 1878 executions, and though Thibaw may have been unpopular with many in court circles, his policies were only an intensification, if anything, of the reform process begun under this father. They were also a damage control exercise, attempting to cope with the economic and social forces un-leashed by a quarter-century of growing international economic ties and radical changes in the whole structure of government. The vilification of

[29] The stories of Yanaung, Supayalat, Mi Hkin-gyi and others at Thibaw's court form the backdrop to F. Tennyson Jesse's novel *The Lacquer Lady* (London, 1929), which was based in part on interviews with surviving courtiers.   [30] *MMOS*, vol. II, pp. 241–6.
[31] *Ibid.*

Thibaw was in many ways the work of Rangoon-based commercial interests which had been, throughout the 1870s, pressing for intervention. For
several years prior to Mindon's death, they had already been warning that
'at no former time has the population of Burma been so poor or so
poverty-stricken as they are known to be at present' and predicting a crisis
'as the situation had reached beyond even Burmese endurance'.[32] Conditions were worsening, not because of political intrigues and repression in
Mandalay, but because external conditions were changing ever more
quickly and the Burmese state remained unable to meet these new and, by
this point, perhaps impossible challenges.

The central problem facing Thibaw's government was that of revenue,
which was steadily worsening as the Mandalay treasury became caught
between its own budgetary needs, British demands for free trade and fear
of the consequences of increased taxation over the countryside.[33] In the
search for new, politically feasible sources of revenue, the government
initially turned to the institution of new monopolies on the export of
selected commodities. British traders complained that this move ran contrary to the 1867 treaty, but the treaty itself had already lapsed after ten
years. But the resulting protests from Rangoon were so strong, that the
monopolies were quietly dropped within a few months.[34] The government
then turned to the sale of new concessions to both local and foreign firms.
Concessions mainly in the area of forestry had already been sold to British
companies, most notably the Bombay Burma Trading Corporation.

An increasing number of smaller concessions, not only in forestry but
also for example in mining and oil production were also sold to local
businessmen. The most notable of these was the *thuhtay* banker, Moola
Ismail, a Muslim, and the nephew of another prominent Muslim *thuhtay*,
Moola Ibrahim. The latter had been active in court circles since at least the
mid-1850s when he was mentioned in Yule's reports.[35] Many other local
businessmen-concessionaires seem also to have been Mandalay-based
Muslims, normally referred to in Burmese sources, however, under Burmese names.[36] In the final years of Thibaw's reign, he also held the coveted

[32] Sladen Diary, 19 June 1869, Papers of Sir Edward Sladen.

[33] For a detailed discussion of revenue administration under Thibaw, see *MMOS*, vol. III,
pp. 39–47.

[34] *Correspondence Relating to the Affairs of Upper Burmah 1880–85*, London, 1885,
p. 14.   [35] *MMOS*, vol. III, p. 144. Some sources say he was Moola Ibrahim's son.

[36] Revenue and Agriculture Departure Proceedings (Upper Burma) (hereafter RAR),
January–June 1886, no. 1; another example was the '*kala*' Po Myint, who bought a

post of revenue minister. Merchants were then paying 10,000 rupees per year and bankers 40,000 rupees per year for *thuhtay* status and the resulting access to various monopolies and licences. Moola Ismail, with government encouragement, also built the new Mandalay market, or Zegyo. This was located outside the city walls, and designed by a resident Italian architect.

Despite continued attempts to regularise the *thathameda* tax regime, related administrative problems plagued the government until the very end, when, just before the war, a new tax code attempting to clarify the *thathameda* was promulgated.[37] In addition to all the various complications of administering the tax, problems which took the British more than ten years to finally resolve, was the inability of the royal agencies to rein in local taxation in many areas. Neither could they end the seepage of tax revenues through various administrative layers, though the Thibaw government attempted to confront this problem head on. Several royal orders expressly prohibited the levying of customary fees[38] and others called for closer supervision of hereditary local office-holders. The government also turned to the easier but much more desperate solution of farming out revenue from state lands (but not, it seems, the *thathameda*). These state lands included crown estates belonging to the incumbent monarch. They also included prebendal estates which had been granted to crown service families in return for service but which now, with the introduction of cash salaries, required holders to pay rent. While initially this revenue was paid in kind, under the tax farming system, payment had to be made in cash, the determination of the equivalent cash demand being said to have been less than generous.[39]

By increasingly turning to tax farming, Burmese government policy had begun to turn full circle as crown agencies, which had taken much of revenue administration away from hereditary local officials, were now feeling pressurised into handing revenue administration back. Critically, however, revenue administration was not being handed back under the old system, to the various *myothugyi* and crown service chiefs, but to the highest bidders. These included some gentry leaders, but also many more

---

five-year forestry concession for 200,000 rupees, including 50,000 up front (*KBZ*, vol. III, p. 610).   [37] *MMOS*, vol III, pp. 33–9.

[38] *KBZ*, vol. III, p. 589.

[39] J.A. Stewart, *Burma Gazetteer – Kyauksè District* (hereafter *Kyauksè Gazetteer*), Rangoon, 1925, vol. I, p. 126.

members of the Mandalay aristocracy and *thuhtay* enjoying court patronage. Most of the tax farms were over estates close to Mandalay. In Kyauksè, for example, rents from all crown land in 1884 were farmed out to a chief secretary of the court, the Ywaza of Windaing, for payment of ten lakh rupees per year.[40] He in turn sub-let revenue collection to several other officials and local hereditary officers, such as the Thugyi of Sulègon who farmed the irrigation tax from the Thindi canal for 4,000 rupees.[41]

Another quite novel attempt to shore up state finances was the introduction of a national lottery in 1878.[42] This was apparently the brainchild of the Myoza of Yaw, who had played the French lottery while in Paris. The lottery at once became very popular, initially offering a possible 10,000 rupee win for a two rupee ticket, rising later to a possible 50,000 rupee win for a five rupee ticket. The lottery is mentioned in numerous contemporary plays,[43] was condemned by many distinguished monks as state support for gambling, and is remembered in contemporary Burmese sources as an important cause of popular unrest and even the eventual downfall of the kingdom.[44] The administration of the lottery quickly spun out of control, as various officials and members of Thibaw's own entourage became directly involved and vied for sales through their own personally owned booths. Less and less income then ended up in state coffers. People from surrounding towns were said to have travelled to Mandalay to purchase tickets and families lost their entire savings in what was described by Burmese and British observers alike as a 'craze' which dominated the city for many months.[45] Realising the problems which had ensued, the government finally terminated the lottery experiment in 1880.[46]

At the same time as attempting to increase state revenues, Thibaw's ministers also tried to relieve the burden of taxation in the countryside, possibly out of an awareness that increased taxation had begun to stir considerable discontent. Late in Mindon's reign or early in Thibaw's, *thathameda* assessment had risen to a fairly uniform rate of ten rupees per

---

[40] 'Instructions to Civil Officers in Burma', *Burma Home Proceedings* (hereafter BHP), March 1886.   [41] *Kyauksè Gazetteer*, vol. I, p. 126.

[42] *KBZ*, vol. III, p. 517.

[43] Plays in which the lottery is mentioned include *Konmara, Shwelin, Bandu* and *Kaka*. See Hla Pe, *Konmara Pya Zat*, p. 25.   [44] *MMOS*, vol. II, p. 224.

[45] *KBZ*, vol. III, pp. 517–18.   [46] *Ibid.*, p. 566.

household. Different rates within each community were determined locally. But by the early 1880s, revenue assessments, in most if not all areas, appear to have been significantly reduced. In Alon, for example, *thathameda* demand was less than half that under Mindon, with assessment down from ten to six rupees.[47] The fall in revenue from the countryside was also related to increasing tax evasion as will be discussed below. But by 1883, the Court of Ava was also aware that taxation was becoming a politically explosive issue and in one order expressly banned punishment for underpayment.[48]

In addition to reductions in the *thathameda*, the government in 1884 enacted a number of other pro-trade policies. Following a meeting between Thibaw and leading businessmen, the government announced a repeal of twenty-three internal tariffs on trade as well as substantial reduction of many other tariffs, 'in the interests of economic progress and development'. At the same time, however, ministers called for a 'more disciplined collection' of remaining taxes.[49] Noting the importance in several of its last orders of promoting 'vigorous buying and selling'[50] the government, despite its severe fiscal situation, also completely exempted key market towns such as Bhamo from the payment of *thathameda*.[51] Half-hearted attempts to encourage an expansion of agricultural production were also made and in one of the very last royal orders before annexation, the government granted limited ownership rights to cultivators reclaiming state lands, exempting them from tax and allowing inheritance, but prohibiting sales.[52]

The final attempt by the ailing government to shore up its financial position was to borrow money. Receiving credit from firms and traders in Calcutta and Rangoon for various purchases had been common under Mindon. But it seems only under Thibaw that the government began borrowing large amounts of cash from private individuals. Moola Ismail lent the government 160,000 rupees, for example, in the early 1880s.[53] By around this time, the government had also begun planning for the establishment of a 'Royal Bank of Burma'. The idea was that initial capitalisation would come from a European partner bank. The new bank would then lend money to private Burmese businessmen as well as to the

---

[47] Lower Chindwin Gazetteer, p. 161.   [48] *ROB*, 30 November 1883.

[49] *KBZ*, vol. III, pp. 643–4.   [50] *ROB*, 12 August 1881.

[51] *Ibid.*, 8 October 1885; *KBZ*, vol. III, pp. 568–9.   [52] *ROB*, 16 January 1885.

[53] 'Lease of the Zegyo Bazaar', BHP, December 1887.

treasury.[54] Negotiations had taken place in Paris in 1885 for the establishment of a joint Franco-Burmese bank, but no final agreement was made prior to the outbreak of war.

Beyond revenues, Thibaw's government was also facing increasing problems with administrative disorder in the countryside. This was a continuation of trends which had begun under Mindon. The first major problem related to local hereditary offices, those of the *myothugyi* and various crown service chiefs. The Burmese state in the early 1880s was in no position to completely revamp local administration, in the manner the British were to do ten years later. Early modern political structures at the *myo* level and below therefore needed to be fitted into emerging new national institutions and policies. If the goal of the post-1878 government was to create a more bureaucratic state based on cash revenues, local authority would have to become rationalised and more territorially based. This was attempted by creating a new layer of centrally appointed officials, the 'district commissioners', or *hkayaing wuns*, as well as strengthening the older *myowun* and subordinate offices but without any real effort fundamentally to reform lower-level hereditary positions.

This neglect of the gentry encouraged the increasing penetration by outsiders of still important local hereditary offices as well as much infighting among local elite families over chiefly position. The last proper accounting of local hereditary offices and office-holders had taken place in 1805. By the early 1880s, in many areas, two or more persons were claiming the same chiefly position.[55] In other areas, outsiders, not of the traditional chiefly family, had taken over the local office, either through the intervention of a friendly *myowun* or other Mandalay official, or by buying the office directly from the old family. By annexation, British sources said that some rural offices were changing hands as often as every few months.[56] *Myothugyi* offices could also allegedly be purchased from some of Thibaw's less than high-minded *aides-de-camp*.[57] Despite a call in

[54] India Foreign (Secret) Proceedings (hereafter ISP), 1885, no. 178, 23 September 1885. See also Joseph Dautremer, *Burma Under British Rule* (trans. from French by George Scott), London, 1913, pp. 7–75. Apparently plans for a national bank had begun as early as 1873 under Mindon. See 'Mandalay Diary', IFP, 25 February 1873.

[55] *KBZ*, vol. III, pp. 585–6 says that there were now four or five claimants for many offices.

[56] *GUBSS*, vol. II, p. 370. See also R.R. Langham-Carter, 'Burmese Rule on the Toungoo Frontier', *JBRS*, 27 (1937), 15–33, for a detailed look at local administration around this time.   [57] *MMOS*, vol. II, pp. 241–6.

1882 for all chiefs to submit fresh papers stating their hereditary claims to office, it does not seem that these practices were in any way attenuated. Only one subsequent royal order actually dismissed a chief, the Myothugyi of Ahmyint, for not being of the hereditary governing family.[58] Far from Mandalay's grip, however, other gentry leaders were apparently capturing provincial office previously reserved for Ava officials. In 1879, for example, Naymyo Thamada Raza, the Myothugyi of Myede, was made *myowun* of his home town, erasing the old bifurcation of power between hereditary chief and appointed provincial governor.

The second major problem was the status of prebendal estates. As we have seen, by the early 1880s, the process begun under Mindon of replacing the early modern system of *appanages* and prebendal land-holdings with cash revenues and cash salaries had largely succeeded, in the sense that the *appanage* system was abolished. But the reforms had not succeeded in the sense that officials now contented themselves with only their nominal cash incomes. Instead, the reforms had thrown into disorder the earlier tenure system and Thibaw's government was able to make no real headway towards redefining land ownership to conform with a more bureaucratised state at the centre. The net result was a large-scale selling and mortgaging of state lands and the growing prominence of non-local traders and money-lenders throughout the countryside.[59]

As already mentioned, the main innovation of the Thibaw government in the area of local administration was the creation of a new layer of administration, that of the 'district' (*hkayaing*).[60] These districts, which numbered ten altogether, were modelled on British Indian districts such as those in Lower Burma. By placing fairly senior officials in charge of these districts (as *hkayaing wun*) with judicial and administrative authority over the several *myowun* in their territory, the direction of policy became that of further centralisation, rather than any resuscitation of more local institutions. The new *hkayaing wun* were noblemen of fairly high status in Mandalay and needed quite a lot of encouragement before actually travelling to their district seat, much less touring around their district as they were also called on to do. Their main brief was to check

[58] *ROB*, 20 June 1883; *GUBSS*, vol. II, p. 93.

[59] *MMOS*, vol. II, pp. 128–30.

[60] *ROB*, 29 February 1884; *KBZ*, vol. III, p. 631. See also Langham-Carter, 'Burmese Rule on the Toungoo Frontier'.

growing banditry. They were given a small military detachment, thus increasing the number of army posts around the country, and were specifically charged with investigating banditry and restoring order. In addition, *myo* offices were instructed to be more diligent in reporting judicial cases to Mandalay. The government also expressed concern over both the number of magistrates serving on provincial benches and the length of time it was taking them to adjudicate the growing pile of land and inheritance disputes.[61]

Efforts to modernise Burma's military accelerated under Thibaw. By 1879, the year war seemed momentarily imminent, Calcutta commissioned several British intelligence reports on Burmese military preparedness.[62] These reports stated that the army had made the transition to a 'professional' standing army, with an increasingly elaborate system of ranks, uniforms and local commands. European drill practices were copied with moderate success and several military parades were held around the palace compound. The British estimated the standing army as totalling approximately 15,650 men, including 8,800 troops of the Household Guards and 2,500 cavalry.[63] Considerable attention continued to be given to the running and expansion of local armaments factories, which could now produce ammunition and minor explosives. A small river force of 4,000 was also established, with fairly elaborate plans made for the blocking of any hostile British force coming up the Irrawaddy. Several forts were constructed along the river and an apparently successful experiment in underwater explosions was conducted in 1882. In all these efforts Thibaw continued his father's policy of employing Italian, as well as a few French, advisors and military engineers.[64]

Despite all the work of the Thibaw government in attempting to modernise further the Burmese state, more traditional obligations were far from forgotten. Mindon had left behind a much revered legacy as Buddhist patron, and Thibaw, the former monk, did try to live up to people's expectations. He presided over the many, almost daily, ceremonial functions and also made large personal donations to new monasteries and other religious establishments. Early in his reign, Thibaw met with leading *sayadaw* to discuss the state of the religion,[65] and followed with several attempts to further encourage Sangha discipline.[66] His government ex-

---

[61] *ROB*, 27 February 1884, 17 March 1882.   [62] IFP, January 1878, pp. 223–5.
[63] *GUBSS*, vol. II, pp. 498–9.   [64] *KBZ*, vol. III, pp. 541–2.   [65] *Ibid.*, p. 651.
[66] *ROB*, 22 June 1882, 18 May 1883, 23 May 1884.

plicitly condemned 'heretical' (*alleikzi*) practices (perhaps related to the emergence of 'millenarian figures', described below) and criticised popular support for these 'so-called' monks.[67]

One important act of merit took place in July 1883, when he ordered the enumeration of all slaves in Mandalay. Slaves, slave owners and slave sellers were all summoned to determine the facts of each case and the amount of indebtedness which had led to each of the slave's bonded status. Thibaw then paid 40,000 rupees towards their emancipation. Of the freed slaves, over 1,000 became Buddhist monks and novices. Two hundred of these entered the Thudhamma monastery in Mandalay and offerings were made to them by the king himself.[68] New legislation was passed to protect animals, proscribing not only the killing but also the caging of animals.[69]

Collapsing royal authority

The precipitous decline of the Thibaw government's authority over large parts of the kingdom in the 1880s came first and most dramatically in the Shan states. Within a year or so of the death of Mindon, tax revenues fell close to zero and only constant military campaigns prevented the complete ouster of Burmese forces.[70] Unrest in the Shan states had been brewing for some time, with occasional rebellions, normally by one or more of the four dozen hereditary *sawbwa*. These *sawbwa* apparently saw Thibaw's succession and related infighting in Mandalay as their best opportunity in a while to overturn Burmese authority. Many local chiefs had made surreptitious contact with the British Assistant Resident at Bhamo or with Rangoon, and many of the most eastern tributaries were coming under the shadow of French expansion along the lower Mekong. Within this volatile context, Thibaw's decision to break with tradition and not take the daughters of the *sawbwa* as his minor wives could only have come as a shock. Many then refused to attend the first regular homage ceremony in 1878 and raised the standard of rebellion.[71] The initial focus of the Shan revolt was Mong Nai, one of the largest towns in

[67] *Ibid.*, 22 June 1882, 18 May 1883.   [68] *KBZ*, vol. III, p. 607; *GUBSS*, vol. I, p. 94.
[69] *KBZ*, vol. III, p. 552.
[70] *MMOS*, vol. II, p. 224. See also Saimong Mangrai, *The Shan States and the British Annexation*, Ithaca, 1965, pp. 101–28. On problems with payment of the *thathameda* tax, see especially pp. 103–5.   [71] *KBZ*, vol. III, pp. 545–7.

the eastern hills. An expedition was immediately sent out to deal with what the relevant royal order termed these 'uncivilised' (*mayinchay*) *sawbwa*.

For six years, thousands of Burmese troops were sent in campaign after campaign against the Sawbwa of Mong Nai as well as against the several other *sawbwa* who came to fight alongside him.[72] During the course of one such campaign, in 1881, the Mong Nai Sawbwa managed to overwhelm the local garrison, killing the commander and over 400 soldiers. While the town of Mong Nai was finally captured in 1882, the Sawbwa himself was able to flee further east to Keng Tung. Keng Tung had become a refuge for the Sawbwa of Yauksauk, Mai Nong, and others and was itself now far from the grip of declining royal power.[73] Other *sawbwa*, such as the Sawbwa of Hsenwi, decided not to take sides and instead fled to British territory, returning only after annexation in 1885.[74]

A number of very prominent noblemen were lost to the incessant campaigning, including the Myoza of Pagan, a court *wundauk*. He had died in an abortive attempt to seize the town of Mai Nong in 1885 after the local chief had refused to recognise Thibaw's authority. Many of the losses were due to malaria and other hardships rather than combat. The governor of Pahkangyi, Maha Mindin Minkaung, was then appointed commanding general for the entire theatre, but he too soon died of illness. The commander of the main cavalry regiments, Mingyi Maha Minkaung Kyawdin, the most senior military officer in the regular army, then took to the field himself.[75]

By the time of the Third Anglo-Burmese War, many if not most of the *sawbwa* had decided to join together in a formal alliance aimed at replacing Thibaw, not with a Shan prince, but with his cousin, the Burmese Limbin Prince. Limbin was the son of the assassinated Kanaung Prince who had been living in British territory and who now agreed to join forces with the rebel *sawbwa*. The Shan revolt thereby turned from a localised rebellion into a direct challenge against the Mandalay government. The following extract, part of a letter from the Keng Tung Sawbwa to the Hsipaw Sawbwa, provides an interesting insight into the motivations behind the revolt:

---

[72] *Ibid.*, vol. III, pp. 602, 617–23.
[73] IFP, 30 January 1885; *KBZ*, vol. III, p. 614. See also Saimong Mangrai, *The Padaeng Chronicle and the Jeng Tung State Chronicle Translated*, Ann Arbor, 1981, esp. pp. 272–3.   [74] *KBZ*, vol. III, pp. 567–8.   [75] *Ibid.*, pp. 669–70.

Without a suzerain there will be continual struggle among the *sawbwa*... If there is a suzerain, the interest of the country, of the religion, of all of us, will be protected... If the Limbin Prince becomes King the *thathameda* tax (an unprecedented thing in history) will be remitted, and the *sawbwa* will be required to do obeisance to the King only once in three years.[76]

It seems from this, first of all, that the *sawbwa* were not fighting for complete 'independence' but for increased autonomy under some sort of nominal Burmese sovereignty. Second, the *thathameda* tax was an important source of discontent, perhaps a key cause driving these hereditary local elites into rebellion. We will return to this point in the next chapter, comparing this phenomenon with the causes underlying popular resistance to the British occupation in the Irrawaddy valley in the late 1880s.

By the early 1880s royal authority had also begun to collapse much nearer to home, in the Sagaing Hills, along the Lower Chindwin plain and around the suburbs of Mandalay itself.[77] Burmese sources describe sections of this area coming under the control of large gangs of 'bandits' (*damya*), and several of the new district commissioners were replaced, presumably for not dealing effectively with them. New appointments were given first fifty, and then one hundred soldiers and ordered to travel around their districts and suppress the lawlessness.[78] By 1883 the situation had become so bad that no district commissioner could be posted to either Sagaing or Alon because of the complete breakdown of government authority.

The cream of the regular army was sent out to areas where the dacoits were most active. Three hundred of the North Marabin regiment together with the elite Natshinyway ('chosen by the gods') were sent to Alon. The latter regiment had been reorganised under Mindon and comprised specially selected men over six feet tall. The Linzin Regiment, descendants of men brought from the Lao court at Vientiane, were sent to Tabayin. All, however, found themselves the constant victims of ambush by increasingly daring bandit gangs.[79] Official reports stated that all military efforts to suppress the bandits had failed, and that 'if one were captured, two would appear to take his place'. The government believed that trade and the economy in general was beginning to suffer as a result.[80]

[76] Quoted in Ni Ni Myint, *Burma's Struggle Against British Imperialism: 1885–1889*, Rangoon, 1983, p. 107.
[77] *Correspondence Relating to the Affairs of Upper Burmah 1880–85*, p. 51.
[78] KBZ, vol. III, p. 671.   [79] *Ibid.*, p. 696.   [80] *Ibid.*

In June of 1885, the king chaired a special meeting, attended by all senior government ministers and military officers, to discuss the insurgency. The meeting agreed to dispatch Mingyi Thiri Maha Zeyya Kyawdin, the Myoza of Salay. He was a Privy Councillor and also in charge of the royal river forces and, as such, was more commonly known as the Hléthin *atwinwun*. His mission was to be a fact-finding one, though he would travel with a sizeable escort. After several weeks in the worst-hit areas north of the Chindwin, he returned to present a dire picture of the situation.

He said:

> In attempting to fight and capture these bandits, we must remember that they are not headquartered at any particular place. Instead, they live in remote settlements far from government posts, attacking and then retreating into the forest. I believe that some do wish to return to life in the towns and villages but are afraid of being convicted as criminals and receiving harsh sentences. I recommend that we declare a general amnesty, and place the returned dacoits under the responsibility of the local chief or local officials. Heavy penalties would then be imposed on anyone caught after the amnesty deadline.[81]

The policy then agreed by the Hluttaw was one made from a position of weakness. An amnesty was declared and those bandits who turned themselves in were registered and tattooed, their right arm being tattooed with their name and their left with the warning 'beware' (*thadi-hta*).[82] Unfortunately, we know very little about these bandits, their aims or motivations, their social background or their relationship with local communities or Buddhist monasteries. In 1875, Mindon's government had compiled a list of senior gentry office-holders which categorised twenty out of approximately two hundred as being in 'rebellion', indicating that state control had begun to falter as early as the mid-1870s. This also suggested that some of the leaders of these bandit groups were former *myothugyi* and other chiefs.[83]

Revolts against the state also came under religious leadership. Generally, Buddhist monks did not 'go into rebellion' until after the British takeover. What we do see at this time, however, is the emergence of what we might term 'millenarian figures', though this is a very preliminary categorisation as we have very little information beyond their actual

---

[81] *Ibid.*, pp. 696–9.   [82] *Ibid.*, pp. 697–9.   [83] *ROB*, 9 January 1875.

self-given titles. One such figure, named 'Buddha Thiwali', operated around Singu with 200 men and carried not only the red, green and yellow flags of the nobility and the Sangha but also the white umbrella of royalty.[84] Both cavalry units and river forces under the Hlèthin Atwinwun were sent to capture him but without success. In Mogaung, another similar figure appeared, calling himself Min Taya, or the 'Just Ruler'.[85]

In areas somewhat further from Mandalay but still in the Irrawaddy valley, we hear less of armed revolts against the government by either bandits or millenarian figures. Instead, local elites, *myothugyi* and others, simply stopped paying revenue.[86] If we compare revenue collected in 1869 with revenue demand in 1885, we see firstly that in 1885 demand was greater in areas close to Mandalay. For the suburbs of Mandalay, for example, revenue collected in 1869 was 90,000 rupees whereas demand in 1885 was 120,000 rupees. In Dabessway, Paleik and Kyauksè, tax demand increased from 144,000 rupees to 232,000 rupees. Other increases were all either in areas close by (Sagaing, Ava) or in large towns along the Irrawaddy (Pahkangyi, Pagan) which presumably remained under relatively strong state control. This is not to say that all these places paid the demanded amounts, but that at least some enumeration of households was able to take place.

But in many other areas, some not very far away, revenue demand decreased precipitously or even dropped to zero. Places where revenue demand fell included, ominously, most of the major military recruiting grounds such as the Shwépyi Yanaung area, the home of major cavalry regiments. Here, taxes collected in 1869 amounted to 168,880 rupees but demand in 1885 was only 131,050 rupees. In the Lower Chindwin, where much banditry was taking place, the fall was even greater. Demand in Alon, Tabayin and Amyint, the heartland of the Konbaung dynasty, fell to only about half of that collected earlier. In places further away, such as Salin and Minbu, revenue demand in 1885 was zero. Revenue was also down to zero in nearly all the major Shan towns, in all the important north-eastern trading towns such as Bhamo and mining towns such as

---

[84] *KBZ*, vol. III, p. 608.   [85] *Ibid.*, p. 629.

[86] This is mentioned in a number of British sources, mainly gazetteers written after annexation. The main source, however, appears to be *GUBSS*, vol. II, pp. 419–21. Without giving many statistics, *MMOS*, vol. II, pp. 126–34 describes population decline in many areas, a decline which is based on a significantly lower number of households paying taxes in 1885 than in previous years, which I would attribute only partially to emigration and mainly to tax evasion.

Mogok, as well as in dozens of small towns across the country. Overall, only 200,000 households were assessed in 1885, as compared to 400,000 in the last years of Mindon.[87] By this time the number of 'chiefs in rebellion' had grown to a substantial percentage, particularly in places along the middle Irrawaddy such as Salin and Taungdwingyi, where hereditary authority remained intact and where rebel chiefs took their communities with them. In Kyaukse, Sagaing and other nearby areas, taxation necessarily increased to shore up disappearing revenues. Proximity to Mandalay changed the nature of the local response to one of banditry or religious revolt and not gentry-led resistance.[88]

The extent to which armed revolts and unrest were actually taking place in the countryside may also be judged from the huge numbers of people who fled to British territory in the year or so immediately preceding British intervention. What had been an economically driven migration, both seasonal and permanent, and mainly of cultivators, had turned into a flood of refugees. As many as 50,000 left in 1885 alone, including several thousand a month in the run-up to the final war. One contemporary Burmese source states that not only had the government's revenue base shrunk dramatically by the mid-1880s with unrest becoming endemic throughout the countryside, but that the army too was becoming smaller, presumably also as a result of emigration and the falling away of areas from state control. The crown was able to muster only 6,849 men during the call-up for the Third Anglo-Burmese War. Even factoring in the two or three thousand men likely to have been committed to the Shan campaigns, this still represented a considerable drop from British estimates of 15,000 seven years before, or 50,000 from the early 1860s.[89]

Attacks also began from across the border. In December 1884, Bhamo, the second most important town in the country, was captured by 2,000 Chinese and Jingpaw freebooters crossing from the north.[90] There was little resistance from the Burmese garrison of 300 men, and the town was looted and set on fire. The counter-attack was led by the Maha Mintin Minhla Thihathu, Master of the King's Barges. Arriving by steamer with heavy guns and nearly 2,000 men, he was still only able to recapture the town after a sustained month-long siege.[91] The Jingpaw, or *Kachin* as the

[87] *MMOS*, vol. II, p. 127.

[88] See *GUBSS*, vol. II, pp. 419–21, for a comparison of revenue demand in 1869 and 1885.   [89] *MMOS*, vol. II, pp. 128–30.   [90] IFP, nos. 205–14, March 1885.

[91] *KBZ*, vol. III, pp. 695–6.

Burmese called them, continued however to raid into the lowlands, creating generally unsettled conditions throughout the north and practically ending cross-border trade with Yunnan.[92] By the few months preceding the British intervention, even the Manipuris seemed to be joining in, and British observers reported limited incursions by the Maharaja of Manipur's men across the disputed border into the Kubo valley.[93]

By late 1885, the violence had spread to Mandalay itself. Late in the year, during the annual Thadingyut festival, 200 prisoners were killed in what the military alleged was a failed breakout. The attempted escape was said to have been orchestrated by the dacoit leader Nga Yan Min, whose body was kept on display for three days in order to quell rumours that he had managed to flee the city.[94] British observers believed the escape was engineered by prison warders as an excuse to execute the 150 or so political prisoners being held.[95] Stories spread throughout the capital about the imminent arrival of either the Myingun Prince or the Nyaungyan Prince to depose Thibaw, with or without foreign help. The Myingun Prince had left Saigon in late 1884 for Bangkok and had begun preparations for an attack into Upper Burma. Soon after, all inhabitants of Mandalay were required to present themselves and provide information on their address and occupation to the city governor and prisons director.

All through these difficult times, the royal couple continued to celebrate in grand style. The feasts and festivals accompanying the ear-boring ceremonies of their eldest daughter (their only son having died in infancy), for example, lasted for several days and involved thousands of people. Preparations were placed under the charge of the treasury minister, the Myoza of Paukmyaing, and other high officials were involved. The ministers in charge of Chinese and Indian affairs, in what must have been a somewhat pedestrian task for such important grandees of the court, were instructed to organise Chinese and Indian food for the occasion.[96] Gifts were given out by the royal family, Siamese dancers entertained large crowds of ordinary people, and more than 2,000 court *ponna* presided over the relevant rituals.

The royal couple were also keen shoppers and sent close aides on numerous trips to Rangoon and Calcutta to buy cloth and other consumer

---

[92] IFP, January 1878, pp. 223–5.   [93] IFP, nos. 47–51, 59–61, August 1885.

[94] *KBZ*, vol. III, pp. 664–5.

[95] *Correspondence Relating to the Affairs of Upper Burma 1880–1885*, Secret Letter 56, 24 March 1885.   [96] *KBZ*, vol. III, pp. 668–9.

goods. In late 1885, in one of her last acts as queen, Supayalat sent offerings to the Shwedagon Pagoda in Rangoon and to the white elephant at Pegu. She also dispatched three royal retainers, including the court tailor Shwedaung Kyaw. They were given 70,000 rupees to spend and returned with boxes of the latest Rangoon fashions as well as with 'interesting and unusual new things'.[97] Though the signs of impending disaster continued, Thibaw's court took heart in the capture of a baby white elephant in the southern forests along the Toungoo frontier, a special palace being built for the animal and preparations for his grand welcoming to Mandalay being placed under the charge of the Taingda Mingyi himself.[98]

Around the time of Lord Churchill's fateful ultimatum in November 1885, a Parsee drama troupe from Bombay had arrived in the royal city and performed to packed audiences at the new, European-style theatre just outside the main palace complex. During the cool autumn evenings, from the open-air theatre, the assembled aristocrats, and the royal couple on occasion, could have seen in the distance the Shan hills, where nearly half the army remained bogged down in bloody fighting. But even closer to home, royal authority, once so strong across the valley and the uplands, was now in tatters. Everyone expected a new British assault. Many hoped the growing crisis would bring back the Prince of Myingun or the Prince of Nyaungyan. No one could have thought that within weeks, the kingdom's thousand-year-old monarchy would disappear for ever.

Explaining the crisis of the Burmese state

The crisis of the Burmese state during the several years immediately preceding colonial rule manifested itself most visibly in the disintegration of royal power over much of the countryside. In some areas control was lost to local hereditary elites who refused to continue to recognise the authority of Mandalay. This was the case throughout the Shan hills and also in some areas within the Irrawaddy valley relatively far from the capital. In areas closer to Mandalay, control was lost to an assortment of bandits and millenarian figures, as well as perhaps some hereditary gentry leaders. In addition the fall in state revenues reached 'crisis' proportions. This is not to say that there was a general economic crisis in Upper Burma during these years; our economic information is much too sketchy to state

---

[97] *Ibid.*, pp. 702, 704.   [98] *Ibid.*, pp. 691–4.

definitively the extent of decline if any in economic production, much less reach any conclusions about popular welfare. But there was though most certainly a *political* crisis, one which in its form bears some similarity to that of the mid-eighteenth century, but which was caused by very different factors and which led not to a royal reconsolidation, but to a direct colonial administration.

Conventional historiography on this period tends to discount any economic explanation for the political crisis under Thibaw by simply referring to the considerable expansion of trade which took place between Upper and Lower Burma in the last years of Burmese independence. From 1878 to 1885, there was indeed a significant expansion in trade, from approximately 44 million rupees in 1878/9 to more than 50 million rupees in 1884/5.[99] The only exception was a short-lived but precipitous decline in the very early years of Thibaw's government from 1878 to 1882.[100] This early fall in trade is largely attributed to growing political uncertainties following the withdrawal of the British Residency and popular rumours of impending war. Certainly rice harvests seem to have been quite good at this time, and British reports observed that rice shipments had substantially decreased. According to these reports, abundant harvests during these years had reduced imports to 'a minimum' and rice was sold in Upper Burma 'at even cheaper rates that those ruling within British territory'.[101] The fall in trade was also attributed by Rangoon to the government's desperate attempt to gain revenue through new monopolies.[102] The government had established new monopolies on the export of betel nut, raw and manufactured silk, sugar, cheroot leaves and several other goods. Many were sold in November 1881 for a total 120,000 rupees, including many to Thibaw's cohorts such as the Myoza of Yanaung. A new monopoly on the export of hides and cutch was sold to Moola Ismail. As a result, many middlemen attempted to sell only to the home market, rather than at fixed prices for export, causing in turn a depressed market for producers.[103] The treaty of 1867, according to some British interpretations, prohibited such monopolies, but the treaty had

[99] Compiled from *RAB* 1878/9–1885/6.

[100] It should be noted that the value for imports (in comparison with earlier values) is lower than it would be were it not for the significant lowering of tariffs by Thibaw's government. See *Correspondence Relating to the Affairs of Upper Burma 1880–85*, December 1885, p. 44.   [101] *RAB*, 1880/1, p. 84.

[102] See *GUBSS*, vol. II, pp. 419–21, for a comparison of revenue demand in 1869 and 1885.   [103] *RAB*, 1881/2, p. 80.

lapsed after ten years in 1878. Nevertheless, the monopolies ignited such a furore among the Rangoon business community that the government then felt compelled to abolish many within the year. Trade as a result picked up and then continued to grow right up to annexation.[104]

But what this narrow focus on total trade figures hides completely is that Upper Burma was actually trading at a large and increasing *deficit* throughout this period. This in turn resulted in a net outflow of 'treasure', mainly silver, as much as 4 million rupees per year between 1878 and 1884. The real amount of silver leaving the country could have been much more, given restrictions on the Burmese side against the export of silver, the difficulty of registering land (as opposed to river-borne) trade, and the technically illegal flight of people during these years, people who must have also carried with them silver or other capital.

The final three years of Thibaw's reign were also years of very poor rice harvests in some areas, particularly the Lower Chindwin where food supplies bordered on famine conditions. We might assume that Upper Burma incurred this large deficit particularly in years of bad harvests, but the fit is quite rough and certainly many other factors must have been involved. While in 1880/1 and 1881/2, the country imported only 5–6,000 tonnes of rice a year, this figure climbed to 40,000 tonnes in 1882/3, 87,000 tonnes in 1884/5 and 96,000 tonnes in 1885/6.

The cost of this rice to the economy is difficult to calculate given its different prices at various stages of transport, prices which are not available over the entire time-span. The price of rice generally, however, had increased by well over 50 per cent over the course of Thibaw's incumbency. In the worst years (1882–4), when the entire rice crop was lost in the Lower Chindwin and around Mandalay, the price was reported to have even gone beyond 120 rupees per basket, this at a time when most annual incomes were considerably less.[105]

What the emphasis on increases in the value of bilateral trade also does not reveal was the precipitous fall in world commodity prices in the 1870s and early 1880s. This included the prices of nearly all of Upper Burma's principal exports, while the price of rice, the main import, increased considerably during this time. This dramatic change in Upper Burma's terms of trade came almost at the same time as the change in regime and

[104] *Ibid.*, 1882/3, p. 93.
[105] Cheng Siok-Hwa, *The Rice Industry of Burma (1852–1940)*, Kuala Lumpur, 1968, p. 73.

provided an all important backdrop to the political events of the next few years – increasing crime and administrative collapse in parts of the countryside, British intervention and annexation, and the widespread resistance to the colonial regime.

One sector of the economy badly hit during this time was the cotton industry. This was partially the result of several consecutive years of poor cotton harvests around 1880. But world prices as well began to fall, combining with the poor harvests to produce extreme hardship for cotton producers in areas such as Myingyan and Magwé, traditionally among the poorest parts of the valley. Manufacturers of cotton goods also suffered considerably as cheap British products began aggressively to establish themselves in even fairly remote markets. Mindon's cotton mills had been able to stave off foreign competition to some extent in the early 1870s. But by the late 1870s all British reports stated that the industry was now in terminal decline because of the preference throughout the country for the less durable but much cheaper British cloth.[106]

While both yarn and piece-good imports were negatively affected by the general downturn in trade in 1881/2 (see below), piece-good imports bounced back, while the import of yarn, for local manufacture, continued to decline. This fits well with the drop in the export of Upper Burma cotton piece-goods to Lower Burma from a total value of 1,645,000 rupees in 1878/9 to 970,000 rupees in 1885/6.[107] Silk manufacturing was also said to be in decline, partly because of the 'unsettled state of affairs in Mandalay' where the industry was based but mainly because this industry was weakened by continuing competition from European silk manufacturers.[108] Colonial reports also stated that imports of British crockery were damaging the sale of locally made lacquerware.[109]

The oil industry was a further sector where a significant decline was reported. Mindon had personally acquired direct control over 120 oil wells at Taungdwingyi through marriage to a member of a Twinzayo family. He then acquired a further seventeen wells through local mortgages to the crown.[110] Oil was becoming more valuable as a result of the increasing demands of foreign markets. But by the early 1870s, though there were about 150 wells worked at Yénangyaung with a daily production of 15,000 viss, there were also many abandoned wells and wells

---

[106] *RAB*, 1884/5, p. 36; 1885/6, p. 37. [107] See also analysis in *ibid.*, 1884/5, p. 36.
[108] *Ibid.*, 1880/1, pp. 81–5. [109] *RTC*, 1876/7, p. 31.
[110] Penzer, *The Mineral Resources of Burma*, p. 128.

producing very small quantities. The total yield was 60,000 viss per year and the king's income was 400,000 rupees.[111] A downturn in production, which had been growing steadily throughout the first part of the century, began around 1873 and lasted until right after British annexation. Possibly, this post-1873 downturn in production was the result of Mindon's intervention in the trade and the resulting depression of prices. It may also have been simply an exhaustion of supply at the level of technology then locally available. Other more local industries experienced more long-term falls in production. The iron and brass industries were said to have declined as a result of diminishing royal spending on religious construction.[112] There was also a marked decline in handicraft production, for example of paper, pottery, lacquerware and rockets for fireworks[113] as a direct consequence of competition from British products.

Speculation also increasingly affected the economy. As the economy became more nationally integrated, financial shocks emanating from Mandalay as a result of speculation severely affected trade on several occasions. For example, in 1869 a squeeze on credit led to a sudden depression of economic activity. This was in turn caused by the political uncertainty surrounding the imminent establishment of Sladen's residency.[114] This proved to be only a temporary stagnation but demonstrates both the extent to which speculation in Mandalay affected the entire country, and the pivotal importance of British influence. The weakness of the Burmese state by the 1870s was one which would be increasingly seen as a cause of economic instability. For foreign firms doing business in Upper Burma and through Upper Burma to China, this situation where trade could be so easily disrupted by the policies of an independent Burmese regime was a situation which demanded change. This was the commercial argument for annexation. By now the Burmese had more or less given in to demands to end intervention in trade and to grant unlimited access to British firms. The main problem remaining for British commerce was the inherent instability of the political situation at the centre. This made the environment for increased investment much more

[111] Aparna Mukerjee, *British Colonial Policy in Burma: An Aspect of Colonialism in South-East Asia 1840–1885*, Delhi, p. 21.
[112] Tun Wai, *Economic Development*, p. 39.
[113] Charles Forbes, *British Burma and its People*, 1878, pp. 110–11.
[114] Sladen Diary, 19 June 1869, Sladen Papers.

Table 1. Ngapi *imports by Upper Burma*

Year	Volume in mounds	Value in thousand rupees
1879/80	516,166	2,045
1880/1	575,243	2,338
1881/2	491,293	2,046

risky than many businessmen coping with the world depression would have cared to accept.

Exactly how all this was affecting the economy as a whole or personal incomes is impossible to know. Perhaps the best (though still problematic) index we have for a fall in popular incomes at this time is the fall in the importation of *ngapi*. *Ngapi* was the fermented fish paste which was and is as much a dietary staple as rice (together with tea), but which was (unlike rice) almost entirely imported from Lower Burma. Looking at *ngapi* imports, we find that indeed the volume and value of consumption did fall from 1880/1 (table 1). Unfortunately, there are no statistics on *ngapi* alone after 1881/2, but the category of 'provisions' in which it was included also continued to fall at least to 1883/4.[115]

At the same time, while the price of rice increased during the Thibaw period, the price of many cash crops – sesame, wheat and cotton in particular – dropped dramatically. Wages for skilled labour rose to keep pace with the rice inflation but wages for unskilled labour, representing in part new migrants from depressed rural areas, fell very low. Those few rice producers who escaped the poor harvests of 1883–5 and avoided as well increasing taxes might have enjoyed a rise in real income. The vast majority, however, especially those dependent after thirty years of integration into the new world economy on cash-cropping, would have been severely hit by the reversal in the country's terms of trade.

Two further aspects of trade which contributed to the worsening economic picture must also be noted. One was the relative fall in the price of silver, Upper Burma's currency, to that of gold. This change in the relative value of silver, and thus pounds sterling, to gold affected not only Burma but also other regional trading partners such as India, China and Siam.[116] The second was the economic crisis in China which also began in the

---

[115] *RAB*, 1883/4, p. 33.
[116] Fransisco O. Ramirez (ed.), *Rethinking the Nineteenth Century: Contradictions and Movements*, New York, 1988.

mid-1870s with a series of natural disasters and was then followed by a nationwide tightening of the money supply and a soaring trade deficit. In 1883, a financial panic in Shanghai set off a collapse of commodity prices throughout the country, a severe depression which did not end until the turn of the century.[117] Though Upper Burma's trade with Yunnan was not as important in the 1880s as it had been earlier in the century, the sudden contraction of the Chinese market may have further exacerbated an already bad situation at home. We should also note the possible effects the war in the Shan hills might have had. Trade is reported to have come to a standstill, and this may have pushed up the price of tea (which was imported from the eastern tributary of Tawng Peng), a staple commodity. The fighting almost certainly cut off the key domestic source of silver, exacerbating the squeeze on liquidity.

The final area of economic change which may have fuelled the political crisis was the interrelationship between taxation, indebtedness, money supply and general economic growth and trade. The introduction and rise in the rates of the *thathameda* tax until at least the early years of Thibaw's rule placed pressure on the rural economy to produce increasing amounts of cash. The tax was perhaps collected in kind at the source but was said to have been paid in cash at the township or at least at the provincial level. We have no concrete figures on indebtedness, but considerable anecdotal evidence exists from royal orders (and later British reports) of widespread indebtedness on the part of cultivators and others. As we have seen, by the late 1870s, if not earlier, Upper Burma was trading at a large deficit with Lower Burma, a deficit paid for in silver. Later British reports also stated that whereas the total issue of Burmese rupees was 253.5 lakhs from 1865 to 1868, the value dropped to only 8 lakhs in the period 1869–78, and to only 2.5 lakhs in the period 1879–85, that is, under Thibaw.[118] Quite possibly, the very poor harvests of 1883–86, which forced people to buy imported rice at all-time high prices, came at a time of increasing cash scarcity and thus high interest rates, pushing many who were already in a precarious position into a desperate situation. This in turn was a key factor behind the huge flight of people to Lower Burma, tax evasion and outright rebellion as well as the ongoing revolt in the Shan hills.

In summary, while it is difficult to make a rigorous case for overall

[117] Hao Yen-p'ing, *The Commercial Revolution in Nineteenth Century China: The Rise of Sino-Western Mercantile Capitalism*, Berkeley, 1986, pp. 324–8.

[118] Proceedings of the Finance Departments (Upper Burma), July 1886, nos. 1–2.

increasing economic hardship, it appears clear that the two or three decades prior to annexation were times of rapid economic change. More people became producers for world markets and attendant dependence on international prices and structural changes in the economy fuelled emigration, weakened traditional bonds and threw up new groups of traders, money-lenders, and concessionaires 'cashing in' on Upper Burma's insertion into the world economy. The early 1880s, with their poor rice harvests and increasing trade deficit, were a difficult time for ordinary people, including those who had become heavily indebted and were now perhaps paying higher interest rates.

One contemporary Burmese source, the *Myanma Min Okchokpon Sadan*, by a former Hluttaw official, ascribed the collapse of state authority to a number of factors. These included the inability of local officials to provide basic security of person; unfair taxation practices where poorer people without official connections bore the brunt of *thathameda* demands; the growing position of self-serving traders and other *thuhtay*; the neglect of irrigation works as hereditary irrigation officers lost their position; money-lenders combining with local officials to demand from poor people exorbitant interest rates; and finally, the loss of position by hereditary leaders. All these reasons seem to agree well with the economic history described above.[119] This is not however to suggest that economic changes were alone responsible directly, or even indirectly, for the political crisis under Thibaw. Many other possible factors remain unexplored. These might have included both material factors, such as demographic change and the impact of new technologies such as improved transportation, and other less tangible factors, such as changes in popular attitudes towards a dynasty defeated in two successive British wars. But it seems very probable that the growing integration of the Irrawaddy valley's economy with global markets under a British informal empire had contributed to increasing economic difficulties which in turn helped to cause the final fall of Mandalay.

[119] *MMOS*, vol. II, pp. 128–30.

8 | War and occupation

The colonial officer and writer V.C. Scott O'Conner, who had lived in Upper Burma in the 1890s explained: 'The Burmese Court ... were too proud and too weak to make the concessions that could alone serve as the basis for conciliation. Its own resources were too slender to sustain its great pretensions... The result was war.'[1]

Others have echoed this assessment. The viceroy, Lord Dufferin, in a telegram to Rangoon, complained of the Burmese kingdom's 'molluscous consistency' which made informal empire over the Court of Ava near impossible. In many ways, this analysis of the reasons behind Britain's decision to impose direct rule over the kingdom of Burma in 1885 was correct and relates to many of the processes discussed in earlier chapters. Specifically, we have seen that, on the one hand, the development of a political and fiscal crisis of the Burmese state led to a precipitous decline of its authority within its nominal borders. This 'weakness' was in turn the consequence of a variety of factors related both to British imperialism and local responses to changing international conditions. On the other hand, the Burmese government, like the shell of a mollusc, remained 'hard' and impervious to informal control. Half a century after defeat in the First Anglo-Burmese War, the 'pride' and 'great pretensions' of the Court of Ava, though diminished, remained strong. Local patriotism, born in an age of conquest, had hardened under the shadow of British expansion. The best local collaborator for the British empire would have been at once strong internally and appreciative of its external weakness. The Burmese were neither. They were losing their grasp on villages just outside Mandalay and still insisting on their rights as an equal power with Britain.

The road to Mandalay

From the mid-1870s onwards, official circles in London and Calcutta and the European business community in Rangoon had been discussing with

---

[1] V. C. Scott O'Conner, *Mandalay and other Cities of the Past in Burma*, London, 1907, p. 26.

increasing seriousness the possibility of further intervention in Upper Burma. Military intervention could either establish a protectorate under a suitable Burmese prince or lead to outright annexation.[2] British policy-makers believed that some sort of intervention was inevitable but preferred the first option of simply replacing Thibaw, who was seen as incompetent and unfriendly. Through a new treaty the kingdom would then be turned into a protected state of British India. When Mindon died in 1878, Lord Lytton, the viceroy, telegraphed the British Resident at Mandalay and instructed him 'to intimate to Ministers that general recognition and support of the Heir-Apparent [Thibaw] will be proportioned in degree to his adoption of a new policy towards the British Government, especially free access to the King and greater consideration and influence of the Resident'.[3] The death of Mindon, always judged a strong figure, was considered an opportunity to arrest worsening relations and finally 're-solve the Burma problem'.

The continual pressure of British business interests on government at various levels was one factor influencing official thinking in the direction of more formal empire in Upper Burma. British commercial concerns in Burma were growing. The problems caused by an independent Burmese economic policy on a market made less profitable by the world depression were becoming more apparent. The Chief Commissioner of British Burma argued:

> Mandalay may be said to be the pivot on which the trade usually turns. If there are no disturbing elements at Mandalay, everything works smoothly, but if there is the slightest derangement the merchants refuse to send goods up country except for cash payment. Credit is stopped and commerce is immediately depressed in consequence ... the only satisfactory guarantee against these recurring derangements of commerce and revenue [would be] a complete revision of British relations with Upper Burma.[4]

British commercial expansion in the context of global economic difficulties had turned more aggressive. For the Bombay Burma Trading Corporation and the other big merchant houses of Rangoon, the distortions to the 'free market' and the fluctuations in trade caused by an enfeebled but unpredictable Court of Ava were now impossible to tolerate. Profits from business in British Burma, with the vast expansion of rice cultivation, were substantial and the thought of even greater profits in

---

[2] SarDesai, *British Trade*, p. 202.
[3] Quoted in Woodman, *The Making of Burma*, pp. 214–15.   [4] ISP, August 1879, p. 16.

Upper Burma and through Upper Burma to China were enticing. Unqualified annexation was the preferred option of Rangoon-based European firms who saw no reason why the business-friendly environment of Lower Burma should not be extended to Mandalay and beyond.

The re-emergence of Anglo-French rivalry in South-east Asia and growing French interest in Thibaw's kingdom was a second reason for moving from informal to formal empire. French power on the mainland had developed rapidly as a result of a victorious war against the Vietnamese and Chinese in 1882 and the subsequent establishment of French protectorates over Tongking, Annam, Cambodia and Laos. Over the early 1880s the Burmese government had adopted a high-risk strategy of courting French and other European assistance in the hope that this would make difficult further British expansion. In early 1885, a Burmese embassy sent to Paris signed a formal treaty of friendship with the French government. Other agreements, between private French interests and Mandalay, were also negotiated following the signing of the treaty, perhaps with official mediation from the Quai d'Orsay. They included agreements for the French to build and manage a new railway from Hanoi to Mandalay, control the ruby mines and, perhaps most importantly, establish a jointly owned Royal Bank of Burma. This bank would have lent money both to the government at preferential interest rates and would have represented the first formal relationship between Western finance and the Burmese state. The news of these agreements and rumours of 'secret clauses' caused significant alarm in official circles in both Rangoon and Calcutta, and Sir Charles Bernard, the Chief Commissioner, warned that 'if Ava refuses to stop the treaty, annexation will be inevitable'.[5]

In addition, the political situation in Mandalay was giving the pro-intervention side more ammunition. The massacres surrounding the alleged prison breakout in 1884 were vividly reported in the English-language press as was growing lawlessness. Even with the paucity of the information available (given the absence of a Resident in Mandalay), it was becoming clear to British officials that events in Upper Burma had taken an even more unstable turn. Refugees from persecution and economic hardship were streaming into British territory and the breakdown in state control over peripheral areas was threatening to affect law and order along the northern borders of Lower Burma.

[5] Bernard to Viceroy, 27 July 1885, ISP.

British military intervention, when it did come in 1885, took place, therefore, within the context of increasing exasperation on the part of both Calcutta and London with the unwillingness or inability of the Mandalay government adequately to accommodate British commercial expansion and to keep out foreign political influence in what was perceived as a British sphere of influence. The unrest apparent in Thibaw's kingdom only added to already sufficient justifications for ending Burmese sovereignty.

The actual pretext for the declaration of war in October 1885 was a dispute between the Burmese government and the Bombay Burma Trading Company over illegal logging.[6] The company had allegedly been logging in areas beyond their agreed licence and the provincial governor had demanded compensation. The company refused and appealed to Mandalay. The government met at the most senior level to discuss the dispute. All three chief ministers – the Kinwun, Taingda and Taunggwin Mingyis – were present as were the king's Privy Councillors and other high officials. Mr Andreino represented the company together with a Burmese aide, Maung Aung Ba. On 22 October, while these deliberations were continuing, Calcutta intervened and issued an ultimatum. The British Indian government demanded not only that the Hluttaw overturn the provincial ruling, but that Mandalay hand over all future foreign relations to their control.[7]

The Burmese clearly understood the choices being laid before them. The special meeting was held on the first day of the new moon of Tasaungmon. The king and all his ministers were in attendance. Many argued that the country was now faced with the possible loss of its independence, and that British policy was a direct threat both to Buddhism and to 'the traditions of the kingdom' (*naing-ngan daw dalay htonsan*).[8] The hardliners in the government, led by the Taingda Mingyi believed the Burmese had no option but to refuse the British conditions and be prepared to fight. Others were not so sure. Both the Kinwun Mingyi and the Taingda Mingyi's own son-in-law, the Myoza of Kyaukmyaung, argued that any military resistance was hopeless and that the only realistic course was to attempt further negotiations. They then arrived at a consensus and drafted a reply which gave in to all British demands except the last and most important one, the demand to relinquish the kingdom's sovereignty. On

[6] *KBZ*, vol. III, pp. 705–6.   [7] *Ibid.*, pp. 707–8.   [8] *Ibid.*, p. 709.

this point the response was left deliberately vague, stating that the Court of Ava would accept this demand if agreed by France, Italy and Germany, the other European countries with which Mandalay had diplomatic relations. The government was apparently playing for time, perhaps in the hope that France would pressurise Britain into backing down. In Paris, the Burmese ambassador Mingyi Minhla Maha Sithu attempted last-minute negotiations with the India Office while courting the British press. At the same time, preparations for war were begun.

No Burmese response, even an unconditional acceptance of all demands, could have prevented the occupation of Mandalay. British intervention to overthrow Thibaw was by the beginning of November a foregone conclusion, and the Conservative government, on the very eve of general elections, was particularly eager to benefit from a successful colonial war. Lord Randoph Churchill, the Secretary of State for India, was certainly in favour of annexation, writing to Dufferin, the Viceroy, that 'the Government as a body are strongly in favour of annexation pure and simple [and] I think you will be *forced into it* by the difficulty of finding a suitable prince who would have any chance of *maintaining himself or of giving any guarantees of value for good government*'.[9] Thus, the argument for 'annexation pure and simple' was not that this was somehow intrinsically better for British interests, but that the local situation made impossible the establishment of a 'workable' protectorate. In other words, London viewed the past twenty years as a failed test of informal empire. Anything less than annexation would only be a marginal improvement on an already problematic arrangement. Churchill and others perceived a 'crisis' of the Burmese state and thus the costs of propping up that state, even one under formal colonial authority, seemed now to far outweigh the benefits.[10]

Senior Indian civil servants, however, were unanimously against annexation. Sir Charles Aitchison, lieutenant-governor of the Punjab, and Lord Reay, governor of Bombay, both warned against the problems which would arise from military intervention. Aitchison wrote that 'the annex-

---

[9] Churchill to Dufferin, 10 November 1885, Papers of Frederick Temple Hamilton-Temple Blackwood, First Marquess of Dufferin and Ava (hereafter Dufferin Papers), emphasis added.

[10] R.F. Foster, *Lord Randolph Churchill: A Political Life*, London, 1987 more or less portrays Churchill as being the prime force behind the decision for annexation. See also Htin Aung, *Lord Randolph Churchill and the Dancing Peacock*, Delhi, 1990.

ation of Upper Burma is not a thing to be undertaken by Lord Randoph Churchill in the easy-going, jaunty way, in which he seems to have announced it'.[11] They warned of an inevitable popular resistance to annexation, despite all the propaganda about Thibaw's repression; the high cost of maintaining troops in Burma; and the difficulty of administering the various upland areas under Mandalay's nominal sovereignty.

Lord Dufferin wavered on the question of Upper Burma's future, placed as he was between his senior officials and the government in London. But on 3 November, he wrote to Sir Charles Bernard, the Chief Commissioner of British Burma:

> The really important question which it is desirable to settle is whether Upper Burmah should be permanently annexed to Her Majesty's dominions, or converted into a feudatory State. I perceive that you incline to the latter course as does Sir Charles Aitchison and, in this view, Lord Ripon, I see, also coincides. I confess, however, that my own instincts point rather the other way. In the first place, the quality required of a buffer state is that of elasticity and the power of resistance. These characteristics may to a certain extent be said to attach to Afghanistan … [but] Burmah is of a soft and molluscous consistency, and is consequently far less adapted to serve the required purpose.[12]

Again, it was a perception of the Burmese state's 'unsuitability' as a protectorate which was used to justify direct annexation.

In early November a Burma Field Force of about 10,000 troops was organised into three infantry brigades and placed under the command of Major-General Sir Harry Prendergast. Prendergast, a veteran of the Abyssinian campaign of 1867, came from an old India family, both his father and grandfather having served in the East India Company. London was anxious that the campaign be completed as quickly and bloodlessly as possible. Lord Dufferin wrote to Prendergast: 'If your occupation of the capital of Upper Burma could be effected in a bloodless manner, it would be extremely creditable to you, and far more advantageous to the ultimate objects of the Government than any number of victorious encounters in the field.'[13] What these 'ultimate objects' were Dufferin did not spell out clearly, but apparently he and other India officials hoped that a swift removal of Thibaw might still leave their options open without much

[11] Aitchson to McKenzie Wallace, 22 October 1885, Dufferin Papers.
[12] Dufferin to Bernard, 3 November 1885, Dufferin Papers.
[13] Dufferin to Prendergast, 21 October 1885, Dufferin Papers.

further cost or many further problems. The Foreign Office seemed unde-
cided about whether it favoured annexation or not. Part of its official
instructions to Prendergast read:

> You will understand that after you cross the frontier no offer of submission
> can be accepted or can affect the movement of the troops; Mandalay must be
> occupied and Thibaw dethroned... You will be informed hereafter whether
> Burma (Upper) is to be annexed. If so, the Chief Commissioner will go to
> Mandalay and assume civil controls meanwhile ... it is extremely desirable
> [that the aims of the campaign] be attained rather by the display than by the
> use of force.[14]

Back in Mandalay, the king, accompanied by his war ministers, toured
a new armaments factory just outside the city wall and inspected the new
rifles being assembled. A few weeks before, new underwater explosives
had been developed and these were tested in a special tank not far from
the palace. But the army's resources were very thinly stretched, with
several brigades fighting near Bhamo or in the Shan hills. Nevertheless, an
order was sent out to all local officials and hereditary chiefs not to leave
their posts, to guard against banditry and to carry on normal civil administration. The government stressed that no general mobilisation would take
place and that only the regular standing army would be employed to try to
slow the British advance.[15]

The Hléthin Atwinwun had recently been brought back from directing
the anti-insurgent operations in the north-west and given overall charge
of the army. The Lower Irrawaddy Column was placed under the command of the cavalry general Mingyi Thiri Maha Zeyya Kyawdin, recently
returned from the Shan war. The Taungdwingyi Column was headed by
the colonel of the Cachar Horse Regiment, Mingyi Minkaung Mindin
Raza, and the Toungoo Column was headed by the colonel of the Shwelan
Infantry Regiment, Mingyi Maha Minkaung Nawrata.[16]

On 11 November the British expeditionary force crossed the border at
Thayetmyo, in the large flotilla made famous by Rudyard Kipling's verse
and armed with more machine guns than ever before assembled in the
Indian theatre. The main battle of the war took place on 17 November
when Prendergast captured the Italian-designed Minhla fort after heavy
fighting. A few days later they achieved what was to be their decisive
victory, defeating forces under the Hléthin Atwinwun north of Pagan.

[14] Burma Military Proceedings (hereafter BMP), no. 885.   [15] *KBZ*, vol. III, pp. 709–10.
[16] *Ibid.*, p. 710.

After that, the army proceeded almost uncontested up the Irrawaddy. On 27 November, as the flotilla approached Sagaing, the British received and accepted the unconditional surrender of the Burmese government.[17] Mandalay was entered at three in the afternoon the following day.

The complete lack of any real Burmese resistance after Minhla was due in part to the speed of the British advance following the declaration of war. Most contemporary British observers believed that given only a few more days preparation, the Burmese would have mounted a much more aggressive defence.[18] Fortifications had also been built at Ava and Sagaing and further passage upriver was about to be blocked through a scuttling of the king's steamers. Mandalay had been built partly with an eye to just such a British attack and the plan was to defend the city at all costs, while Thibaw and his court retired northwards to Shwébo to direct a guerilla resistance. But the Burmese government, by the time the British had defeated the main army under the Hléthin Atwinwun, concluded that any hope of further resistance was futile. The Kinwun Mingyi successfully counselled Thibaw not to flee north but to agree to all British conditions.[19]

The Kinwun Mingyi and at least some of the ministers also seemed to believe that the worst possible outcome of surrender would be a British occupation of Mandalay and the installation of a rival prince under Calcutta's protection. For the reformists, this was perhaps an acceptable alternative to the status quo. Within the government as well, there appeared to be doubts about the loyalty of the Kinwun Mingyi and his faction to Thibaw and the commander of the Ava fort refused to accept orders from the Myoza of Kyaukmyaung to stand down. Kyaukmyaung, the French-educated diplomat, had arrived by boat to negotiate the final surrender. The Ava commander demanded a personal telegram signed by the king, and was satisfied only when this arrived. At six the next morning, on the eighth day of the waning moon of *Tasaungmon*, the first British troops entered the royal city through the Red Gate.

A ceremonial entrance into Mandalay was followed by a tense first night of occupation. Law and order quickly broke down in parts of the city and many European residents fled for their own safety. The next afternoon, Thibaw was told by Colonel Edward Sladen, the former Resident and now political officer attached to the expedition, that he was to leave immediately for India. After a few frantic hours of packing, Thibaw and

[17] *Ibid.*, pp. 714–21.   [18] Prendergast Diary, 14 November 1885, BMP.
[19] *Further Correspondence Relating to Burmah*, London, 1886, pp. 3–4.

Supayalat appeared at the top of the steps of their summer palace, his entire government prostrate on the ground before him. Prendergast and Sladen stood nearby and escorted the royal couple first to the waiting carriage, and then to the steamer three miles away.[20]

Even then, policy-makers had yet to decide on the future relationship between Upper Burma and British India. If a protectorate was to be established, the obvious candidate for the throne had been the Nyaungyan Prince, Mindon's eldest son, who had escaped and had been living in Calcutta. But he had died earlier that year and so the lack of a 'suitable' candidate for the throne was added to the litany of arguments for annexation. In fact, however, several other possibilities did remain, including Nyaungyan's son, Kalayana, or the Pyinmina Prince, Mindon's youngest son, who had survived the 1878 killings because of his youth. At least twelve sons of Mindon were alive and living in Mandalay and dozens of other lesser princes as well. Prior to the war chief commissioner Bernard had favoured placing Pyinmina on the throne under a British regency. He ruled out the Myingun Prince who had been living in Pondicherry and Saigon for fear that he was now too much under the French thumb. What genuinely convinced British officials in Burma that a protectorate was not a viable option was not this supposed lack of a candidate, but the changing local scene in December. To the new colonial authorities, the weakness of Mandalay's control over the countryside even prior to intervention had become clear. They saw what remained of the Burmese state crumble within these first few weeks of occupation.

An interim attempt was made by Colonel Sladen to govern the country through the Hluttaw. Up until this time it was assumed that whatever the final decision was on the political status of Upper Burma and the retention of the monarchy, the country would be governed through the existing officials and institutions.[21] Sladen, who favoured annexation as opposed to a protectorate, nevertheless believed that rule through indigenous structures was possible and was the cheaper and more efficient alternative. By December, however, the disturbed nature of the countryside had pushed most of the military and many civilians towards the view that soliciting the co-operation of the former Mandalay government was a hopeless task.[22]

[20] *KBZ*, vol. III, pp. 724–6.
[21] Chief Commissioner to the Secretary, India Foreign Department, 26 October 1885, ISP.

There were problems right away with Sladen's efforts to utilise the Burmese nobility. The first was that the Kinwun Mingyi had decided to accompany Thibaw on part of his journey to Madras. This left the British to work for several weeks with the next most senior official, the Taingda Mingyi. This former minister was widely held by Rangoon to be responsible for the political killings under Thibaw and to be violently anti-British. Though seemingly co-operative for a time, information surfaced linking him to armed gangs plotting against the occupying army, and he was eventually arrested and deported to India. The experiment continued, however, and the Hluttaw was given some limited authority in districts around Mandalay. The Hluttaw and Sladen worked together to set up some sort of Burmese police force and to reinforce the position of the *hkayaing wun* (Thibaw's 'district commissioners') in the countryside. Bernard, however, quickly came to oppose working through the Hluttaw. Describing the districts in which they were allowed to retain some power as being in the worst state of any, he stressed the need for pacification efforts to proceed under the direct control of British officers.

The members of the Hluttaw were also very frustrated. The Kinwun Mingyi had returned from Rangoon in December and he had signed a series of letters to the viceroy through Bernard asking for the establishment of a 'constitutional monarchy' under British protection. They argued that the monarchy was an extremely important institution for the Burmese and that with a new king, the disorder in the countryside could be easily ended. They also stressed, however, that under their scheme the king would have no real authority, 'as in Britain', and that they, the ministers, would rule under the direction of a British Resident. They complained that the current arrangement, in which they had no control over the administration of the capital and only limited authority in nearby districts, deprived them of any popular legitimacy.[23] They could not, they said, be expected to be effective under the existing arrangements.[24] They asked to be given full authority under Sladen's general direction or be relieved entirely of their responsibility.[25]

---

[22] Edmund Charles Browne, *The Coming of the Great Queen: A Narrative of the Acquisition of Burma*, London, 1888, pp. 228–9.

[23] Hluttaw to the Chief Commissioner, 1 January 1886, BHP.

[24] 'Paper from Certain Ministers to the Chief Commissioner', 30 December 1885, BHP.

[25] Ministers to the Chief Commissioner through Sladen, 10 January 1886, BHP; Sladen to Chief Commissioner, 2 January 1886, BHP.

Bernard, while willing to keep options open for London as long as possible, believed that any handover of internal authority to a Burmese regime would have to await the completion of pacification as British troops could not be expected to operate under the directions of a Burmese government.[26] He was in general very sceptical of the benefits of working through the Hluttaw and finally secured the agreement of Lord Dufferin to cease working through the council in January.[27] Some senior officials including the Kinwun Mingyi were retained as advisors. But essentially by late January, the British had decided not to work through a protected monarchy, nor through the Mandalay nobility nor through the royal agencies which they had controlled.[28]

What British officials now faced was the task of creating an almost entirely new administration, a task most knew would be extremely difficult. Brigadier-General Sir George White, who was one of Prendergast's deputies remarked in what proved to be a prophetic statement:

> [The Ministers] pass resolutions and threaten to resign if not granted 'home rule'. But the district over which they preside [i.e. around Mandalay] is the most disturbed in the country. Our annexation must be followed by a rain [sic] of district officers all over the country, civilians whose courts must be hedged in by British bayonets for a long time to come.[29]

On 1 January 1886, the British government formally announced the annexation of Upper Burma to the Queen's dominions. On 12 February, Lord Dufferin, accompanied by the commander-in-chief of the British Indian Army and many other senior officials, visited Mandalay to see the situation first-hand. The former ministers of the Hluttaw gave the visiting party quite a cold welcome. No Burmese official gave any sort of formal address or welcome to the viceroy and his party and they remained standing throughout the meeting, a mark of considerable disrespect in the Burmese context.[30] As a result of his visit, Lord Dufferin came to the

---

[26] Chief Commissioner to the Secretary, India Foreign Department, 11 January 1886, BHP.

[27] Chief Commissioner to the Secretary, India Foreign Department, 10 January 1886, BHP; 'Officering Upper Burma' by Bernard, 25 January 1886, BHP. Sladen thought Bernard was being unfair towards the Hluttaw in his criticisms and wrote directly on this to Calcutta. See 'Memorandum by Sladen', 12 January 1886, BHP.

[28] *Further Correspondence Relating to Burmah*, pp. 43–5; 'Departure of the Hlethin Atwinwun', IFP (Upper Burma), April 1886.

[29] White to Mrs White, 3 January 1886, Papers of Sir Herbert Thirkell White.

[30] For a description of the event, see *The Times*, 15 February 1885.

conclusion that no formula other than direct rule was possible. He subsequently argued that 'a puppet king of the Burmese type would prove a very expensive, troublesome and contumacious fiction' and that given the state of the country, keeping the Burmese royal family would 'impose upon us all the trouble, anxiety, and cost of British occupation, without securing us any corresponding advantages in the present…'[31] Before he left, Lord Dufferin formally abolished the Hluttaw and, on 1 March, placed the entire country except for the Shan states under British administration as part of British India.

But though the decision was finally taken against retaining the monarchy and for direct rule, there still remained all sorts of possibilities as to the structure of the new colonial 'state' and its 'foundations' within local society. That is to say, direct rule could still have taken many different forms. In the Shan states, for example, British sovereignty still meant only indirect rule through the local *sawbwa* with only minimal interference by the British Superintendent. In the early modern period, the counterparts of the *sawbwa* in the Irrawaddy basin were, in many ways, the *myothugyi*. They were the leaders of local communities and had been the critical intermediary group between Ava and the Irrawaddy countryside. But why did the colonial regime then not base their new state on this institution? Why was not only the monarchy and nobility swept away but also the gentry, the hereditary leaders of the countryside?

The conventional explanation for the British decision to install a completely new 'Indian' bureaucracy right down to the village level was that many of the *myothugyi* and other local leaders died or were wiped out as a class as a result of the fighting which followed annexation. But while a few did join the resistance, the decision was based much more on the weakness of their position within their own charges. This weakness was in turn the result of the several preceding decades of economic and social change which left local elites in many parts of Upper Burma with only a fraction of the authority and influence which they had commanded at the beginning of the century. One contemporary commentator contrasted the situation in the Shan states leading to 'indirect' rule and the situation in Upper Burma: it was not a case of dealing with disintegrated masses like the rebel bands and bandit gangs, but with large organised tribal units, each under the moral and administrative control of an individual ruler.[32]

---

[31] Quoted in Woodman, *The Making of Burma*, p. 246.
[32] Nisbit, *Burma*, vol. I, p. 234.

It was this breakdown of the 'moral and administrative control' of local Burmese elites in the course of the nineteenth century, particularly in the decade prior to British intervention in 1885, which largely determined the nature of the colonial state. In summary, the British decided on the establishment of formal empire as a result of the inability of the Burmese state to accommodate effectively their commercial and strategic concerns. This intervention led not to the establishment of a protected princely state but to direct colonial rule because the political crisis of the preceding decade had greatly reduced the ability of Mandalay to govern the country. In the countryside, longer-term processes of social change had in many places critically reduced the power of gentry leaders, and thus they in turn were offered little or no place in the new regime.

The resistance

The Secretary for Upper Burma wrote to the Chief Commissioner: 'The people of this country have not, as was by some expected, welcomed us as deliverers from tyranny.'[33] This remark is illustrated by the fact that the formal annexation of Upper Burma by British India was followed by over two years of violent fighting, requiring at its peak in 1886–7 over 40,000 British and Indian troops and military police. The resistance to British forces was overwhelmingly rural and enjoyed substantial popular support.[34] Immediately following the occupation of Mandalay in late 1885, the army established ten military posts along the Irrawaddy and around Yamèthin. Then for a while they refrained from mounting any offensive operations against the guerrilla bands which were now gaining control throughout the valley. Some skirmishes did take place, but they were generally initiated by the guerrillas in attacks on British positions. By January, however, the security situation had clearly deteriorated to an extent which warranted a more proactive policy. One official reported to Calcutta: 'More definite information arrives daily of increasing bodies of rebels and dacoits. These are something more than mere marauders, and follow the standards of pretenders. A general feeling of insecurity and

[33] Secretary for Upper Burma to Chief Commissioner to the Secretary to Government of India, Home Department, 19 October 1886, quoted in *History of the Third Burmese War (1885, 1886, 1887)*, Period One, Calcutta, 1887.

[34] Charles Crosthwaithe, *The Pacification of Burma*, London, 1912, pp. 19–23.

systematic terrorism obtains around, and has even penetrated Manda-lay.'[35] The task of turning the tide fell on the shoulders of Sir Charles Crosthwaithe, who was appointed Chief Commissioner of Burma in March 1886. A number of different tactics were tried. Some local Burmese officials in areas close to the initial occupation were approached for help and temporarily reconfirmed in their position. Ex-ministers in Mandalay, especially the Kinwun Mingyi, were also coaxed into lending their services and some did use their influence to persuade appointed provincial figures, the *hkayaing wun* and *myowun*, to serve the new regime. But, by and large, the structures emanating from Mandalay were of little use and Crosthwaithe soon decided on a 'close military occupation of the coun-try', followed by the introduction of a generally all-new administrative apparatus.[36]

By early 1886, after the decision to impose permanent direct rule had been made, Sir Charles took the offensive, launching a 'pacification' operation which was not fully complete in the lowlands for another two years. It would be another five years before the upland areas, the newly named Chin, Kachin and Shan hills were entirely subdued. The problem for the British was that what had been an anarchic situation in the countryside during the last years of Thibaw's rule, aggravated by the power vacuum created by Mandalay's surrender, was now quickly turning into an organised and certainly passionate resistance against colonial rule. The imposition of direct rule would perhaps have resulted in such a resistance whatever had been British policy during the cold season of 1885–6. But sentiment against the new regime was undoubtedly made worse by the series of extremely repressive or insensitive measures which were undertaken and which seemed to confirm predictions that British occupation would soon result in the destruction of Burmese society, religion and culture.

A few days after Thibaw's exile, the white elephant kept in the palace, an object of considerable respect and an emblem of royal authority, died. Though a proper cremation attended by court Brahmins was allowed, the elephant was unceremoniously dragged by Indian troops out through the (inauspicious) western gate in full sight of the public. Just as disquieting to the Burmese, the main halls of the Eastern and Western Palaces were

---

[35] White to Secretary, India Military Department, 2 January 1886, BMP.
[36] *GUBSS*, vol. II, p. 118.

turned into an Anglican chapel and the Upper Burma Club respectively. What British attempts there were to accommodate local ideas and sensitivities were few and far between and were usually unsuccessful. The Chief Commissioner's offices were placed in the royal palace, but in the seven-roofed Pyathat and not the nine-roofed Myénan which was the symbol of sovereignty. Efforts were made by the British to ring the gong in the Bahosi tower to discourage rebellion when they were told that silence might make people think no government was in power, but were then stopped after a few days when they were told people would now think that a *Burmese* government was still in charge.[37]

More seriously, rumours spread, some reported in the English press, of the purposeful destruction of the royal library by British troops on the first night of the occupation, of ill-treatment of Buddhist monks and monasteries, of ill-treatment of Burmese women, and of the summary execution of suspected rebels and sympathisers. After January, as British forces began to try to move out from Mandalay and other riverine posts, fighting intensified and guerilla armies of up to a few thousand strong began coalescing throughout the country. In Lower Burma, events in the north triggered unrest, which quickly spread throughout the delta.

By the first day of the Burmese new year, 15 April 1886, the British were faced with what appeared to be an organised countrywide campaign to evict them from Upper Burma and restore a Burmese prince to the throne. On that day, rebel armies combined to attack all major military posts up and down the Irrawaddy. In Mandalay, twenty or so armed guerrillas succeeded in entering the royal compound, setting several fires and killing two Scottish doctors.[38] But the campaign proved unsuccessful, and by mid-year, the British had gained the upper hand.[39]

The upper hand was gained in large part thorough the large-scale

---

[37] White, *Civil Servant in Burma*, p. 165.

[38] *RAB*, 1885/6, 8–9. The British seemed to think this attack on Mandalay city was the work of followers of the Myingun Prince. See *RAB*, 1885/6, 7–8.

[39] The several narratives of these events might be divided into three groups: those by British officials serving at the time, including especially Sir Charles Crosthwaithe, *The Pacification of Burma*; but also Sir Herbert White, *A Civil Servant in Burma*; those by contemporary civilian observers who were much more critical of British actions such as Grattan Geary, *Burma After the Conquest*, London, 1886; and J. Nisbit, *Burma Under British Rule and Before*, London, 1901; and Burmese narratives, the most recent of which is Ni Ni Myint, *Burma's Struggle Against British Imperialism, 1885–1889*, Rangoon, 1983.

forced relocation of people, cutting off guerrillas from their basis of support. British magistrates were given wide-ranging powers to move 'suspected sympathisers' and these powers were used quite liberally.[40] Even in Mandalay, 6,000 houses, belonging mainly to the nobility, their dependants and retainers, were moved outside the city walls.[41] In the countryside, entire villages suspected of sympathising with the guerrillas were burnt and their inhabitants moved, often dozens of miles away.[42] Of the forced relocations, Crosthwaithe, the architect of 'pacification' policy, called the effect 'magical'.[43]

On top of this came a widespread famine, largely man-made, resulting from the fighting and the inability of many cultivators to harvest their crop.[44] The forced relocations were coupled with a programme of disarmament or the redistribution of arms to trusted local officials who were then held personally responsible.[45] The forced relocations were also linked to a more ruthless turn in conduct. *The Times* ran a series of critical articles describing the summary execution of suspected rebels, and questions were asked in Parliament, but no real disciplinary action was ever taken against those publicly mentioned as being the worst offenders. Crosthwaithe, in a revealing justification of his policies, wrote that the rebels displayed a 'ruthless and savage cruelty that might have made a North American Indian in his worst time weep for human nature'. But he then went on to write: 'As they [the villagers] would not [give information on the rebels], the only course open was to make them fear us more than the bandits.'[46]

A large number of weapons were collected in late 1886 and 1887. In Yê-U district, for example, a total of 1,088 guns were collected of which 148 were captured in action. Subsequently 192 licences to possess guns were granted, with a maximum of five per village. British reports proudly stated that there was no instance in which licensed guns then fell back into the hands of guerrillas. Of the guerrillas who surrendered 96 were classified as 'leaders' and 474 as 'ordinary', indicating the fractured nature of resistance organisation by this time. Most were released on bail of

[40] Crosthwaithe, *Pacification of Burma*, p. 23.   [41] Nisbit, *Burma*, vol. II, p. 118.

[42] *RAB*, 1885/6, p. 6.   [43] Crosthwaithe, *Pacification of Burma*, p. 105.

[44] Geary, *Burma, After the Conquest*, pp. 51–2. British intelligence had predicted famine conditions prior to the beginning of the war. See Bernard to Secretary, India Foreign Department, 25 October 1885, ISP.

[45] *GUBSS*, vol. II, 143; Crosthwaithe, *Pacification of Burma*, pp. 80–3.

[46] Crosthwaithe, *Pacification of Burma*, pp. 103–4.

200–500 rupees and many were then allowed to take office under British government as 'headmen'. Official reports say that while 'some served well, a few endangered life and property in service'. Half of those who surrendered had been branded professional bandits by Burmese officials before annexation. Of captured bandits, three were officially executed. The rest were imprisoned for terms up to life.[47]

Crosthwaithe wrote in his memoirs that 'in some districts there was not merely a system of brigandage; it was a system, a long established system, of government by brigands';[48] and that 'in a district where there was little activity on the part of British officers, and where the chief civil officer failed to get information, very little was heard of the bandits, simply because the people were paying tribute to the leaders, who did not need to use coercion'.[49] In addition, British reports of the uprising suggest that there were a considerable number of attacks against local officials, especially those who had been appointed by the crown.[50] While many may have been targeted as British collaborators, some of these attacks may have been motivated by grievances or conflicts originating under Burmese rule.

These remarks help to confirm that in some areas at least, for several years prior to annexation, authority had effectively passed away from those recognised by the Court of Ava either to gentry leaders 'in rebellion', or 'brigands' – popular figures who successfully usurped power from official authority whether local or Mandalay-appointed. Perhaps, the gentry leaders who became most actively involved in the resistance were those whose political authority had weakened as a result of economic change and administrative reform and who were unable (unlike some local elites) to find new power and position through money-lending, private land ownership, or trade. These may have included crown service chiefs who had seen much of their old status vanish with the abolition of the early modern system of labour control.

The uprising may be seen as a coming together of three distinct though related elements: banditry, rising patriotic sentiment, and millenarianism. The first was a continuation of the collapse of political authority in the countryside which had at least begun by the late 1870s. In some areas hereditary rural chiefs themselves had gone into rebellion. In other areas, especially around the capital, new bandit leaders emerged who sup-

[47] *GUBSS*, vol. II, p. 144.   [48] Crosthwaithe, *Pacification of Burma*, p. 103.
[49] *Ibid.*, p. 104.   [50] *Ibid.*, p. 83.

planted what was left of traditional gentry authority as well as the provincial appointees of the Mandalay state. The most 'disturbed' areas immediately following annexation were the same ones mentioned in Burmese sources as having been the centres of banditry and lawlessness – those areas right around Mandalay.[51] Among the most prominent of these bandits turned resistance leaders were Hla U in the Lower Chindwin, Bo Po Tok in the Ava area, Maung Cho in Pagan, Nga To and Nga Yaing in the islands of the Irrawaddy above Mandalay, Nga Zeya in the hills above the capital, Kyaw Zaw in Kyauksè and the Shan foothills, and Yan Nyun in Myingyan.[52] Here, armed opposition to the Burmese state, especially in the area near the capital, simply carried over into attacks on British forces in the early months of the opposition.

The second element was a patriotic resistance to British rule, in which some princes and others in the old aristocracy took part. This resistance was often passive, with members of the Hluttaw, for example, pretending to co-operate but in fact obstructing attempts to consolidate the British position. In a few cases princes and noblemen did actually go over to the 'other side' and came to head existing armed bands or perhaps new groups which gathered around them at this time. Because of their prominence, these princes and noblemen who joined the resistance are the most remembered, giving the impression of a large-scale resistance by the aristocracy. But actually, there does not seem to be much evidence that many from the old regime, including those from the army, openly resisted the new rulers. Very few if any of the thirty-odd *myowun* were active participants in the resistance, and neither any of the ten *hkyaing wun* nor the numerous Mandalay ministers did anything more than perhaps be involved in behind-the-scenes activities.[53] The elite cavalry units as well, including those in the Shwébo area, the home of the royal family, were also uninvolved in armed resistance and several of their officers lent immediate help to British suppression efforts.[54]

But the inclusion of a few aristocrats in the resistance did add a 'patriotic' character to the anti-colonial fighting. For example the

---

[51] Places mentioned in *KBZ*, vol. III, pp. 697–8 are Ava, Chindwin, Sagaing and Yadantheinhka (Shwébo) *hkayaing*. These are the same places mentioned in early British reports. See, for example, *RAB*, 1885/6, pp. 8–9; Chief Commissioner to the Secretary, India Foreign Department, 10 January 1886, BHP.

[52] *GUBSS*, vol. II, p. 120.

[53] See 'Departure of the Hlethin *Atwinwun*', IFP (Upper Burma), April 1886.

[54] White, *Civil Servant in Burma*, pp. 129, 160.

Myinzaing Prince, a son of Mindon who escaped massacre because of his youth, became, for a short time, virtually a 'national' leader against the foreign occupation. Only sixteen years old, he had been persuaded to leave his monastic school in Mandalay and take on the nominal leadership of the anti-British efforts by his close friend, a grandson of the Taingda Mingyi.[55] The Burmese New Year's Day attack on the Mandalay fort, now Fort Dufferin, had been intended to signal the beginning of his campaign. After basing himself near Kyaukse, he was, for a few months, a focal point for much of the uprising, with subversive networks, including networks of Buddhist monks, extending as far as Rangoon and Akyab in Arakan. By August, however, he had been forced by the British to retreat into the Shan foothills, where he later died of fever, his death signalling the end of attempts to organise a national-level campaign of opposition against the new colonial authorities.[56]

We have, unfortunately, very little Burmese material which would shed light on the internal dynamics of the uprising or even ways in which leaders tried to win over popular support or instil patriotic feeling, if that was indeed the case. We do have some statements issued by a few of the most prominent resistance leaders such as the Myinzaing Prince and these are similar to the Shan statements supporting rebellion mentioned in the last chapter. One states:

> towns and villages, fields and forests, hills, rivers and streams throughout the land have been measured and assessed, and taxes have been imposed and collected; that paper has been exchanged for silver and metal coins have been given currency as though they were silver; that there have been schemes for making the people, lay and clerical, die sudden deaths through disease [and] that the Religion of the Lord Buddha is in decline, and monks are in distress...'

and that he (Saw Yan Paing, a minor prince) had to attempt to restore the monarchy with himself as king.[57] Even if much of the rank and file in the resistance were not motivated by patriotic sentiment, many of the Mandalay elite who joined the rebels or who refused to co-operate with the new authorities certainly were. They were motivated not only by a simple desire to defend the old dynasty, but to protect their imagined Burmese 'nation' and its religious beliefs and traditions.

---

[55] *RAB*, 1885/6, pp. 11–12; Ni Ni Myint, *Burma's Struggle*, pp. 45–9.

[56] Maung Tha Aung and Maung Mya Din, 'The Pacification of Burma: A Vernacular History' (edited by H.R. Alexander), *JBRS*, 25 (1936), 80–136.

[57] Quoted in Ni Ni Myint, *Burma's Struggle*, appendix F.

The record of participation in the resistance on the part of the gentry is fairly mixed. On the one hand, a number of the *myothugyi* were reported by the British to have 'gone over to the rebels', not initially, but by the late spring of 1886.[58] These included the Myothugyi of Mekkaya and the Myothugyi of Myobin. But in most areas, the majority of local hereditary leaders are not reported to have actively assisted the resistance. A few, such as the Thwéthaukgyi of Tabayin, a well-known crown service chief, proved especially helpful to British authorities during this time.[59]

The third element, least understood but perhaps most important, was the surfacing of the 'millenarian' beliefs mentioned in earlier chapters.[60] Contemporary accounts also mention the widespread participation of Buddhist monks. Sir Herbert White, then serving under the Chief Commissioner, while dismissing most of the resistance as comprising 'gangs of bandits pure and simple', wrote also that 'wherever there was an appearance of organised resistance, Buddhist monks were among the chiefs'.[61] Monks in the resistance included U Oktama (the Myayanhkaing Pongyi) who for a time held nearly all of the Minbu area as well as U Parama along the middle Irrawaddy. In addition were other figures, who may also have been monks but who assumed 'millenarian' titles such as Buddha Raza, Thinga Raza, Dhamma Raza and Setkya Mintha. They are also mentioned in British reports but without any further explanation as to their role or aims.[62] Some, such as the so-called Buddha Raza seemed to particularly target officials of the old regime, in one raid, for example, carrying off the old royal governor of Meiktila and his wife.[63] In some areas, reports mention '*pongyi* (monk) risings',[64] while other reports attribute to

---

[58] These included, for example, the Mekkaya Myothugyi in Kyauksè (see Inspection Notes by the Chief Commissioner, Kyauksè District, 11 April 1886, BHP); the Myobin Myothugyi near Pagan (see Summary Correspondence on Minhla and Taungdwingyi, August 1886 BHP); and the Myogyi Myothugyi in the Lower Chindwin (see Fryer to the Chief Secretary to the Chief Commissioner, 4 January 1888, BHP).

[59] India Judicial Proceedings (Upper Burma), November 1886.

[60] On millenarian revolts in South-east Asia generally, with some reference to Upper Burma, see Reynaldo Ileto, 'Religion and Anti-Colonial Movements', in *Cambridge History of Southeast Asia*, vol. II, Cambridge, 1992, pp. 197–249. Also see Michael Adas, *Prophets of Rebellion: Millenarian Protest Movements Against European Colonial Order*, Chapel Hill, 1979, which includes a section on the 1930s' Saya San rebellion in Lower Burma (pp. 34–40).   [61] White, *Civil Servant in Burma*, p. 161.

[62] J.G. Scott, *Burma: From Earliest Times to the Present Day*, London, 1924.

[63] Inspection Notes by the Chief Commissioner, Yamèthin District, 2 June 1886, BHP.

[64] 'Summary Correspondence on Minhla and Taungdwingyi', August 1886, BHP.

shadowy individual leaders quite large followings as well as royal pretensions.[65]

A brief comparison with contemporary developments in the Shan states is useful. Here, as mentioned in the last chapter, many Shan chiefs or *sawbwa*, of which there were a few dozen of various ranks, had gone into rebellion, refusing to acknowledge Thibaw's kingship and instead trying to band together into a confederation in support of the Limbin Prince, a member of the Burmese royal family. Following British intervention and the takeover of Mandalay in 1885, however, the same Shan chiefs turned their rebellion against the Court of Ava into an organised resistance against the new colonial authorities. Within the new context, they added rhetoric about the defence of 'Buddhism and Tradition' to existing complaints about the *thathameda* tax and efforts towards political centralisation.

This is very much what happened in parts of the Irrawaddy valley, but on a more local scale. In other words, in some areas, where early modern institutions of local leadership, meaning the *myothugyi* and other chiefs, retained a local following and where conditions had turned these local elites against the crown, the gentry effectively overthrew royal authority in the late 1870s and early 1880s. In other areas, however, where traditional leadership had largely collapsed or become very weak, other types of local leaders, monks, millenarian figures and bandits came to fill the vacuum and similarly overthrew central authority (represented by the increasingly embattled *hkayaing wun* and *myowun*) and became the 'government by brigands' described by White.

In other words, the political crisis at the centre coupled with longer processes of social change led to three different local situations: in the only minimally integrated Shan states, entire sub-states under their own rulers broke away and were eventually co-opted under indirect colonial rule as semi-autonomous principalities. In the 'core' area of Upper Burma around the capital, hereditary elites had become so weakened by the 1880s that they became politically irrelevant or were actually replaced by royal appointees or other outsiders. In these areas, resistance to the old state was taken up by an assortment of popular figures unrelated to the state. In the peripheral areas of Upper Burma itself, the situation was somewhere in between, and some gentry leaders were still strong enough

---

[65] *RAB*, 1885/6, p. 17.

to exploit the weakness of the centre, and resisted increased tax demands, with a few later participating in the anti-British resistance.

When Prendergast's army arrived in Mandalay, however, and Thibaw was taken away, a cross-section of these local leaders, new and old, came to find common cause, as did the Shan chiefs, with displaced individuals of the old regime who were looking to resist the imposition of direct colonial rule and place a new Burmese king on the throne.

The colonial state

When the resistance had finally been overcome in the lowlands British policy-makers found themselves faced with the task of restoring government to a society which had experienced more than ten years of upheaval and many more of rapid social change. In the more remote areas of the Kachin Hills fighting would continue well into the 1890s; and in the Wa Hills along the Chinese border some parts were not 'pacified' until the 1930s. In the early nineteenth century, the Irrawaddy valley had been the demographic, economic, cultural and political centre of an empire which had reached from Assam and Manipur to Siam. By the turn of this century, the Irrawaddy valley had not only lost its sovereignty but had come to be overshadowed in all those areas by the delta, its erstwhile frontier, now centred on Rangoon.

This process, through which Lower Burma, the less important half of the country had been first annexed, transformed economically under a colonial administration, and then reunited with Upper Burma as a much more dominant partner, was a critical part of the country's colonial experience. Not only were Upper Burma's ports and rice surplus seized in 1853, but, in the following thirty years, Lower Burma grew as a sort of 'alternative Burma' which sapped the legitimacy of Mandalay, allowed an unprecedented flight of cultivators, produced a new source of Burmese culture, especially through printed books, and threw up a new class of indigenous administrators, schooled by the British and who retained only very limited family and other connections with the old elites in the north.

By the early 1890s, the administration of Upper Burma had become almost fully integrated with that of Lower Burma and, as a result, with the rest of British India.[66] The structure of the new colonial state was the

---

[66] British administration has been discussed in detail in several books, mainly by former officials. See for example F.S.V. Donnison, *Public Administration in Burma: A Study*

familiar one of other Indian provinces, headed by a Chief Commissioner until 1897, and then by a Lieutenant-Governor, based in Rangoon. The former dominions of Mindon and Thibaw were divided primarily into two parts. The first part was 'Burma Proper', was ruled directly from Rangoon, and had three divisions (Mandalay, Magwé and Sagaing), each under its own divisional commissioner, and thirteen districts, under a deputy commissioner. The second part was the Shan states and the upland areas ruled 'indirectly' from Rangoon. The Shan chiefs were not 'protected princes' on the Indian model enjoying a special treaty arrangement with Calcutta, but were simply being allowed by the new colonial power a large degree of local autonomy. Mandalay itself retained no special status and all separate 'Upper Burma' institutions, such as the Upper Burma High Court, had been abolished by the turn of the century.

Backing up the new colonial state through the 1890s was a strong military presence. The British army garrison in Upper Burma numbered approximately 7,000, with 3,000 British and 4,000 Indian troops. In addition there were over 10,000 military police,[67] nearly all Indian, with some Karens but almost no Burmese, as well as over 7,000 civil police, predominantly Burmese, with some Karens and Indians.[68] Pacification efforts had also led to a rapid expansion of prison facilities. Mandalay Central Jail had opened in 1887 for about 1,000 inmates, and another large jail was built soon after in Myingyan together with thirty smaller ones by 1895. Serious overcrowding of these new jails, however, led authorities to transport some prisoners to the Andaman Islands, 1,000 a year from all of Burma. Compared with Lower Burma, however, the level of crime in Upper Burma was markedly low until after 1900.[69] Corporal punishment was also employed, one report stating that 'whipping was used to relieve accommodation pressure'. Other punishments included solitary confinement with reduced food as well as tortures named the 'treadmill' and the 'shot drill'.[70]

The upper ranks of the new state were all, of course, at this time British.

of Development During the British Connection, London, 1953; and Robert Taylor, The State in Burma, London, 1987, pp. 66–147.

[67] Having reached a high of 17,000 in the late 1880s. See RAB, 1887/8, p. 19.

[68] Government of Burma, Economic and Social Board, Office of the Prime Minister, A Study of the Social and Economic History of Burma (The British Period). Part V: Burma Under the Chief Commissioners 1886–7 to 1896–7 (hereafter SEHB), Rangoon, 1957, p. 5; RAB, 1887/8, p. 71.   [69] RAB, 1895/6, p. 19.

[70] Nisbit, Burma, vol. I, pp. 236–8.

Most of Thibaw's senior officials and other members of Mandalay's nobility, including fairly young officials who had been trained abroad, had slipped quietly into oblivion by the late 1880s. The Kinwun Mingyi was retained as an advisor to the government and then as a member of the Lieutenant-Governor's Council and produced at the request of Rangoon his *Digest of Burmese Buddhist Law* in 1887. A dozen others received pensions and a few official decorations, but practically all of the top ranks of the *ancien régime* retired completely from public service soon after Sladen's failed attempts to work through the Hluttaw.[71] While a few of the old nobility had acquired some private wealth,[72] for others the most important aspects of their difference from the rest of society – their residence within the old royal city walls and the exclusivity of their sumptuary rights – entirely disappeared.

In line with long-standing British Indian policy of non-intervention in indigenous religious affairs, the relationship between the state and the Buddhist Sangha was effectively severed at annexation. Some officials were aware of the critical role which had been played by the Burmese state and in particular the king in support of Buddhism and a minor debate ensured as to how best to fill this vacuum. Many Burmese had long warned that British rule would inevitably bring about the disestablishment of Buddhism and there was no real expectation that the new colonial authorities would fulfil traditional functions.[73]

The British knew that a major function of the reigning monarch was to appoint the head of the Sangha, the Thathanabaing. They were also worried about possible Chinese annoyance over the annexation of Upper Burma. As a result Rangoon toyed with the idea of inviting the Qing emperor to nominate the successor to Thibaw's Thathanabaing, the Taungdaw Sayadaw. This proposal was vigorously criticised by the former Mandalay ministers who were aghast at the notion of being considered somehow a tributary of China and tried to provide documentary evidence against the idea. British officials then quietly dropped the whole idea, and on the death of the Taungdaw Sayadaw in 1895, no successor was

---

[71] For a list of those who continued to serve as advisors through the late 1880s, see *Further Correspondence Relating to Burmah*, pp. 43–5.

[72] The Hlèthin Atwinwun, for example, invested some of the wealth he had gained from office to enter into business deals with firms based in Calcutta. 'Departure of the Hlethin *Atwinwun* from Mandalay', Upper Burma Proceedings (Foreign Department), April 1886.   [73] Geary, *Burma, After the Conquest*, pp. 105–9, 114–15.

appointed for several years.[74] In addition, the abolition of royal structures meant the disappearance of the various state agencies which provided secular support for the authority of the Thathanabaing and his Thudhamma Council.[75] Ecclesiastical courts were also no longer formally recognised, though in practice British courts tended to uphold the decisions of the Thudhamma Council on all internal Sangha disciplinary matters.[76]

The search for local intermediaries

Though the military suppression of the resistance consumed the energies of most colonial officers on the ground throughout 1886 and 1887, much thought was also given to the final nature of local administration and the extent to which British rule could realistically expect to work through local elites and indigenous institutions and practices. An important factor in this debate was, naturally, the experience in Lower Burma over the preceding thirty years. Once the decision for annexation was made, the assumption was that there would be an integrated Lower and Upper Burma administration.[77] But the administration of Lower Burma was also at this time coming under fundamental review and the sympathetic rebellion there in 1886 had come as a profound shock to many British administrators.[78] The result was an increasing prejudice against reliance on all things Burmese and the belief that attempts to work through the *myothugyi*, or 'circle headmen' as they were known, had decidedly failed.

When the British had taken over the administration of Lower Burma in 1853 following the Second Anglo-Burmese War, many hereditary *myothugyi* as well as crown-appointed officials had retreated north to Burmese territory. Others participated in the several years of resistance in much the same way as their Upper Burma counterparts did thirty years

---

[74] See Smith, *Religion and Politics*, pp. 45–56.

[75] Several leading members of the Sangha had approached the new colonial government in early 1886 for a continuation of state support in return for preaching submission in the countryside. This was rejected. See Smith, *Religion and Politics*, p. 46.

[76] The precedent-setting case was U Teza v. U Pyinna, in which a lower court had ruled against the Thudhamma Council's decision. The appellate courts, however (the Court of the Judicial Commissioner), overturned this decision, ruling that the area claimed by the Thathanabaing and the Council was 'moderate' and in all internal matters the Sangha should be allowed autonomy. See 'U Teza v. U Pyinna', in Upper Burma Rulings, 1892–6, vol. II, pp. 66–7.

[77] White to the Secretary, India Foreign Department, India Home Proceedings (Upper Burma) (hereafter IHP), July 1886.   [78] *RAB*, 1886/7, p. 10.

later. An attempt was made, nevertheless, to work through the *myothugyi* who were largely seen as the backbone of local society. But while appreciating the importance of these local leaders, their real functions and role in early modern society were not fully understood, and the British attempt to fit them into the framework of an increasingly standardised Indian bureaucracy, as territorially based revenue collectors, was probably doomed to failure. While as late as 1868, the 'circle headmen' were still being viewed as the foundations upon which colonial administration rested,[79] by 1881, their system of government was said to have 'outlived the society which had produced it'.[80]

The 1886–7 uprising in Lower Burma as well as the intensity of the resistance in Upper Burma contributed to a British decision not to recruit Burmese into either the Indian Army or the military police. The British had already come to class the Burmese as one of the 'non-martial' races of the empire. This was in part the result of failed experiments earlier in the century to establish Burmese and Arakanese battalions; on the basis of these experiments, the Burmese were assessed as lacking in soldierly discipline. The 1886–7 rebellion in Lower Burma, in which the Burmese police and military police overwhelmingly sided against the colonial authorities made this classification permanent and led directly to a strengthening of the Indian element in the force. Rangoon began a search for new recruits from among the Karen (who had remained 'loyal') as well as from among the so-called 'war-like races' of the newly acquired Kachin and Chin Hills.[81]

In the area of local administration, Sir Charles Bernard, who was Chief Commissioner in 1886–7, and other colonial officials in Burma appeared to still appreciate the need (if only for purposes of financial expediency) to maintain, as much as possible, indigenous structures and personnel. Some believed that the *myothugyi* would have to play a key role in this effort but that something, though it was not clear quite what, had gone wrong with attempts in Lower Burma to integrate them into the colonial state.

Bernard toured much of Upper Burma in 1886 and early 1887 to assess first-hand the workings of the new colonial regime and to participate directly in the appointment of Burmese administrators. His reports help to shed considerable light on the final transition away from the early modern

---

[79] *Ibid.*, 1868/9, p. 34.   [80] *Ibid.*, 1881/2, p. 46.
[81] *Ibid.*, 1886/7, p. 9. See also, for example, Donald MacKenzie Smeaton, *The Loyal Karens of Burma*, London, 1887.

gentry-based system and towards the much more centrally controlled bureaucratic structures which remain with us today. Just prior to the beginning of his tour, Bernard issued his 'Instructions to Civil Officers in Burma'. While this document continued to espouse the position that support for hereditary local leaders was desirable, the instructions also allowed civil officers on the ground considerable discretion to decide who should remain in office and who should go.[82] The instructions stated that the 'thugyis and myothugyis' were the most important agency for maintaining order, but that though most had submitted, 'some are still heading rebel bands and by reason of their local influence, materially prevent the pacification of the country'. Rangoon would thus allow 'removals and new appointments'.

In fact, many *myothugyi* were removed for a variety of reasons other than outright 'rebellion' against the British authorities. Over the course of the next several months, many changes, on an *ad hoc* basis, would be made, both in terms of the actual people holding local offices and in the nature and jurisdiction of the offices themselves. This was done, however, outside of any clear policy as to how either properly to reinvigorate or to phase out what remained of the old system.

Three different processes were at work. The first was an attempt to regularise the system in place. For example, the British believed that in Upper Burma, there existed *thugyi* or 'village headmen', *myothugyi* or 'circle headmen', as well as centrally appointed *myowun* and, occasionally, *myo-ok*. The *myo-ok* or 'township officer' was a British invention in Lower Burma, copied in places by Mindon's government. Colonial officers on the ground, however, in addition to these various categories of local officials also saw numerous others – such as *myingaung* and *thwéthaukgyi* – mainly various crown service chiefs. These had somehow to be fitted into a more 'regular' system.[83] In Yamèthin, for example, on finding many *myingaung*, or hereditary cavalry officers, the district officer asked them to select one to be representative and made him the new *myo-ok*.[84] Similarly, in Madeinbin, the influential local *thwéthaukgyi* (an hereditary infantry officer) became the local *myo-ok*.[85]

Secondly, the all-important category of 'myothugyi' and that of 'myo-

[82] BHP, March 1886.
[83] White to India Foreign Dept. Secretary, July 1886, IHP.
[84] Inspection Notes by the Chief Commissioner – Yamèthin District, 2 June 1886, BHP.
[85] White to India Foreign Dept. Secretary, July 1886, IHP.

ok' overlapped, and this apparent duplication in function needed to be resolved.[86] The new colonial administrators naturally saw a need to fully establish the township officer in Upper Burma and this meant either that the incumbent *myothugyi* became that officer (such as happened in Pyinmina,[87] Kyaukpadaung, Pin[88] and Yénangyaung[89]), would be removed entirely and replaced by the existing or a newly appointed *myo-ok* (such as in Myinhkondaing[90] or Bhamo[91]) or would be 'pushed down' to the level of 'village headman'. All three of these transitions took place in the late 1880s. In a few areas, it appears that only a *myo-ok* already existed and that this individual was perfectly acceptable and was kept in office.[92]

The third process at work was the replacement of local officers as a result of their participation in the armed resistance to British rule. Up to around April 1886, it appears that many hereditary local leaders as well as appointed *myowun* and others did submit to British authority. But in the summer of 1886 a few actively took part in the fighting against the British. Others, such as those around Meiktila, ran away, rather than actively taking a stand one way or another.[93] These *myothugyi* and others were then replaced, sometimes by members of the same family (such as in Yé-U),[94] sometimes by *myo-ok* as part of the process described above, or sometimes by other 'influential men' or 'men elected by the people' who were hastily selected on the spot by the touring Bernard or by the district commissioner.[95] In Shwegu, the *myothugyi* proved 'undesirable' and was replaced by a *nahkan* (a provincial reporter) from the nearby Bhamo court.[96]

The old Burmese positions of *hkayaing wun*, or 'district commissioner',

[86] Note by R.H. Pilcher, Kyauksè Deputy Commissioner, 27 April 1886, BHP.
[87] Inspection Notes by the Chief Commissioner – Ningyan District, 27 April 1886, BHP.
[88] Inspection Notes by the Chief Commissioner – Pagan District, June 1886, BHP.
[89] Inspection Notes by the Chief Commissioner – Minhla District, 6 June 1886, BHP.
[90] Inspection Notes by the Chief Commissioner – Kyauksè District, 11 April 1886, BHP.
[91] G.W. Dawson, *Burma Gazetteer – Bhamo District* (hereafter *Bhamo Gazetteer*), 2 vols., Rangoon, 1912, vol. A, pp. 61–70.
[92] Inspection Notes by the Chief Commissioner – Minhla District, 6 June 1886, BHP.
[93] Captain G.S. Eyre (Pagan Deputy Commissioner) to the Chief Secretary to the Chief Commissioner, Mandalay, 10 April 1886, BHP.
[94] F.W.R. Fryer (Commissioner of the Central Division, Upper Burma) to the Chief Secretary to the Chief Commissioner, 4 January 1888, BHP.
[95] Captain G.S. Eyre (Pagan Deputy Commissioner) to the Chief Secretary to the Chief Commissioner, Mandalay, 10 April 1886, BHP.
[96] *Bhamo Gazetteer*, vol. A, pp. 61–70.

and *myowun* were centrally appointed positions, and were more or less easily replaced by the district and sub-divisional officers. None of the *hkayaing wun*, being quite senior officials based in large part in Mandalay and not in their districts, lasted very long after annexation. The record of the *myowun*, however, was somewhat mixed. Many preferred to leave of their own accord. Those that stayed were usually those who were natives of their charge, and were eventually made *myo-ok* or given some other new designation.[97] For example, in Sagaing district, the governor of Myinhmu was originally from the area and was considered to be of some help in the campaign against the resistance leader Hla-U. Nearby, the governor of Sagaing was reported to be a 'Mandalay man of no local influence' who retired soon after the British arrival.[98]

Finally, many boundaries, representing the jurisdictions of the various new *myo-ok* and others, were drawn up or redrawn during this hectic time. Whatever remained of the 'personal', as opposed to the 'territorial', nature of gentry leadership in the last years of the Burmese kingdom, local offices were now assumed to be completely territorial and were revised as such. In Kyaukse, for example, nearly all the *myothugyi* jurisdictions had towns and villages added or subtracted, over a period of a few months, without any real explanation being reported.[99] Other *myothugyi* jurisdictions were enlarged; sometimes two were combined. The Myothugyi of Pyaungbya, for example, received neighbouring Myogyi in the Lower Chindwin after that *myothugyi* went over to the rebels.[100]

These appointments and dismissals created a semi-functioning administration in the countryside, one which came to approach that of Indian bureaucratic norms and the reformed administration in Lower Burma. The *myo-ok* township officer was quickly replacing the *myothugyi* but the possibility of reviving and using the *myothugyi* still remained. Policy varied from district to district, and it was recognised that the entire issue of local administration still needed to be settled.[101] It was for Sir Charles Crosthwaithe, who as we have seen succeeded Bernard as the new Chief Commissioner in mid-1887, to make the final decision against continued

[97] *Myo-ok* came in seven grades with pay ranging from 50 rupees to 300 rupees per month.

[98] Inspection Notes by the Chief Commissioner – Sagaing District, 2 April 1886, BHP.

[99] Note by R.H. Pilcher, Kyaukse Deputy Commissioner, 27 April 1886, BHP.

[100] F.W.R. Fryer (Commissioner of the Central Division, Upper Burma) to the Chief Secretary to the Chief Commissioner, 4 January 1888, BHP.

[101] BHP, March 1888.

gentry-based administration. This he did through the drafting and implementation of the Upper Burma Village Regulation which proved so useful
in crushing Burmese resistance.[102] This regulation, which was largely
conceived to aid the pacification campaign, also came to change permanently the nature of Burmese government.

Through the regulation, Crosthwaithe dealt the final death blow to the
old system of local government by essentially removing the position of
myothugyi and creating the new bureaucratically appointed and controlled village headman. He wrote, ironically, that the regulation gave 'position and powers which [headmen] have exercised under the *ancien regime* as near as may be . . .'. Crosthwaithe somehow seemed to believe that
the *myothugyi* were the creations of recent troubles under Thibaw and
that they were the expansion of one village headman's authority at the
expense of others during a period of anarchy. He seemed to believe that
the village headman was the real local authority and began a policy,
carried out until completion around the time of the First World War, of
dismantling the 'circles'. As a result, British officials then began either
dismissing *myothugyi*, making them head of only their main village or
town, or waiting until they died and not appointing a successor.

Crosthwaithe explained:

> in Burma there are no hereditary leaders of the people. There is no hereditary
> aristocracy outside the royal family and their descendants rapidly merge with
> the people . . . The really stable part of the administration on which everything
> rested was the village, the headmanship of which was by custom hereditary,
> but not necessarily in the direct line.[103]

His real motivations, however, are much better summarised in his
Report on the Revenue Administration of Burma for 1889/90 in which he
stated that circumstances required the 'establishment of a system which
will work to some extent irrespective of the personnel of the officers
administering it'.[104] Crosthwaithe's period in office thus represented the
final end of the power of the *myothugyi* and crown service chiefs and the
early modern system of government which they represented. As we have
seen, their position had already undergone considerable change over the
preceding half-century. Whether or not the gentry could have been resus-
citated as a class under colonial rule is not known. But these decisions of

---

[102] *RAB*, 1889/90, p. 14.   [103] Crosthwaithe, *Pacification of Burma*, p. 4.
[104] *Report on the Revenue Administration of Burma* (hereafter *RAR*), 1889/90, p. 2.

the early British administration soon ended what was left of their position in local society.

What little remained of their old prerogatives and authority faded away over the 1890s as the colonial state moved to a more effective consolidation of power. In the judicial sphere, colonial officers continued attempts to find them a role, with suggestions that 'superior headmen' be allowed to try cases worth up to 50 rupees. But only a handful were able to make this transition to colonial judge. The experiment was soon ended with the note that 'few were competent to observe regular procedure'.[105] Some British officers hoped that these old rural chiefs and other local *lugyi* (or 'big people') could 'arbitrate' disputes without these disputes having to be referred to civil courts. The feeling was that some sort of arbitration was the 'traditional system'. But even here, by the mid-1890s, most British officers on the ground were against any encouragement of arbitration, one explaining that 'when people come to court they prefer to get the court's decision. When asked why they do not go to the lugyis, the reply is we cannot agree with the lugyis, we do not trust the lugyis, we want an order from the court, etc . . .'.[106]

These and other similar remarks suggest that colonial officials quickly grew impatient of trying to create a small space for 'traditional' government within the context of the very substantial changes in the whole manner of governance which had taken place. That is to say the whole basis of the gentry's position had gone, and British administrators on the ground soon gave up trying to prop up the old chief's position solely in the area of judicial administration, believing that the effort was not really in anyone's interest, including that of the local population.

The Shan states provide an interesting comparison for the proposition that the British decision to impose a centralised bureaucracy was not necessarily the one which they would ordinarily have preferred. The Shan rulers, the hereditary *sawbwa*, were, in many ways, the counterparts of the Burmese *myothugyi*. But, as we have seen, whereas the *myothugyi* came under increasing control from the centre, the *sawbwa* were able to maintain a large degree of autonomy and local power. Thus, despite some resistance to the imposition of colonial authority, the British were faced in the Shan states with a much more familiar situation – a clearly visible class

---

[105] *Report on the Administration of Civil Justice in Burma* (hereafter *RCJB*), 1890, p. 6.
[106] *RCJB*, 1891, p. 9.

of hereditary local 'chiefs' through which to govern cheaply and effect-ively. Following the suppression of insurgency, by late 1888, nearly all the various *sawbwa* had submitted.[107] Under the Shan States Act[108] of that year, the indirect control of the British superintendent was regularised, and by the following year a series of agreements had been reached limiting the authority of the *sawbwa* and asserting British rights to the forests and mineral resources of the area.[109] This sort of accommodation between British authority and local power-holders was much more the norm in the history of late-nineteenth-century imperialism. In the Irrawaddy valley, it was the host of local factors discussed, precipitating the crisis of the Burmese state, which led to such an unusually radical overhaul of govern-ment and indigenous elites by the new colonial power.

While it is possible that Crosthwaithe was entirely motivated by his desire to destroy the Burmese resistance and saw the formation of the village system as the best way to achieve that objective, it may also be useful to consider the state of colonial knowledge regarding Burmese society. After over half a century of close contact with Burma, various interpretations about the country and its people had developed. These interpretations, however, were naturally based much more on the areas which had earlier come under British occupation – Arakan, the Tennas-serim and the delta – which would have had the effect of presenting 'frontier' conditions as the norm. It must be remembered that compared with the Irrawaddy valley, particularly the area around the capital, many early modern structures and institutions would have been much weaker in the areas forming Lower Burma, local communities being much younger and perhaps less under the influence of hereditary elites. This being said, a certain amount of British intelligence about Burmese society was of course gathered in the valley as well. But for reasons which are not completely clear, most British scholarship by the 1870s had come to view Burmese society as a mix of oriental despotism and a sort of rural egalitarianism. There seemed to be little notion of any intermediate class between the royal family and ordinary cultivators, and this view was quite explicitly spelled out in many official documents. One report, for example, stated that all officials in the kingdom were only temporary, holding office at the king's pleasure, and contrasting this Burmese royal

---

[107] BHP, September 1888. [108] *Burma Gazette*, 17 November 1888, pp. 3, 115.
[109] *GUBSS*, vol. II, pp. 313–16.

absolutism with the supposedly more diffuse power structure of the Mahrattas.[110]

Following annexation, this interpretation became the accepted orthodoxy, and both Scott's official *Gazetteer of Upper Burma and the Shan States* and Nisbit's unofficial *Burma Under British Rule and Before* echoed this view.[111] Even the historian G.E. Harvey, who wrote extensively on the organisation of early modern Burmese society, contradicted his own studies and stated that 'the largest unit the Burmese could systematise was the village community. Beyond that they failed to build, and so the highest structure of central government inevitably fell in the form of despotism, which is anarchy – the negation of system.'[112] Crosthwaithe's pacification policy had, if not engendered, at least strongly reinforced, the dominant school of colonialist thinking.

[110] 'Mr T. Wheeler's Memorandum on the Political Status of Ava', in 'Correspondence Relating to Burmah', IFP, 1874, 7.

[111] Scott, though defending Crosthwaithe's position, however argued that 'Burma has nowhere any village communities as the expression is understood in India ... No Burman village held rights of any kind against the State', *GUBSS*, vol. II, p. 429.

[112] G.E. Harvey, *History of Burma: From the Earliest Times to 10 March 1824 – The Beginning of the English Conquest*, London, 1925 (reprint 1967), p. 329.

9 | A colonial society

From the fall of Mandalay to the turn of the century, the Kingdom of Ava was reintegrated with its erstwhile southern frontier as well as its old imperial possession of Arakan. Together, they formed 'Burma'. But in this process of reintegration, old royal structures and old aristocratic elites had no say. Instead, the web of institutions and processes which bound the new country together were fashioned in Rangoon and Calcutta, by British policy-makers, with little or no accommodation with the collapsed and largely discredited Konbaung regime.

The early colonial period in the Irrawaddy valley represented an end of attempts to reform the early modern state. As a consequence, many aspects of early modern social and economic organisation, already in decline, disappeared entirely. Existing institutions such as the Hluttaw were supplanted by an imported British Indian bureaucracy, and local offices, both hereditary and appointed, were largely extinguished. The changes were more than institutional, as they also led to a complete transformation in the rationale of government and the ceremonies and symbols used to legitimate state authority. Gone was the role of the state in supporting Buddhism and the Buddhist Sangha, as well as in patronising the cultural activities which made up Ava's 'great tradition'. The British in India had, over the course of the late nineteenth century, attempted to invent a new 'traditional' place for their authority over local society.[1] But practically no such effort was made in Burma, beyond a few court costumes retained for the governor's durbars and the creation of minor Burmese titles as rewards for service to the colonial Raj.

In some respects, however, colonial policies represented an intensification of trends already underway prior to annexation. The centralised and bureaucratic nature of the colonial state completed, albeit much more quickly and effectively, efforts begun under Mindon and Thibaw to centralise and bureaucratise their administrations. In the area of land and revenue policies, the capacity of the colonial state to gather information

---

[1] Bernard S. Cohn, 'Representing Authority in Victorian India', in Eric Hobsbawm and Terence Ranger (eds.), *The Invention of Tradition*, Cambridge, 1983, pp. 165–209.

and taxes far exceeded that of the Burmese. But the general direction of policies was not dissimilar to the efforts of the later Konbaung kings to move away from early modern structures based on labour obligations to one more suited to a cash-based economy dependent on foreign trade. This chapter on the early British occupation aims to survey fairly broadly the impact of these colonial policies on Irrawaddy valley society, the final act of the valley's transition from the centre of empire to a part of modern Burma.

Places and peoples

The early colonial occupation of the old kingdom presided, first of all, over the fixing of Burma as a political and geographic entity on the world map. The political boundaries of twentieth-century Burma are, of course, entirely colonial creations. As we have seen, the Court of Ava saw little need for anything but the vaguest of borders, as her authority waned gradually over hills and forests. The first precise boundaries were drawn up in the aftermath of the First Anglo-Burmese War, demarcating the lines between Arakan, the Burmese Kingdom and the Tennasserim. Arakan's administrative boundary with Bengal was also drawn, as was the Tennasserim's boundary with an equally unmapped Siam. These became modern-day Burma's international frontiers. Similarly, a series of discussions led to a fixed border with Manipur, now a British Indian principality. Over the first couple of decades of colonial rule in Upper Burma, the remainder of the new country's frontiers were carefully negotiated and surveyed: in deciding what was Assam, Burma, Tibet and China, the diplomats and cartographers of Fort Williams set the Indian–Burmese–Chinese borders of today.[2] Modern Burma thus included the entire heartland of the old kingdom, the dry zone, 'Thunaparanta and Tampradipa' or the land of the Myanma. But the map also included some, though not all, of her erstwhile tributaries and frontier regions, as well as places never even claimed let alone ruled by the Court of Ava. Remote Rawang and Lisu communities living near the Himalayan ranges around Fort Hertz were now under Rangoon's authority, while Manipur and Assam formed their own province of British India.

In 1891, five years after the British annexation, the first India census to

[2] See especially Woodman, *The Making of Burma*, pp. 205–335.

include Upper Burma reckoned the population of this new entity at just over 3 million.[3] The population was found to be overwhelmingly rural, with only 12 per cent living in a total of twenty-four towns of over 5,000 people, and the remainder spread over 11,000 villages. Mandalay was the only city in the entire country; it had a population of 180,000, which was believed to have fallen from perhaps 200,000 since the war. The next largest town, Pakkoku, had a population of around 15,000. Salin, Myingyan, Bhamo and the rest were found to be just under 10,000, though in these towns as well a significant number of people are believed to have left in the mid-1880s for Lower Burma, with some only now beginning to return. The second census, which took place ten years later in 1901, revealed a further decline in the urban population of Upper Burma,[4] and twelve out of the nineteen towns listed showed a decrease in population.[5] The only ones to show any significant increases were Bhamo on the China frontier, and Meiktila and Yamèthin on the new railway line between Rangoon and Mandalay.[6] Mandalay itself continued to fall in population, down by about another 5,000. A total of 372,000 people had been listed in the earlier census as residing in Lower Burma but having been born in Upper Burma.[7] In 1901 this figure was 399,000, indicating a still substantial migration south. Whatever seasonal aspect to this migration had existed in the past, entire families were now emigrating permanently.[8]

The decline in the urban population would have been even greater had it not been for the immigration of Europeans, Indians and Chinese to Mandalay and other towns. A total of 21,000 people were listed in 1901 as having been foreign-born.[9] Though no distinction was made as to whether individuals had immigrated before or after annexation, the vast majority of Indians and Europeans must have arrived under British rule. In Mandalay, for example, the 'Buddhist' population (more or less the same as the 'Burmese' population) fell by nearly 8,000, but was partly compensated by

---

[3] The total area used as 'Upper Burma' in the census was somewhat larger than the area which has been used throughout this book; the census included predominantly Shan areas such as the Upper Chindwin valley, which have not been considered. It did not, however, include the Shan states themselves.

[4] *Census of India, 1901* Burma Report 14 (hereafter *Census of India* with year and page or table number). Comparisons between the 1891 and 1901 censuses are not very easy as many of the categories used were changed, as well as territorial boundaries.

[5] *Ibid.*

[6] *Ibid.*, p. 25. The population decreases were most marked in Amarapura, Shwébo, Kyauksè, Myingyan and Pagan.   [7] *Ibid.*, table XI.   [8] *Ibid.*   [9] *Ibid.*

a rise of nearly 2,000 'Hindus' and 1,000 'Muslims'.[10] Overall, however, Upper Burma registered a 12 per cent increase in population, which reached a total of 3.7 million. There are, unfortunately, no figures on birth and death rates, and a portion of this increase may have been the repatriation of refugees from Lower Burma after 1891. The overall 'Indian' population was at this time still very low, less than 1 per cent, and was concentrated in Mandalay and in the frontier towns of Bhamo and Myitkyina. Unlike in Lower Burma, a large immigrant presence was never a major consequence of British rule.[11]

We know little from these censuses about the internal breakdown of the population classed as 'Burmese'. We do not know at all, for example, whether the majority of migrants from the north to the delta were former crown servants or what percentage of the population saw themselves as *thuhtay*. Instead, the authors of the 1891 and 1901 censuses simply squeezed the people of the Irrawaddy valley into existing British Indian categories. In Sagaing district, for example, the census table on 'caste' reports 41 people as 'Kayastha', 113 as 'Parayan', 50 as 'Banyan', 4 as 'Chhatri', 24 as 'Reddhi', 47 as 'Musalman Dhobi', 114 as 'Chetti' and 241,837 as 'Burmese'.[12]

Descendants of captives and immigrants from Chiang Mai, Vientiane, Arakan, Manipur and Pegu, noblemen and pagoda slaves, *myothugyi* and their retainers, crown servants and *athi*, all were now 'Burman-Buddhists' together.

A British market

Early colonial rule ended the possibility of a significant French penetration of the economy and removed the aristocracy from their protected and privileged market positions. The late 1890s also witnessed a rapid expansion in Britain's commercial presence in Upper Burma. This was assisted by the major infrastructural developments which were undertaken by the new colonial state. These infrastructural developments cost over £12 million over the first ten years of the British occupation and were almost £5 million more than total revenue from Upper Burma during this time. They averaged more than £600,000 per year exclusive of salaries,[13] and may have played a role in arresting the economic decline of the Thibaw

---

[10] *Ibid.*, p. 27.   [11] *Ibid.* Subsidiary table II-A.
[12] *Census of India, 1891*, vol. II, table XVI.   [13] Nisbit, *Burma*, vol. II, p. 246.

years. The developments permitted an early intensification of British economic activity, particularly in resource extraction sectors such as forestry and oil production. They may also have helped to end the anti-colonial resistance by assisting economic growth and providing temporary work.

While revenue demanded from Upper Burma climbed steadily during these years, from 149,000 rupees in 1886/7 to 875,000 rupees in 1896/7, the amount expended on public works (over a million rupees a year every year after 1887) far exceeded taxation, with Lower Burma providing the deficit financing. This expenditure on public works included, firstly, spending in the area of transportation. The expansion of Upper Burma's transportation infrastructure very early on was given major impetus by its usefulness to the British military during the 'pacification' campaign, both in providing increased mobility to British forces and also in providing work to large numbers of people who might otherwise have remained in areas outside of government control.

Upper Burma's railways were built during the 1880s and 1890s and were the most important and lasting of all infrastructural developments. Construction was begun as early as 1887 on the main line from Rangoon to Mandalay, reaching Mandalay in 1889[14] and other more remote areas, including the northern Shan states near the China border, by the turn of the century. The railways were then sold to the private Burma Railways Company in 1896, after approximately five million pounds had been expended from local revenues.[15] On the rivers, the Irrawaddy Flotilla Company had already come to enjoy a near monopoly on steamer traffic in the Irrawaddy valley and this continued throughout the early colonial period with services now expanded from Rangoon to Mandalay and Bhamo. In 1896, a new four times a week service was inaugurated between Katha, along the new railway line, and Bhamo on the China border.[16]

The second area of infrastructural development was irrigation, and the first irrigation survey was conducted in 1890. As with transportation, irrigation work also provided employment for considerable numbers of people and in 1888–9 construction projects were incorporated into the famine relief effort in Meiktila and Yamèthin.[17] In 1892 extensive work was also begun in Mandalay and Shwébo and then in Myingyan, Minbu and

[14] See Maung Shein, 'Burma Railways 1874–1914', *JBRS* 44 (1961).
[15] *RAB*, 1895/6, p. 11.   [16] *Ibid*., 1896/7, p. 11.   [17] *Ibid*., November 1889, nos. 1–3.

Kyauksè, and in total, the area irrigated was increased by 500,000 acres from 230,000 in 1891 to 740,000 in 1921.[18] The third area of development was the post and telegraph system, where Mindon's telegraph system was taken over, rebuilt, and English substituted for Burmese.[19]

The final area of infrastructural development for the new colonial economy was the establishment of a more modern system of currency and banking, where the somewhat unstable Burmese 'peacock' rupee was replaced with the British Indian rupee in 1886/7. Colonial officials found that the Burmese rupee was worth 12 per mille less than the Indian rupee but the government decided to accept them for exchange at par up to 31 March 1888 and then at a discount for another two years. The circulation of paper currency rapidly expanded from 1,567 lakhs in 1886 to 3,201 in 1887 and then doubled again by 1893.[20]

Major British banks based in Rangoon quickly established branches in Mandalay, but mainly to cater to foreign firms. In the countryside, changes in agricultural finance are difficult to see and British reports are mainly concerned with possible inroads by Chettiyar money-lenders from South India whose extensive activities in Lower Burma had already begun to worry colonial authorities. The reports state, however, that most agricultural loans were still from other Burmese, the majority of whom were not professional money-lenders but were traders and other townspeople or simply better-off relatives.[21] The exceptions were 'frontier' trading and mining towns such as Mogok where significant Indian communities had already emerged and where Indian bankers were now able to turn to the British courts to recover money from an increasingly indebted Burmese and Shan population.[22]

All these changes in infrastructure as well as the general stability enjoyed throughout Upper Burma by 1890 led to a long period of expanding trade and economic growth, certainly through the turn of the century. According to the 1891 census, the vast majority of the population were employed in the agricultural sector. Only in Mandalay district did agriculturists not exceed three-quarters of the total population. 'Commerce' was found to be the occupation of over 10 per cent of the people in Mandalay district and of approximately 2 to 3 per cent of the population in every other district.

[18] A. Ireland, *The Province of Burma*, 2 vols., Boston, 1907, vol. III, pp. 669–70.
[19] *SEHB*, p. 29.   [20] Burma Finance Proceedings (Upper Burma), July 1886.
[21] *RCJB*, 1896, p. 4.   [22] *Ibid*.

Despite the growth in population and the return of many refugees and others from Lower Burma, by the late 1880s, wages of both skilled and unskilled labourers had risen well above their depressed levels under Thibaw, wages for unskilled workers rising from 1 anna a day to 6 annas a day, while the rise in wages for others was much less dramatic. There was considerable internal variation with wages being significantly higher for both skilled and unskilled labour in the frontier town of Bhamo and ruby mines town of Mogok.[23] At the same time, however, the price of rice fell considerably while the prices of all of Upper Burma's major crops, including millet, sesame, wheat, peas, cotton, tea and tobacco rose considerably. The areas dependent on rice production around the capital – Kyauksè and Shwébo – may have had any fall in farm-gate prices for their product offset by lower taxes. Lower real taxes would have resulted from the removal of aristocratic control over their erstwhile estates, while income may have increased from improvements in irrigation and transport. In Salin, the other rice-growing area, tenants of the local landowning class (see below) may not have fared so well, a possibility evidenced by the continued flight of cultivators from there to the delta during early British rule. On the other hand, for cultivators in Mandalay, where tobacco was increasingly grown, and Myingyan which grew cotton, tobacco and wheat, the relative change in prices could only have been welcome.[24] Indeed, most official reports around this time note that more stable market conditions encouraged a move away from rice farming in areas not particularly suited for rice, and towards other cash crops, intensifying a trend which had only just begun under Burmese rule.

Profits from the 'backdoor' China trade never lived up to pre-colonial expectations. Partly as a result of continuing instability in China throughout the 1890s, trade remained insignificant, at least relative to maritime trade, both for Upper Burma's growing economy and for British firms.[25] The trade amounted to about 30 lakh rupees[26] in 1895, increasing to over 50 lakhs in 1900. Indian yarns and European manufactured goods were exported and raw silk was still the primary import.[27] By 1891/2, trade between the two Burmas had reached a total value of over 60 million rupees, or more than twice the average in the early 1880s prior to the war.

Statistics on the rice trade between the two Burmas were kept until

[23] *RAB*, 1888/9, appendix, p. ccii.   [24] *Ibid.*, p. cc.   [25] *Ibid.*, 1901/2, pp. 62–3.
[26] *Ibid.*, 1895–6, p. 51.   [27] *Ibid.*, 1901–2, pp. 62–3.

1896 and basically demonstrate a continuing dependence on imports from the delta, amounts fluctuating with variations in the agricultural performance of the north, with 50,000 to 155,000 tonnes being imported every year to 1896.[28] Thus Upper Burma's economy remained, unsurprisingly, an importer mainly of finished products through Lower Burma from Britain and India, as well as an exporter of primary goods. One change in this period between annexation and the turn of the century was the increased reliance on the export of timber and oil, the two goods now essentially under the control of large British firms.

The oil industry was one sector which underwent considerable change and expansion in the early years of British rule. Production throughout the early modern period had, as we have seen, been in the hands of the *twinzayo* ruling class, and the *twinzayo* seem to have faced increasingly difficult economic circumstances by the 1870s. Mindon was able to buy some of their wells and several wells under royal ownership were then leased to the *thuhtay* Moola Ismail, but most of the wells at annexation seem to have still belonged to the *twinzayo* families. By 1888, however, the new Burmah Oil Company had taken over the wells inherited by Thibaw from his father and the company then bought most of the wells remaining in the hands of the *twinzayo* and thus established a near monopoly on exports.[29] Production increased dramatically with the introduction of new machinery, with Americans from Texas running the operation from the 1900s, and Burmah Oil's annual output increasing from only 2.3 million gallons to 10 million in 1893, 57 million in 1903, 123 million in 1908 and 200 million in 1913.[30]

The market remained heavily protected, the colonial government turning down drilling requests from the Colonial Oil Company of New Jersey and the Anglo-American Company of Britain, both Standard Oil subsidiaries, and from the 1890s on, Burmah Oil accounted for 75 per cent of oil production and 85 per cent of refined products, 80 per cent of these products being destined for the rest of India.[31]

[28] *Ibid.*, 1898–9, p. 40.
[29] J.G. Scott, *Burma: A Handbook of Practical Information*, London, 1921, pp. 241–6.
[30] T.A.B. Corley, *A History of the Burmah Oil Company: 1886–1924*, London, 1983; Aye Hlaing, 'Trends of Economic Growth and Income Distribution in Burma, 1870–1940', *JBRS*, 47(1964), 57–108.
[31] *Report on the Petroleum Industry in Upper Burma from the End of the Last Century to the Beginning of 1891*, Rangoon, 1892. See also Nobuyoshi Nishizawa, *Economic Development of Burma in Colonial Times*, Hiroshima, 1991, pp. 65–9.

British officials and businessmen alike also had great faith in the country's mineral potential, particularly in precious stones.[32] As with the China trade, however, the profits derived from Burma's mines never lived up to pre-annexation expectations.[33] Forestry was the other area in which British firms supplanted local businessmen. Whereas some Burmese businessmen had managed to operate logging firms in competition with the Bombay Burma Trading Company in the early 1880s, by the turn of the century nearly all leases had been given to British firms, these firms being given strong preference by the state in the selection process.[34] By the turn of the century, five British firms – Bombay Burma, Steel Brothers and Co., MacGregor and Co., Foucar and Co. and T.D. Findlay and Son – accounted for more than 75 per cent of all teak extraction, and exports rose from 50,000 tonnes in 1888/9 to 100,000 the following year to 150,000 by the end of the 1890s.[35]

Of the old court banker *thuhtay* we have little information. The most important of the Mandalay *thuhtay* at annexation, Moola Ismail, appears to have maintained some of his commercial position into the 1890s despite new British competition. He retained for example his control over the main Mandalay market, the Zegyo.[36] He also came to own large landed estates in the Lower Chindwin and prospected for oil at minor oil-fields outside the main Yénangyaung wells dominated by Burmah Oil.[37]

Changing the countryside

Early economic change was not limited to an increased British commercial presence. The late 1880s and 1890s also witnessed the fashioning of new structures of land revenue and tenure, which seemingly followed tradition, but which involved a much greater degree of state supervision and private ownership than had hitherto existed. The state moved firmly away from one dependent upon trade tariffs and labour control to one of

[32] *RAB*, 1886/7, p. 24.

[33] *Ibid.*, 1896/7, p. 8. See also Robert Vicant Turrell, 'Conquest and Concession: The Case of the Burma Ruby Mines', *MAS*, 22 (1988), 145–63 on the political intrigues in London and Calcutta surrounding Burma's ruby monopoly.

[34] Aung Tun Thet, *Burmese Entrepreneurship*, pp. 64–5.   [35] *SEHB*, p. 36.

[36] 'Lease of the Zegyo Bazaar', December 1887, BHP. On Moola Ismail's market, see also Geary, *Burma, After the Conquest*.

[37] *Report on Settlement Operations in the Shwébo District*, p. 31.

which the primary source of taxation was an agrarian countryside of small privately owned lands.

Until the mid-1890s and the first regular settlement operations, colonial knowledge of the Burmese land and revenue system remained extremely rudimentary.[38] Policy-makers knew that the primary Burmese tax was the *thathameda* household tax and that there existed 'royal lands' which paid rent to the state, but did not know much more. Given the decision to administer the country directly and given the cost of that administration, devising an effective taxation scheme could not wait for several years of exhaustive research. For the first two years after annexation, when the suppression of resistance was the paramount concern, revenue was simply collected on an *ad hoc* basis where possible.[39] District officers, whether civilian or military, would ascertain approximately what the Burmese revenue demand would have been from a particular area and solicit the co-operation of local chiefs in securing that amount. But this netted very little. Despite the lack of much information, administrators in 1889 drafted the Upper Burma Land and Revenue Regulation, and with some modifications, this regulation would remain law past the turn of the century. Essentially, this regulation divided all land in Upper Burma into two categories: 'state' and 'non-state'. 'State lands' were defined as including what the British believed were the following 'Burmese' types of tenure:[40]

> *Ahmudan-sa*, or 'crown service lands'
> *Si-sa*, or 'cavalry lands'
> *Thugyi-sa*, or 'headman's lands'
> *Wun-sa*, or 'senior official's lands'
> *Min-mye*, or 'royal lands'
> Waste land
> Abandoned land

'Non-state land' was defined as including:[41]

> *Dama-ugya*, or land which had been cleared by the current occupant or his parent
> *Bobabaing*, or land which had been cleared by the occupant's

---

[38] *Report on Settlement Operations in the Mandalay District*, pp. 24–7.
[39] *RAB*, 1885/6, Revenue Section.
[40] *The Upper Burma Land Revenue Manual* (hereafter *LRM*), Rangoon, 1900, pp. 9–12.
[41] *Ibid.*, pp. 12–13.

ancestors and had remained in the family
Wuttankan, or 'glebe land'

This twofold division of the land was made on the understanding that state land in 'Burmese times' paid rent to the royal treasury above and beyond any ordinary assessment. It was ruled that state land could not be inherited or transferred, but that cultivators working such land as tenants of the government could also not be ejected except for default on rent.[42] Cultivators working state land would pay 'rent' to the government at varying rates.[43] The nominal Burmese assessment of state land was said to have been one-quarter of the produce but in practice varied from around a tenth to a quarter, and these rates of assessment were generally maintained.[44]

The British also believed that they had inherited Mindon's *thathameda* taxation system and unravelling the intricacies of the old *thathameda* administration also took several years.[45] After considerable discussion on the merits and demerits of this system, it was eventually decided after several years of experimentation that this 'household' tax would remain and would remain somewhat flexible, in that rates would be allowed to vary depending on the wealth of the area, but not to the same extent as under Burmese rule. Also, local community leaders would actively participate in ascribing individual household shares. Once the annual *thathameda* for a given township was decided (normally at ten rupees per household), rates on individual households would depend on income, ranging from just one rupee to over fifteen. This was another departure from the Burmese method, in which assessment was based on wealth or property rather than income. Some exemptions were allowed. But the system whereby an entire 'destitute' class of people (*dokkhita*) was recognised and exempted, was not continued.[46]

In addition to the rent on 'state land' and the *thathameda*, colonial authorities also decided to impose a tax on 'non-state' land.[47] By the late 1890s it had become clear to the British that the Burmese state imposed no tax on 'non-state' land, which had many of the attributes of private property, and that there was thus no land revenue. This break with local tradition was made in line with the long-standing British Indian concept

[42] *Ibid.*, pp. 9–12.   [43] *Ibid.*, pp. 46–7.
[44] *Report on Settlement Operations in the Mandalay District*, pp. 24–5.
[45] *Ibid.*, pp. 24–7.   [46] *LRM*, pp. 43–5.   [47] *RAB*, 1899/1900.

of the state being the ultimate owner of the land or was justified in part by citing the Burmese notion of the king as the 'lord of water and earth' (*yé-myé shin*). Thus, what had been an abstract Burmese theory of government, never practised, in this way became a codified and enforced reality under the British administration. This triple system of taxation – the *thathameda*, 'rent' on 'state land' and general land revenue – proved fairly unwieldy in the early years and was constantly modified throughout the 1890s as more and more settlement operations were carried out. Fairly elaborate formulae were devised for calculating the revenue owed, but as a general principle, the amount paid as land revenue was deducted from *thathameda* obligations.[48] By the turn of the century, the regulation was finally simplified by ending all distinctions between the payment of rent on state land and revenue on non-state land, all lands now being liable to payment of the land revenue.[49]

Attempts at implementing these new policies were very confused, not surprisingly as the inherited Burmese system, originally complex and varied, had itself been undergoing radical but not fully completed reform. Now, added onto this, was a hectic attempt, based on partial information, to restructure but not completely replace this system with one which fitted into British Indian norms. A key problem was simply trying to distinguish 'state' from 'non-state' land.[50] In theory, all tenures should have fitted easily into one of the several categories listed above. In fact, the Burmese state had never really been able to completely control land use, in particular in areas at any distance from the capital. Categories of tenure tended to blur into one another and changed with distance from the capital or provincial centres of state authority. The past ten years of upheaval had added even more complex elements. In Shwébo, for example, it was found that most of the land was 'originally' *bobabaing*, or ancestral, but that 'recently' the land had been confiscated by Mandalay and handed over to various members of the royal family or nobility, causing much local dissatisfaction. Here, it was decided that the land would remain 'state land' but assigned back to the original owners on payment of 'a moderate annual revenue'.

Gaining the necessary information to make a proper distinction at

[48] *LRM*, p. 62.

[49] 'Upper Burma Land Revenue Regulation of 1901', *RAB*, 1901/2, p. 18.

[50] Note by Burgess to the Commissioner of the Northern Division on Shwébo, July 1886, *RAB*.

times proved an insurmountable problem. Over much of the Lower Chindwin plain, for example, both the local chief's 'official' or 'state' land and his 'private' or 'non-state' land was simply known as the 'the chief's land' (*thugyi-myê*), and no amount of inquiry could reveal any further difference in tenure.[51] In other areas, however, officials reported a fairly clear distinction.[52] This 'clarity' of distinction, however, may in part be related to the zealousness with which some settlement officers tried to identify land as belonging to the state, believing that this would bring higher revenues. Whatever the case, by the mid-1890s a total of 1.5 million acres were declared 'state land', dispersed over 270,000 holdings, compared with only one million acres declared 'non-state' over 890,000 holdings.[53] Later settlement officers tended to become less concerned over 'finding' state land, as the difference in income derived from the two types of land became insignificant. In the first regular settlement operation in the Lower Chindwin, for example, land occupied by former military families was allowed as 'non-state', with the explanation that these tenures possessed full rights of inheritance and transfer, the key tests of whether property was to be seen as 'private'. On the other hand 'official' land controlled by the Myothugyi of Monywa and members of the royal family was classified as 'state.' *Appanages* were considered only 'titular' and claims to these estates were classed 'non-state'.[54]

In codifying and enforcing a system of land revenue based on a division of state and non-state land and on a *thathameda* assessment, British policy-makers apparently thought that they were modifying local norms. Instead, they were pushing Mindon and Thibaw's agrarian reforms much further than either regime had dared, creating for the first time a structure of genuinely private ownership, entirely free of gentry or aristocratic control or involvement. The result was a decade of confusion and competition. The new colonial courts were quickly put to work.

The *Reports on Civil Administration* of the 1890s tell a story in which Burmese people, realising that all land was in effect becoming 'private', became quickly familiar with the colonial judicial system,[55] and then fought intensely through the courts for ownership of land. It was also a story in which British magistrates found themselves making these

---

[51] *Report on the First Regular Settlement of Operations in the Lower Chindwin District*, pp. 41–7.   [52] *Yamèthin Gazetteer*, vol. I, p. 130.
[53] Ireland, *Province of Burma*, vol. I, p. 602.   [54] *Lower Chindwin Gazetteer*, pp. 180–1.
[55] *RCJB*, 1896, p. 6.

decisions regarding ownership based on very limited information. The rise in litigation was very rapid. The first report for Upper Burma, which was published in 1890, five years after annexation and less than three years after the 'pacification' of the countryside, noted an increasing number of civil suits, over 7,000 in 1889 and over 9,000 in 1890, the majority being for breach of contract and over land, with the numbers beginning to decline only after 1895.[56]

Throughout the reports, the British expressed repeated surprise at the amount of litigation and the extent to which members of sometimes quite small communities were challenging one another in court.[57] Suggesting a certain absence of the communal spirit which pre-colonial villages were supposed to have displayed, one report stated that 'a Burman who has a little money at his command to spend on litigation is not indisposed to use it to gain an advantage over his poorer neighbour who has not the means of engaging in a prolonged contest in the Courts'.[58]

The sort of cases brought before British civil courts may be usefully divided into two types. The first type comprised suits for the division of ancestral property, in which land declared 'non-state', that is mainly *bobabaing* land, had risen in value in many areas and was now being fought over by various heirs.[59] This sort of litigation was noted to be more common in areas such as the Lower Chindwin and Sagaing where recent improvements in irrigation and transportation had led to economic growth and where much of the land, including, as we have seen, old crown service land, had become classified as privately owned.[60] The second type of case was of suits for the redemption of land which had been mortgaged.[61]

Thus, after ten years or so of very uncertain political conditions, economic decline and then foreign intervention and war, the extent to which the economy had become commercialised now demonstrated itself in the extent to which individuals were eager to use the new courts to establish ownership claims. There may have been an appreciation early on, once British power was firmly in place, that whatever hereditary rights to the control of land based on office still remained up to 1885, the early modern system of tenure was now definitely past. A solid claim to ownership could now be made.

These reports also reveal that British courts may have been manipu-

---

[56] *Ibid.*, 1890.   [57] Burma Judicial Proceedings (hereafter BJP), August 1886, no. 7.
[58] *RCJB*, 1891, p. 5.   [59] *Ibid.*, 1890, p. 3.   [60] *Ibid.*, 1891, p. 4.   [61] *Ibid.*, 1890, p. 3.

lated by different local class interests. As we have seen, gentry leaders had managed in some areas to maintain their authority through reappointments by the colonial regime to local office. In the 1891 report, it was suggested for the first time that newly appointed Burmese officials were using the courts to further their own commercial interests, and the Commissioner of the Southern Division, which included Salin, argued strongly in favour of British or at least non-Upper Burman subdivisional officers trying all land cases where possible, noting also that litigation in Minbu rose when land suits were 'disposed of by disinterested tribunal'.[62]

In most other places, however, the impact of the British courts was reversed, and members of the old ruling lineages lost control over land to their former tenants. In Pagan, for example, the British categorised the estates of the old minthas of Pagan, the *min-myay*, as 'land held by the village community'.[63] Here it seems clear that the establishment of British courts reinforced existing trends and further undermined old elites whose influence still rested on their early modern prerogatives. In other areas, the biggest winners were outsiders, traders and money-lenders.[64]

How all this affected popular welfare is difficult to judge. Certainly, the colonial state was able to extract much greater revenue from the countryside than the Burmese state ever could, even in the best years of Mindon's reign (estimated at around 50 lakh rupees); it amounted to over 100 lakh rupees a year by 1889. The vast majority of revenue was from the *thathameda* assessment, together with rents on state lands and income from forestry concessions.[65]

What is easier to see are certain shifts in the tax burden. The first was geographic. Mandalay, which had been exempt from the *thathameda*, was taxed for the first time in 1886/7 against strong local opposition.[66] As British reports stated, however, this new taxation may have been more than compensated by the lifting of many restrictions and tariffs on trade.[67] On the other hand, under Burmese rule, areas close to the capital and other centres of authority generally paid more tax simply because they were more accessible. As the new colonial state reached all areas almost

[62] *Ibid.*, 1891, p. 5.   [63] *Ibid.*, 1894, p. 4.   [64] *Ibid.*, 1894, p. 5.

[65] *RAB*, 1898/9, p. 80.

[66] Burgess (Commissioner of the Northern Division) to the Chief Secretary for Upper Burma to the Chief Commissioner, 21 December 1887, BHP.

[67] Burgess (Commissioner of the Northern Division) to the Secretary for Upper Burma to the Chief Commissioner, *RAR*, October 1886; Burgess to the Chief Secretary to the Chief Commissioner, 21 December 1887, BHP.

equally, this distinction would have disappeared, helping poorer cultivators in Kyauksè but worsening the burden of more distant communities who had been paying only a nominal tribute to their Konbaung overlords.

The second shift in the tax burden related to social status and proximity to the Mandalay aristocracy. Members of both the Mandalay aristocracy and local gentry elites, who had been completely exempt from any revenue obligations, received no exemptions under British administration. The only minor exceptions left were some officials, such as township officers and village headmen. Tax exemption under Burmese rule had extended not only to the nobility and their extended families but also to members of elite military units such as the Linzin Guards regiment based in Kyauksè.[68] While the British continued to depend in some areas on local elites for tax assessment this sort of class bias may have continued, but the situation soon changed. For example, in Minbu, it was stated that taxation of state land more than doubled after the Land Records Department took over assessment from the local headmen in the late 1890s.[69] Just as disastrous for many in both the old aristocracy and the gentry was the loss of their position in the taxation process itself. The state crisis of the late 1870s and early 1880s resulted in the government turning increasingly to informal taxation, including especially the creation of tax farms. These lucrative concessions were ended. Though many members of the royal family and nobility petitioned colonial authorities early after annexation for some sort of compensation, no compensation was ever made.[70]

The third shift related to economic hardship. Tax exemption on account of 'destitution' or temporary economic difficulties, an important and often used royal prerogative, became rare. While the British did relax *thathameda* demands during times of extreme hardship, such as during the drought and famine in Meiktila and Yamèthin in 1897–8,[71] these exemptions appear to have been much more infrequent and to have been made in response only to very severe conditions. In addition, they were assessed much more formally and not on the personal *ad hoc* basis with which Burmese exceptions appeared to have been decided.

The Shan states, in significant contrast again, seem to have enjoyed a definite *absolute* reduction in revenue demand, at least on average, under

---

[68] S. Westlake, *Report on Settlement Operations in the Kyauksè District, Season 1890–1891 and Part of Season 1891–1892* (hereafter *Report on Settlement Operations in the Kyauksè District*), Rangoon, 1892, p. 25.   [69] *RAB*, 1898/9, p. 81.
[70] *RAB*, June 1887.   [71] *RAB*, 1898/9, p. 80.

British administration.[72] The total Shan states assessment was only £18,000 at the turn of the century, compared with £30,000 under Burmese rule. It should be noted that, at least under Thibaw, assessment came only from a few states and so there was considerable internal variation in the amount of tax paid. Some areas had come to pay nothing to Mandalay, Burmese sovereignty being completely nominal, while others, closer to Upper Burma proper, would have paid a far greater amount than they eventually did to the new state early in the colonial period. In addition, the Shan states benefited from a lifting of all internal restrictions and imposts on trade in tea, their major export.[73]

The impact on local communities

The early colonial settlement reports and other official records give us our first detailed view of social and economic organisation and change at the local level. For rural society as a whole, the first census undertaken following annexation listed 1.8 per cent of the population as landlords, 64 per cent as landowning cultivators, 26 per cent as tenants and 8 per cent as agricultural labourers. But these figures varied considerably from region to region and, in general, British sources from the 1890s describe quite different conditions in different parts of the Irrawaddy valley. This is what we would expect given differences in early modern local communities, the availability of irrigated land and proximity to the extractive powers of royal agencies and the Mandalay aristocracy. All of the Irrawaddy valley may thus be grouped into three broad categories based on these factors.

The first category comprises the areas right around the capital where the economy was the most commercialised and where Ava aristocrats concentrated their efforts to develop landed estates. In this region, old hereditary office-holders often lost their positions to traders, money-lenders and other outsiders linked to the royal court. In addition, much of this area had been settled by crown servants who had held land on a prebendal basis. But with Mindon's reforms abolishing the crown service system, land-holdings became essentially private. In theory, the former prebendal estates still belonged to the state and thus the occupant was required to pay rent. However, in many cases rent was not paid, or influential individuals from the capital bought the land surreptitiously

---

[72] Nisbit, *Burma*, vol. III, p. 231.   [73] *Ibid.*, p. 121.

and thus established a private holding. The Burmese state was too weak to prevent such transactions from occurring and here we see most visibly the rise of a commercial and land-holding class, composed in part of members of the aristocracy and their friends and clients.

An example of this first category of social change was Kyauksè. In the 1891 census, in strong contrast to the Upper Burma averages, less than 1 per cent of the agricultural population were listed as landlords, while 53 per cent were landowning cultivators, 16 per cent were tenants and 31 per cent were agricultural labourers, by far the highest proportion of agricultural labourers in the country. Kyauksè, throughout the early modern period, was closest to approaching the traditionally conceived model of society, a large portion of the population having been crown servants closely supervised by the state.[74]

This breakdown in early modern social organisation came at a time when an increased population allowed more intensive cultivation. Surplus production was siphoned off quite effectively by Mandalay-based noblemen and their banking partners. Liquidity for economic growth was provided by Mandalay nobility and merchants, channelled only in part through dependent local authorities. As crown service and non-service distinctions were largely ended, aristocrats, as absentee landlords, expanded their private ownership of the best lands. Some of these aristocrats managed to hold on to their new estates under colonial rule with now full and recognised rights of private property. In the first Kyauksè settlement report written in the early 1890s, of twenty large landlords with holdings over 100 acres, four are easily identifiable as members of the former royal family or nobility. They are the widow of the former Myoza of Yaw, the widow of a former commander of the Household Guards, the former foreign minister, the Myoza of Kyaukmyaung, and the Pintha Princess.[75]

A similar example of this category was Sagaing, across the river from Mandalay. Much of this land had also been crown service land in the early modern period, but became essentially privately owned by former servicemen – cultivators who now paid rent. But being close to the capital, here too members of the Mandalay elite had attempted to secure some control over agricultural production, translating that control, at least in some cases, into outright private ownership under British rule. The settlement officer states that:

[74] *Kyauksè Gazetteer*, p. 126.
[75] *Report on Settlement Operations in the Kyauksè District*, p. 68.

[In Sagaing], large landholdings were exceptional. As a rule they have been accumulated by purchase by mortgages which have been lost sight of. The official classes furnish several of the largest holders. In Ava and Chaungu considerable areas are held by members of the Burmese Royal Family, in some instances with titles that will not bear close scrutiny.[76]

In other areas close to the capital, British policies entirely reversed the inroads made by aristocrats and other outsiders. For example, in the slightly richer and irrigated Mu valley, control over land by the Mandalay elite was not recognised.[77] Around Shwébo, for example, the British undid the expanding control of princes and noblemen over the best irrigated land, essentially handing the land back to the cultivators themselves.

The fate of my own family around this time is perhaps representative of the middling Mandalay nobility. One of my great-great-great-grandfathers, Maha Mindin Thinhkaya was born in Dabessway, a collection of seven villages just to the west of Ava and close to the old fortified town of Mekkaya. His father had been a court banker and his mother a member of the Mekkaya chiefly line. After a long monastic career, he joined the king's service and eventually rose to become a Chief Secretary to the Hluttaw and court poet (*sasodaw*). He was created the Myoza of Dabessway in the 1840s and married into the minor Yanaung Minzin branch of the royal family. Of his two sons, one Maha Mindin Minkyaw Raza became Keeper of the Privy Armory, while another, my great-great-grandfather Maha Mindin Kyawthu was Thibaw's Privy Treasurer. While neither of these men were given *appanages*, having achieved office only after the reforms of the 1860s, they continued their commercial and financial interests in and around Dabessway. Both retired to the area after the fall of Mandalay, but the early revenue settlements left them with little private land, forcing their sons and grandsons to seek their careers in the new colonial civil service and nationalist politics.

The claims of some local hereditary office-holders and their relatives, however, were treated much more generously, the Myothugyi of Monywa, for example, being left in private ownership of over 3,000 acres and the Myothugyi of Tawbo being granted the 4,000 acres which he was found to control. Other landowners included several *myo-ok* and a former

---

[76] L.M. Parlett, *Report on the Settlement Operations in the Sagaing District, Season 1893–1900* (hereafter *Report on Settlement Operations in the Sagaing District*), Rangoon, 1903, p. 58.

[77] *Report on Settlement Operations in the Shwébo District*, p. 15.

myowun of local origin. Similarly, along the Lower Chindwin, most of the large landowners were found to be former or current *thugyi*.[78]

Thus, in this first category, the region close to the capital, colonial policy aided and consolidated the position of a few of these new business-men-aristocrats while undermining the position of others. In Kyauksè, the new state permitted some of the Mandalay-based estates to remain. In other areas, however, administrators refused to recognise the claims of aristocratic outsiders and handed land back to local people, including the local gentry. This variation could be due in part to the fact that the system of tenure in Thibaw's Burma was still very imperfectly reformed and did not explicitly recognise land bought by outsiders as private property. While the old regime was in place, *de facto* control of land was not a problem. But under the colonial state these 'virtual' estates could be, and were, easily undone.

The second category of social change occurred in Salin, a rich irrigated region in which we see a much greater movement towards the development of a genuine local landlord class.[79] In Salin, unlike the region closest to the capital, the local gentry, given their greater geographic distance and the considerable local resources at their disposal, successfully maintained a certain autonomy from the Court of Ava and transformed their traditional position based on personal loyalty and patronage into a commercial position based on privately owned land. As we have seen, these local gentry families were known as the *thugaung*, a title peculiar to that region.[80] At the time of the first settlement report, they were organised into twenty-eight related families.[81]

At the time of the first settlement in the mid-1890s, the *thugaung* were still maintaining their dominant position. The 1891 census lists Minbu district, of which Salin is a part, as the district with the highest proportion

---

[78] *Report on Settlement Operations in Lower Chindwin District*, p. 23.

[79] Lieberman, *Burmese Administrative Circles*, makes passing reference to Salin as an important regional centre and the site of a *myowun*ship after the administrative reforms of the Restored Toungoo dynasty (pp. 114n, 115, 120).

[80] Judson's Dictionary, translates *thugaung* as 'a respectable person, one above the commonality'. The phrase *thugaung pyu*, used in the Mandalay court, means 'to confer an office of dignity and emolument upon one (as a king)'; *Judson's Burmese–English Dictionary*, Rangoon, 1853 (reprint 1966).

[81] O.S. Parons, *Report on the Settlement Operations in the Minbu District, Season 1893–1897* (hereafter *Report on Settlement Operations in the Minbu District*), Rangoon, 1900, p. 45.

of tenants and a much lower percentage of agricultural labourers than Kyauksè. One per cent of the district population were landlords, only 34 per cent were landowning cultivators, 61 per cent were tenants and 4 per cent were agricultural labourers.[82] Of the largest land-holding families in Minbu district (which included another sub-division in addition to Salin), the majority listed their occupation as either *thugyi* (headman) or *myo-ok* (colonial township officer) or as *'thugaung*/landlord'. The largest estate was over 1,000 acres and the rest averaged around 300 acres.[83] Most likely, those who became and who listed their position as township officer and village headman were also from the *thugaung* families. In the revision settlement of 1904–7, the largest landowner was still a *thugaung* and the size of *thugaung* land-holdings had grown somewhat larger, averaging over 400 acres, with a few estates well over 1,000 acres.[84]

The third category of social change during this period took place in poorer areas mid-range from the capital. In these areas, commercialisation and Mandalay elite involvement had been relatively minor while the local gentry had not made the sort of expansive transformation to private landlord status achieved by the Salin *thugaung*. The dusty plain around Myingyan, for example, had been partly the home of crown cavalry regiments and partly the home of non-service commoners. Some of the region was tied to the new commercial economy through Myingyan, which is on the Irrawaddy, but the rest was a remote, poor and unirrigated hinterland. Here at the turn of the century, the vast majority of people were still landed cultivators, the 1891 census listing 2 per cent of the population as landlords, 70 per cent as landowning cultivators, 20 per cent as tenants and 8 per cent as agricultural labourers.[85] Small landlords were hereditary village chiefs who had somewhat expanded their estates over the past century but not to the extent of the *thugaung* of Salin.[86]

Thus, we see three different types of social change in Upper Burma towards the turn of the century, based on geographical distance from Mandalay, and the local variant in early modern social organisation: the area around the capital where hereditary office-holders had largely disappeared and the economy was the most heavily commercialised and outsider-dominated; the Salin area, geographically the furthest irrigated area, where the gentry had turned into a powerful landowning class; and the

[82] *Census of India, 1891*, p. 14.   [83] *Ibid.*, pp. 43–4.

[84] *Report on Revision Settlement Operations in the Minbu District*, p. 23.

[85] *Census of India, 1891*.   [86] Furnival, *Political Economy of Burma*, p. 90.

poorer middle area which had experienced only moderate commercialisation and where some local gentry had come to benefit. Colonial policies helped those who had already made the transition to private land-holder – the Salin *thugaung*, a few other rural chiefs and a handful of Mandalay aristocrats – while undercutting the position of others, including many in the capital, who, at annexation, had been able to exploit the agrarian economy only through the still wobbly structures of the Court of Ava.

From kingdom to nation

The death of the Kinwun Mingyi in 1909, the last of the great scholar-noblemen of the Court of Ava, marked the end of a long tradition of early modern learning. Then aged 87, he had lived to see his country transformed, and had outlived many of his younger contemporaries, reformists and royalists alike. He and others like him took with them to their graves an enormous body of knowledge about royal government, social organisation, political thought and kingly ritual. The royal library, as we have seen, was burned to the ground on the first night of the British occupation, and many remaining Pali and Pali-Burmese texts were taken away to the British Museum Library in London. Personal and monastic collections remained, but with each passing year, these palm-leaf manuscripts succumbed to the effects of an unfriendly climate. There was, of course, some continuation in classical knowledge. Many of the royal chronicles would be translated into English, and former court officials such as Pagan U Tin would write new works of history in the old style. But in general a huge chasm had been created. The imagination of Burma, like her new frontiers and administrative apparatus, would be constructed anew under the aegis of British colonial scholarship.

With the exception of Dr Marks' school, schooling in the old kingdom had been exclusively monastic and male. Pali had been taught together with literary Burmese, and learning was focused on Buddhist and Brahmanical texts. After 1885, though there were some attempts by the colonial authorities to maintain monastic education as part of the overall educational system, popular preferences were quickly demonstrated to be in favour of secular schooling and especially of English-language education at an 'Anglo-vernacular' school.[87] Many contemporary observers of

---

[87] Kaung, 'A Survey of the History of Education in Burma before the British Conquest and After', *JBRS*, 46 (1963), 1–112.

this shift, both Burmese and British, were critical of this sudden change, and commented that the entire ethical dimension of education was being wrought away. Many later blamed the decline in monastic teaching for the rise in crime in Upper Burma after the turn of the century.[88] The total number of pupils in 1891, the year of the first census, is believed to have represented approximately 15 per cent of the total school-age population.[89]

Whether or not this expansion of formal schooling led to a rise in literacy during this same period is not clear. The 1891 and 1901 censuses used very different criteria for literacy and this makes any comparison over the ten-year period impossible. Both, however, clearly show an enormous gender disparity in literacy; the 1891 census records a male literacy rate for over-fifteens of around 70 per cent compared with a female literacy rate of only around 3 per cent.[90] The same census listed only 3,000 girls in school as opposed to almost 90,000 boys in both monastic and secular schools. By the turn of the century the percentage of girls in both primary and secondary schools had more than doubled as secular education expanded.[91]

The Buddhist monasteries thus lost their critical role in society as the educators of the ruling elites. But the Sangha easily survived the withdrawal of state patronage and the loss of its key social function, and by the turn of the century Theravada Buddhism had achieved an unparalleled dominance over rival schools of thought. Burma, or the Burmese, and the Singhalese neo-conservative recension were forever linked in local and foreign perceptions. The strict observance of ethical precepts which fundamentalist and mainstream monasteries alike now preached became part of the emerging national identity.

What did not survive the transition to colonial rule, however, were the myriad court-sponsored Brahmanical rituals, the *puja* of Hindu deities and the worship of royal ancestors. *Ponna* lost their separate identity and many of the images of veneration were themselves soon lost, some taken away to museums in Calcutta and elsewhere, and the images of the Konbaung kings and queens being melted down for their gold. Less than a hundred years after Bodawpaya sent for Benares Brahmins and installed images of Ganesh and Skanda in his Amarapura palace, the 'new Burmese' saw these devotional cults as 'Hindu', in opposition to 'Buddhism', and 'foreign'.

[88] Taw Sein Ko, 'A Study in Burmese Sociology', *JBRS*, 10 (1920).
[89] *RAB* 1891/2, p. 17. [90] *Census of India, 1891.* [91] *SEHB*, pp. 21–3.

Other aspects of aristocratic life also disappeared. The old system of noble titles, for example, collapsed and new types of personal names were developed. The titles of the nobility and royal family were not hereditary and the imposition of direct rule led to the ending of all the old Pali-Burmese styles. Gentry and noble lineage names or the names of crown service groups were not then taken as surnames and, instead, the great mass of Burmese were left with only their single personal names. But these personal names became slightly grander and longer and were now often prefixed for men with 'U' meaning maternal uncle and for women with 'Daw' meaning aunt, as a mark of respect. By the early twentieth century, some, particularly in the cities, began to use old noble titles, once coveted and carefully assigned, as their own personal names. Former titles such as *min*, or ruler, were taken as ordinary names, such as in the name of U Kyaw Min, the Arakanese Indian Civil Service officer. The Burmese upper classes thus entered the colonial period with a very precise and complex system of titles and styles and were left with only their personal names, once the mark of a commoner.

The destruction of the royal family and the nobility as a class apart helped to turn colonial imaginings of Burma as an egalitarian rural society into a living reality. Of course, there was a new Burmese-speaking elite, but this elite, throughout the British occupation, was numerically very small and dependent upon the colonial state. Many were men of the south, from Arakan and Pegu, but a sizeable number were descendants of the Ava officialdom. These included nearly all the first Burmese deputy commissioners from Upper Burma such as U Pein and U An Tu; other officials such as U Tin Tut, a graduate of St Catharine's, Cambridge and the first Burmese Indian Civil Service officer; politicians such as Mandalay U Ba U, academics such Dr Htin Aung, later rector of Rangoon University and jurists such as Dr Ba U, later the first post-independence president of Burma. All were sons or grandsons of Mandalay noblemen and many had gone on to receive their education in India or Britain. Some were members of the extended royal family. The author of the final segment of the Konbaungzet chronicle, for example, Pagan U Tin, served the colonial state as a minor official at the turn of the century. He was one of the last great scholars trained in the Burmese classical tradition and was a fourth generation descendant of Bodawpaya, through his son the Prince of Kawlin.[92]

---

[92] *KBZ*, vol. II, pp. 188–9.

The subordinate civil service positions were also filled, to an extent, by sons of old gentry families, though the extent of elite continuity differed from place to place.[93] In some families, one son would attend an English-language school and perhaps receive a clerical or police appointment, while other sons remained in their home towns and villages as the new headmen. For example, the Kinwun Mingyi's father, U Hmo, had been a *thwéthaukgyi*, or hereditary officer, of the elite Natshinyway regiment in the Lower Chindwin. Of his many grandchildren (the Kinwun Mingyi himself had no children), one was the chief clerk at the district office, two were *myo-oks*, one was a member of the Monywa municipal committee and one became a member of the Legislative Assembly under the diarchy of the 1920s and early 1930s.[94]

In general, however, the primary cleavage in the new Burma was not to be one of class but of ethnicity, between those seen as 'foreign' and those seen as 'native', and between the 'native races' themselves. The colonial census and legal codes divided people by religion, language and known caste categories. Thus, the vast majority of people in the Irrawaddy valley were returned as 'Burmese Buddhists'. Others were seen as 'Indian' Hindus or Muslims or as a member of a 'native' minority community. These minority communities in turn were defined in part by the existing classification schema of the Court of Ava and in part through the new science of linguistics. Old court notions of 'Kachins', 'Shans', 'Karens' and others largely remained, and were reinforced or somewhat changed by emergent European theories of language, race and migration.[95] The 'native' races, grouped by their linguistic families, were seen as immigrating in waves from the north, while the 'Indians' from across the sub-continent were the perpetual foreigners of the valley. In local thinking, the inclusion of the English as another *kala* seemed to end around this time. The English were now commonly referred to as *bo*, formerly a military title, and no longer confused with their Bengali, Tamil or Pathan subjects. The peculiar

---

[93] For example, the descendants of the well-known Maha Bandula were members of the subordinate civil service (R.R. Langham-Carter, 'Maha Bandula at Home', *JBRS*, 26 (1936), 122–31); see also Maung Tha Aung and Maung Mya Din, 'Pacification of Upper Burma'. Many of the elite cavalry families mentioned had descendants in the early twentieth century who were township officers, district office clerks or members of the police.

[94] R.R. Langham-Carter, 'The Kinwun Mingyi at Home', *JBRS*, 25 (1935), 121–9.

[95] For a contemporary discussion of language and race in Burma, see *Census of India, 1891*, Burma vol. I, pp. 145–70.

twentieth century divide between 'Europeans', 'Indians', the 'Burmese' and the 'minorities' was firmly set.

Gender relations also underwent a considerable transformation. Burmese men were no longer in positions of great power or authority, except as Buddhist monks, and even those with some power were subordinate to men who were entirely foreign, that is to say European. We have already seen that in early modern Burma, women occupied a clearly subordinate political, economic and ritual status to men. But now the wonderful 'traditional' freedom of Burmese women became part and parcel of colonial thinking about the country and, again, the nationalist imagination. There must have been, by the turn of the century, a considerable demographic shift throughout the Irrawaddy valley and delta in the population balance between men and women. One would suspect, given both the considerable death toll of early Konbaung military campaigns and the legal tolerance of polygamy, that there was a significantly greater number of adult women than men. Under British rule, not only would this imbalance end, but there would be a huge influx of foreign men, mainly from other Indian provinces, but also from Europe and China. As late as the early nineteenth century, foreign men visiting the country were encouraged to take local wives or mistresses.[96] In great contrast, by the early twentieth century, the practice by which British men took Burmese mistresses met with strong disapproval. We might note that the practice also met with some concern in the Rangoon secretariat, where the Chief Commissioner in 1890 sent out a 'confidential circular' calling for these relationships to end. That weekend at the Rangoon Turf Club, one horse was named 'CCCC' and another 'Physiological Necessity'. The practice continued and was to become an issue of early nationalist concern.

All of these changes – the construction of a relatively egalitarian and rural society in the valley, the complete collapse of the old upper classes at Mandalay, the entrenchment of ethnic over class differences – all helped to form the Burma we still know today. Over the course of the nineteenth century, a great transition had been made, from the early modern Ava-based polity of Alaungpaya and his sons, to the radically different Burma of our own time.

[96] See, for example, Pemberton, 'Journey from Munipoor to Ava'.

Conclusion: The making of modern Burma

The deposed King Thibaw of Burma lived in virtual seclusion with his wife and family for the better part of thirty years. They resided in a large rambling house just outside Ratanagiri, a small town along western India's hot and humid Konkan coast. Though not strictly confined to the house, he could only leave his compound with permission, and rarely ventured outside. He took little exercise, ate copious amounts of fried pork, and was surrounded by a still considerable retinue of servants.[1]

On 11 October 1915, just after the long rains had finally ended, the old king's second daughter disappeared without warning to the residence of the Political Officer. She was a friend of the Political Officer's wife, Mrs Head, and had left to solicit her help. For several weeks, the Second Princess, as she was known, had carried on, against her parents express wishes, a relationship with a former royal secretary named Khin Maung Lat. A few years back, her elder sister, the First Princess had married against Thibaw's wishes, an Indian who was employed at the house. This was seen as a most unsuitable match, but the old king and queen later relented and the young couple, with their little daughter, were eventually welcome back. But here Thibaw had drawn the line. Marrying a foreigner was one thing. Marrying a Burmese beneath one's class, a Burmese descended from court retainers and a former servant of the crown, this was beyond the pale. For several years, a succession of British officials, Collectors and Governors had schemed to find eligible partners for Thibaw's four daughters, all of whom were well into their twenties. But the king had rejected all the unmarried Burmese princes British civil servants had proudly produced on a list. At this point, even the Viceroy himself, Lord Minto, and his Foreign Secretary, Sir Louis Dane, became involved. Playing matchmaker, they introduced the princesses to the crown prince of Sikkim, the future *chogyal*. But the heir to the Gangtok throne, though initially declaring some interest, declined any talk of marriage, commenting only that the young women were not fluent in English. So the matter had rested, temporarily.

[1] On Thibaw's exile, see N.S. Desai, *Deposed King Theebaw of Burma in India*, Delhi, 1968.

But now the Second Princess was gone. Thibaw, immediately on hearing the news, had dispatched his car and driver to fetch his runaway daughter. An hour or so later, the black Ford Model T pulled back into the compound and the ex-Lord of the White Elephant rushed out onto the driveway. On seeing the car empty, except for the driver, he realised the princess had refused to come back. He had a heart attack and died days later. He was 58 years old.

His death and the end of the Great War a few years later marked a change in British attitudes towards the Burmese royal family. All senior members of the family – descendants of Tharrawaddy – had been forced to leave Mandalay in 1885–6. Most of them were sent to Lower Burma. Many others were scattered around India. These were now allowed to return, though not to Mandalay, and they remained under careful surveillance and supervision. Supayalat herself lived for nearly ten years in a modest bungalow off Churchill Road in Rangoon, with two daughters, until her death in 1925. Her funeral was seized upon by young nationalists and held in grand style. Thibaw's remains had been cremated and then buried in Ratanagiri, but Supayalat was allowed a royal tomb, at the foot of the Shwédagon Pagoda. But except for this one occasion, and apart for nationalists' marking of the exile of Thibaw on 28 November 1885 as a day of mourning, the returned royal family was largely forgotten. The young politicians of the independence movement looked to Sinn Fein, the Fabian Society, the Indian National Congress and the rise of Japan for their inspiration, and not to the last remnants of the House of Alaungpaya and the lost world which they represented.

In the chapters above, I have tried to paint, in broad and tentative strokes, a portrait of how the old world of the Court of Ava and the Irrawaddy countryside was transformed into the British Burma of the twentieth century. Long-term demographic and commercial processes; the gradual displacement by military force of Ava by Calcutta from the Brahmaputra and Irrawaddy basins; the reaction of the Burmese government to colonial expansion and her own reduced position; contemporary developments in China; the rise and fall of global prices; and other lesser factors: all these contributed to decades of sustained innovation, change and crisis in the territories which became modern Burma.

The transition from the Ava-based imperial polity of the late eighteenth and early nineteenth centuries to the Burma of the colonial and post-colonial period was a product of the interaction between these and other developments discussed above. By 1885, Calcutta was in a strong enough position to decide unilaterally the fate of the rump Ava polity. But the impact of the reforms attempted by the government at Mandalay, together with a long history of problematic bilateral relations, moved Calcutta's hand in the direction of direct rule and in the direction of a radical break with the past. Like a house which had been partly demolished for renovation, but never properly rebuilt for lack of funds, King Mindon's reforms had left the British, as the new owners, with little option but to design the renovations themselves with the materials at hand.

The last stand of a non-European autonomy

Burma is one of a handful of small non-European states which emerged under the shadow of growing Western power and rapid technological change. By the mid-nineteenth century in the many parts of the globe still not under direct colonial rule, existing polities struggled to redefine themselves and equip themselves to survive better within the new international order. Egypt, Persia, Siam and Vietnam are a few of the several other examples of countries whose governments attempted significant programmes of modernisation, only to come under varying degrees of European domination. Anthony Reid, in his introduction to a recent collection of essays on this period, has remarked on the ways in which colonial and nationalist historians have tended to neglect the often far-reaching reforms attempted in these final years of local autonomy.[2]

Of all these other states, Siam stands out as the most interesting contrast, given the long history of cultural exchange and warfare between Siam and Burma and various similarities in religion and political and social institutions. For example, both royal courts, at Ava and Ayuthaya, placed emphasis on elite control of manpower as well as on the role of the monarch as patron of Buddhism.[3] The contrast is all the more intriguing given Siam's success in preserving her nominal sovereignty and a fair degree of autonomy, while Burma succumbed to perhaps the most direct

---

[2] Anthony Reid (ed.), *The Last Stand of Asian Autonomies: Responses to Modernity in the Diverse States of Southeast Asia and Korea, 1750–1900*, London, 1997, pp. 1–27.

[3] Akin Rabibhadana, *The Organization of Thai Society in the Early Bangkok Period, 1782–1873*, Ithaca, 1969; and 'Clientship and Class Structure in the Early Bangkok Period' in G. William Skinner and A. Thomas Kirsch (eds.), *Change and Persistence in Thai Society: Essays in Honor of Lauriston Sharp*, Ithaca, 1975.

rule in all of the small Asian and North African states still independent in the late nineteenth century.

Mindon and his contemporary Mongut both pursued comparable policies of administrative centralisation, economic development and an accommodating approach towards encroaching Western imperialism.[4] Furthermore, the Bowring Treaty, which the Siamese government felt compelled to accept in 1855, was not dissimilar to the commercial treaties under which vastly increased foreign economic penetration and increased Western political influence became possible in Burma. Both states were by the early 1870s faced with the challenges of avoiding financial insolvency without provoking rebellion. They stepped up reform measures, especially the implementation of new systems of taxation which could exploit increases in agricultural production, and pushed through various infrastructure modernisations. But while widespread social unrest and eventually a virtual collapse of state authority followed Mindon's death in 1878, Mongut's death was followed by continued and even more successful programmes of 'modernisation'. In Burma the unrest was followed by a transition to formal empire, while in Siam economic and political reforms continued together with informal arrangements of accommodation with the West.

Two explanations are normally offered to explain the vastly different fates of Burma and Siam. One explanation centres on the nature of the royal succession and the politics within the respective governments. In Burma, Mindon's death led to bitter intra-elite conflict and the emergence of a weak king. Thibaw was surrounded by a reactionary palace clique and instability in his court led to severe repression. In contrast, an orderly succession followed Mongut's death in 1868 and the Bangkok officialdom under Chuan Bunnag governed effectively during the new king's minority. Though Mongut's son and successor Chulalongkorn later regained power for the monarchy, he proved himself to be a man of considerable vision and ability and led Siam successfully into the next century. A second explanation offered is that Siam was permitted to maintain her independence in order to serve as a buffer state between expanding British and French empires. By the late 1880s only Siam remained between British India and French Indochina with neither country enjoying a clear dominance over the Bangkok regime.

---

[4] Charnvit Kasetsiri, *The Rise of Ayudhaya*, Kuala Lumpur, 1976; Hong Lysa, *Thailand in the Nineteenth Century*, Singapore, 1984, pp. 111–30; David Wyatt, *A Short History of Thailand*, New Haven, 1984, pp. 181–212.

But I would argue that an even more important factor was their very different structures of foreign trade. The rump Burmese kingdom's economy under informal empire had become dangerously dependent on the export of a few primary commodities – cotton and teak in particular. At the same time, rice was being imported in ever larger quantities, draining the country of cash. Siam, in strong contrast, was a rice-exporting nation, having faced no similar annexation of its most productive agricultural lands. While Britain had annexed Burma's maritime provinces, Siam had lost only its peripheral holdings in Laos, Cambodia and Malaya. The world depression of the 1870s led to a dramatic decline in the relative prices of nearly all primary commodities, including all of Burma's main exports. However, and very importantly, international rice prices stayed the same or even rose. Thus, at this time of attempted reform, the Siamese state enjoyed the profits of growing international trade. Burma, however, was plunged into increasing economic hardship and fiscal collapse. Even if Thibaw's accession had not been followed by political instability, the Mandalay government by the 1880s would have been extremely hard pressed to avert the crisis which led indirectly to colonial rule.

This contrast between Burma and Siam helps us then to understand the importance of local conditions in the complex dynamic which informed the nature of European expansion. Siam's geopolitical position and the good government it enjoyed under Chulalongkorn were certainly important factors behind its successful strategy to preserve its sovereignty in the age of imperialism. But we might speculate that had Siam faced the sort of political crisis which engulfed Upper Burma in the 1880s, colonial powers might have similarly considered military intervention and perhaps an Anglo-French partition of the kingdom.

Contemporary Egypt was one country where intervention and colonial occupation did take place and a comparison between Egypt and Burma reveals a number of similarities in the local circumstances leading to this intervention. In both cases, efforts by the state to promote economic development failed as the state lost its autonomy to colonial powers and the economy became more fully integrated into global markets. At the turn of the eighteenth century the two countries were both agricultural societies with roughly the same population. In Egypt, under the reigns of Muhammad Ali (1805–49), Said (1854–62) and Ismail (1863–79), efforts were made to reassert weakening central authority, including a modernisation of the army and the bureaucracy and an overhaul of the revenue system.[5] As in Burma, local elites were bypassed as the state began direct collection of taxes through government agents and established a series of monopolies on virtually every type of agricultural produce. The rents thus derived from the state's role in exporting Egyptian commodities and from more efficient taxation were used to finance various modernisation efforts – in industry, infrastructural development, education and the military – and these efforts were seen as vital in developing Egypt into a viable nation-state. These plans never materialised, however, for two main reasons, the weakness of state institutions, i.e. their inability to play the critical roles assigned to them as part of the modernisation drive, and the effects of European commercial and financial expansion.

Muhammad Ali attempted to profit from European trade while at the same time limiting European penetration of the economy. But, as in Upper Burma, pressure soon forced an opening up of the Egyptian market and the abandonment of the state monopolies which had become a critical part of the state revenue structure.[6] The middle of the century witnessed a dramatic expansion of cotton production, especially during the American Civil War. Trade was conducted directly between local landlords and foreign firms and during the same period the import of British products steadily rose. European banks became increasingly involved in the economy and the Egyptian government itself became a borrower from 1862. With economic transformation came also important social changes, including the growth of a landlord and bureaucratic class and a rise in the position of the foreign community. Egypt's bankruptcy in 1875 then precipitated a series of measures imposed by lending institutions which in turn increased European control over the administration.[7] This expanding foreign control then led to a popular 'nationalist' movement which was seen as threatening to European interests and which eventually led in 1882 to British military occupation.[8] Landowners, fearing tax rises, and bureaucrats and army officers, resentful of increasing European control, were among the main constituents of the nationalist reaction to Western expansion.[9]

[5] Roger Owen, *Cotton and the Egyptian Economy 1820–1914*, London, 1969, pp. 352–68; and 'Egypt and Europe: From French Expedition to British Occupation', in Roger Owen and Bob Sutcliffe (eds.), *Studies in the Theory of Imperialism*, London, 1972, pp. 198–200.   [6] Owen, *Cotton*, pp. 200–1.   [7] *Ibid.*, pp. 205–7.
[8] A. Scholch, *Egypt for the Egyptians: The Socio-Political Crisis in Egypt 1878–1882*, London, 1981, p. 303.
[9] R. Robinson and J. Gallagher, 'The Imperialism of Free Trade', *Economic History Review*, 6 (1953), 1–15.

Thus in both Burma and Egypt we see local reactions to European expansion leading to crisis and intervention. In these very similar stories of the failure of informal empire, instability and state insolvency were caused in large part by the revenue restraints imposed by Western countries on indigenous modernising regimes. In both cases as well, the rise and fall of cotton prices and, more generally, dependence on global markets, weakened governments desperate to find the funds with which to finance reform. There were of course a number of critical differences. For example, Western banks played a much greater role in Egypt's economy and, eventually, in the decision for intervention. Other European powers were also more involved, and there were already approximately 100,000 Europeans resident in the country. The khedive Tewfiq and others in the Ottoman-derived Turco-Circassian ruling class, as outsiders themselves, were prepared to collaborate with Britian and the other colonial powers to a much greater extent than the Court of Ava. And finally, there was no large scale rural resistance accompanying the early occupation as there was in the Irrawaddy valley.

At least in part as a result of these differences, Egypt in the 1880s experienced a much less radical break with her past, and even the British occupation itself was undertaken in the name of the Ottoman sultan. In general, however, a comparison between the two cases helps demonstrate the important role played by local conditions on the final form of Western domination and, more specifically, on the interactions between European commercial expansion, local state reactions and the transition to direct colonial rule.

In all of these smaller polities which remained independent into the mid-nineteenth century, notions of modern statehood grappled with existing webs of government and with an ever more militarily superior West. While the final nature of Western domination by the end of the century differed considerably from state to state, in all of these countries, as in Burma, the outcome was determined to a large extent by the local responses to contemporary challenges.

Burma *contra* India

At the same time as Alaungpaya and his sons were creating the largest dominion Ava had ever known, large swathes of the old Mughal empire were coming under British administration. Along the Ganges valley and in Bengal, south India and elsewhere, the East India Company gradually achieved political supremacy after a long commercial and military presence. But in these areas, colonial rule was attenuated by the need for alien administrators to incorporate indigenous elites into new state structures, to better understand local society and to accommodate existing structures of social organisation. In a way, the Ava kingdom might be compared with some of the similar sized Mughal successor states such as Mysore or the Punjab which also existed on the edge of British power, and which eventually came under Company rule.[10] But in at least two important ways, Burma's experience was distinctive.

First is simply the timing. By the time Mindon was beginning his reform initiatives, all of the important independent states in what became India had been absorbed into the British Raj. All had been part of the Mughal polity and were never in a position, as was Mandalay, of attempting to become full members of the late-nineteenth-century international system. Furthermore, their absorption into British India, whether as princely states or under direct rule, took place in a time of relative technological equality, thus compelling colonial policy-makers to find methods of achieving domination which did not rely solely on military coercion. By 1885, industrial England with the resources of all India behind it was easily able to impose an entirely new administration on Upper Burma in a way which would have been impossible either in the Irrawaddy valley or anywhere else just a few decades earlier.

Secondly, Britain's marked superiority *vis-à-vis* Mandalay after 1853, made acceptable a relatively poor knowledge of local conditions. A colonial officer in the 1880s remarked that 'our ideas and customs remain as alien to them, as theirs are to us', a remark unlikely to have been made with reference to polities within what had been the Mughal empire. Very few British officials ever learned Burmese until the twentieth century, and those that did came from an initial and perhaps formative experience somewhere else in the empire. In 1885–6, a combination of relatively poor information and the luxury of largely ignoring local elite groups moved policy-makers towards effecting a much greater departure with the past than nearly anywhere else in the region.

By 1885–6, despite Mandalay's annexation to British India, 'Burma' was already seen as 'essentially' different from the rest of 'India'. As early

---

[10] C.A. Bayly, *Indian Society and the Making of the British Empire*, Cambridge, 1988; *Information and Empire*, Cambridge, 1997; Sugata Bose and Ayesha Jalal, *Modern South Asia: History, Culture and Political Economy*, London, 1997, pp. 48–87.

as the eighteenth century, if not earlier, Ava saw the various peoples to their west as belonging to a different category of descent than the Myanma. The English, as well, often made comparisons between 'Burmese' and 'Indians'. But this distinction was reinforced, rather than dissipated, by the country's incorporation into the Indian empire, leading to separation in 1937, and a very different subsequent history. In part, this was the result of colonial scholarship which viewed India in terms of essential categories such as caste which were not believed to be present in Burma. Burma was seen as an obvious 'other' to India, with Buddhism and an egalitarian social order being viewed as important local characteristics. But on the Burmese side as well, developments pushed towards a distinctive, ethnically based identity. The war of 1824–6 had shorn Ava of all its western possessions, possessions which were under much greater Hindu and Brahmanical influence. In addition, she was reduced to a relatively homogeneous core which, as we have seen, made easier a stronger sense of local patriotism. Local dissatisfaction at the large-scale immigration of labourers and money-lenders from far-away parts of India, as well as the development of a modern Burmese nationalism, then solidified this sense of difference. The Irrawaddy valley's colonial experience made Burma a 'south-east Asian' rather than a 'south Asian' nation.

Reinterpreting modern Burmese history

And what does all this mean for contemporary Burma, a country which has experienced almost incessant armed conflict, international isolation, enduring poverty and the gradual consolidation of military government over the past five decades. Burma is often portrayed as a 'rich country gone wrong', a country which was blessed at independence with everything from a high literacy rate to plentiful natural resources, but which then inexplicably fell far behind less well endowed neighbours such as Korea or Thailand.[11] But while an explanation for Burma's current troubles are well beyond the scope of this book, I would like to point to two colonial legacies, often ignored, which are related to my arguments above. The first is a legacy of institutional weakness. Simply put, the late nineteenth century, as we have seen, witnessed the collapse of many

[11] See, for example, Stan Sesser, 'Burma: A Rich Country Gone Wrong', *New Yorker*, 1990, reprinted in *Lands of Charm and Cruelty: Travels in Southeast Asia*, New York, 1993, pp. 177–239.

important early modern political and social institutions. These were then replaced by colonial institutions, unrooted in local society, which were themselves shattered in the aftermath of the Japanese conquest of 1941–2. With the exception of the Sangha, one is hard pressed to identify any supra-local institution which carried over from pre-colonial through colonial times, and even the Sangha, stripped of its role as educator as well as of royal patronage and supervision, underwent a profound transformation. Unlike Thailand, no older institutions, such as the monarchy, carried over to ballast newer forces in society. And unlike other British Asian possessions at independence, such as India, Ceylon or Malaya, Burma's colonial era structures – the army, police, civil service and judiciary – were singularly fragile, having had barely fifty years of life in the old heartland. Thus Burma at independence faced a weak institutional legacy, a vacuum which the new war-time army was soon able to fill.

The army was able to fill this vacuum in part because of another important legacy: Burmese ethnic nationalism. As we have seen, the transition to a reduced Ava polity, to a core area homogeneous in language and religion, facing imminent foreign domination after decades of her own military expansion, merged easily into a more modern nationalism, still based around a central Myanma identity. But this was an identity which excluded not just 'Indians', as mentioned above, but also many other people living within the boundaries of British Burma. A comparison might be made with Indonesia. In the Dutch East Indies, modern nationalism emerged only well into the colonial period, leading to the construction of perhaps a Javanese-centred but still relatively inclusive national identity. Both the name 'Indonesia' and the new nation's adopted language of Bahasa Indonesia show an inclusiveness lacking in post-colonial 'Myanmar'. In Burma the strength and political dominance of a Burmese/Myanma identity based on older Ava-based memories has never allowed the development of a newer identity which would incorporate the divers peoples inhabiting the modern state. Instead, it has led since 1948 to recurrent warfare, the growth of a large military machine and an army rule which seems unlikely to end.

Bibliography

Primary sources

Pre-colonial and early colonial sources in Burmese

Ba Thein, *Ko Hkayaing Thamaing* (History of Kyauksè), Mandalay, 1910.

Kala, *Maha Yazawindawgyi* (The Great Chronicle), reprint, Rangoon, 1960.

The Kanimyo Sitkè (Mindin Yaza), *Mandalay Yadanapon Mahayazawindaw-gyi* (History of Mandalay), reprint, Rangoon, 1969.

The Kinwun Mingyi, *Kinwun Mingyi London Myo Thwa Nezinhmat Sadan* (London Diary of the Kinwun Mingyi), reprint, Rangoon, 1953.

Pannasami, *Thathanawuntha* (History of the Religion), reprint, London, 1952.

Pe Maung Tin and Furnival, J.S., eds., *Zambudipa Oksaung Kyan*, reprint, Rangoon, 1960.

Pe Maung Tin and Luce, G.H. (trans.), *The Glass Palace Chronicle of the Kings of Burma*, Rangoon, 1910.

Pe Maung Tin and Luce, G.H., eds., *Selections from the Inscriptions of Pagan*, Rangoon, 1928.

Than Tun, ed., *Royal Orders of Burma 1598–1885*, part 9, Kyoto, 1989.

Tin (Mandalay), *Konbaungzet Maha Yazawindawgyi* (Great Royal Chronicle of the Konbaung Dynasty), Rangoon, 1905.

Tin (Pagan), *Myanma Min Okchokpon Sadan* (Documents Relating to the Administration of the Burmese Kings), 5 vols., Rangoon, 1931–3.

Pre-colonial Burmese sources in translation

The Kinwun Mingyi, *Translation of a Digest of the Burmese Buddhist Law Concerning Inheritance and Marriages*, Rangoon, 1903–09.

Sao Saimong Mangrai, *The Padaeng Chronicle and the Jeng Tung State Chronicle Translated*, Ann Arbor, 1981.

Trager, F.N. and Koenig, William, eds., *Burmese Sit-tans, 1764–1826: Records of Rural Life and Administration*, Tucson, 1979.

India Office archives (India Office Library, London)

Correspondence
Secret Correspondence with India.
Political Correspondence with India.
Political and Secret Correspondence with India.

Proceedings
India Foreign (Secret) Proceedings.
India Foreign (Political) Proceedings.
Proceedings of the Finance Departments (Upper Burma).
India Judicial Proceedings (Upper Burma).
Revenue and Agriculture Department Proceedings (Upper Burma).
Burma Finance Proceedings (Upper Burma).
Burma Home Proceedings.
Burma Judicial Proceedings.
Burma Military Proceedings.
Upper Burma Proceedings (Foreign Department).
Upper Burma Rulings.

Manuscript collections (India Office Library, London)

Papers of Frederick Temple Hamilton-Temple Blackwood, First Marquess of
     Dufferin and Ava, Microfilm Reels 516–34.
Papers of Sir Edward Sladen, MSS. Eur. E. 290/12.
Papers of Sir Herbert Thirkell White, MSS. Eur. E. 254.

Government of India official publications: settlement reports

Furnival, J.S., *Report on the Settlement Operations in the Myingyan District,
     Season 1909–1913*, Rangoon, 1915.
Gibson, R.A., *Report on the Settlement Operations in the Meiktila District,
     Season 1896–1898*, Rangoon, 1900.
   *Report on the Settlement Operations in the Yamethin District, Season
     1898–1901*, Rangoon, 1902.
   *Report on the Revision Settlement Operations in the Mandalay District,
     Season 1903–1905*, Rangoon, 1905.
Hertz, W.A., *Report on the Settlement Operations in the Magwe District, Season
     1897–1903*, Rangoon, 1905.
Owens, F.C., *Report on the Settlement Operations in the Pakokku District,
     Season 1905–1910*, Rangoon, 1910.

Parlett, L.M., *Report on the Settlement Operations in the Sagaing District, Season 1893–1900*, Rangoon, 1903.

Parsons, O.S., *Report on the Settlement Operations in the Minbu District, Season 1893–1897*, Rangoon, 1900.

Reynolds, H.O., *Report on the Revision Settlement Operations in the Magwe District, Season 1915–1919*, Rangoon, 1921.

Westlake, S., *Report on the Settlement Operations in the Kyauksè District, Season 1890–1891 and Part of Season 1891–1892*, Rangoon, 1892.

Williamson, A., *Report on the Revision Settlement Operations in the Shwebo District, Season 1918–1923*, Rangoon, 1924.

Government of India official publications: gazetteers

Dawson, G.W., *Burma Gazetteer – Bhamo District*, 2 vols., Rangoon, 1912.

Scott, J.G. and Hardiman, J.P., comps., *Gazetteer of Upper Burma and the Shan States*, 5 vols. in 2 parts, Rangoon, 1900–01 (cited in notes as *GUBSS*).

Searle, H.F., *Burma Gazetteer – Mandalay District*, 2 vols., Rangoon, 1928.

Spearman, H.S., *British Burma Gazetteer*, 2 vols., Rangoon, 1879–80.

Stewart, J.A., *Burma Gazetteer – Kyauksè District*, 2 vols., Rangoon, 1925.

Wilkie, R.S., *Burma Gazetteer –Yamèthin District*, 2 vols., Rangoon, 1934.

Williamson, A., *Burma Gazetteer – Shwebo District*, 2 vols., Rangoon, 1929.

Government of India official publications: annual reports and censuses

Census of India, 1891, Burma Report 9, Rangoon, 1892.

Census of India, 1901, Burma Report 12, Rangoon, 1902.

Report on the Administration of Burma, 1861/2–1909/10.

Annual Statement of the Trade and Navigation of the Province of British Burma Having a Seaborne Trade, 1868/9–1874/5.

Annual Report of Maritime Trade and Customs.

Report on the Inland Trade of Burma.

Report on the Administration of Civil Justice, 1891–1900.

Criminal Justice Report of Lower Burma, 1886–90.

Report on Civil Justice in Burma, 1891–1904.

Report on the Sanitary Administration of Burma, 1890–1900.

Report on the Revenue Administration of Burma.

Government of India official publications: other

History of the Third Burmese War (1885, 1886, 1887), Period One, Calcutta, 1887.

Official Narrative of the Expedition to Explore the Trade Routes to China via Bhamo under the Guidance of Major E.B. Sladen, Political Agent, Mandalay, with Connected Papers, 1871.

Report on the Petroleum Industry in Upper Burma from the End of the Last Century to the Beginning of 1891, Rangoon, 1892.

The Upper Burma Land Revenue Manual, Rangoon, 1900.

British parliamentary publications

Papers Relating to Hostilities with Burma, London, 1852.

Papers Relating to British Burma. Correspondence Relative to the Treaty of the 26th October 1867, London, 1868.

Correspondence Relating to the Affairs of Burmah Since the Death of the Late King, London, 1885.

Correspondence Relating to the Affairs of Upper Burmah 1880–85, London, 1885.

Further Correspondence Relating to Burmah, London, 1886.

Non-British government publications

Government of China, *Chinese Maritime Customs Decennial Reports 1892–1901*.

Pre-colonial and early colonial unpublished sources in English

Phayre, Arthur, 'A Historical Memorandum on the Burma Hunters Family from Beginning to the Present 1866 AD', British Library, Oriental Manuscript, OR3470.

Pre-colonial and early colonial published sources in English

Baird, J.G.A., ed., *Private Letters of the Marquess of Dalhousie*, Edinburgh, 1910.

Black, Charles Drummond, *The Marquess of Dufferin and Ava: Diplomatist, Viceroy, Statesman*, London, 1903.

Brown, R. Grant, *Burma As I Saw It 1889–1917: With a Chapter on Recent Events*, London, 1924.

Browne, Edmund, *The Coming of the Great Queen: A Narrative of the Acquisition of Burma*, London, 1888.

Browne, Horace, *Reminiscences of the Court of Mandalay*, London, 1907.

Burney, Henry, 'On the Population of the Burman Empire', *Journal of the Royal Statistical Society*, 4 (1842), 335–47.

Colbeck, J.A., *Letters from Mandalay*, Knaresborough, 1892.

Collimore, D.H., *The Burmese: What Do They Know of Medicine?*, Madras, 1875.

Cox, Hiram, *Journal of a Residence in the Burman Empire and More Particularly at the Court of Amarapoorah*, London, 1821.

Crawfurd, J., *Journal of an Embassy from the Governor General of India to the Court of Ava in the Year 1826*, London, 1834.

Crosthwaithe, Charles, *The Pacification of Burma*, London, 1912.

Dalrymple, A., *Oriental Repertory*, London, 1808.

Dautremer, Joseph, *Burma under British Rule*, trans. George Scott, London, 1913.

Edmonds, Paul, *Peacocks and Pagodas*, London, 1924.

Ferrars, Max and Bertha, *Burma*, London, 1900.

Fielding-Hall, H., *The Soul of a People*, London, 1898.

Forbes, Charles, *British Burma and its People*, London, 1878.

Fytche, Albert, *Burma Past and Present with Personal Reminiscences of the Country in Two Volumes*, London, 1878.

Geary, Grattan, *Burma, After the Conquest, Viewed in its Political, Social and Commercial Aspects from Mandalay*, London, 1886.

Gouger, H., *Personal Narrative of Two Years' Imprisonment in Burmah*, London, 1860.

Hall, D.G.E., ed., *The Dalhousie–Phayre Correspondence, 1852–56*, London, 1932.

   Michael Symes: Journal of his Second Embassy to the Court of Ava in 1807, London, 1955.

Ireland, A., *The Province of Burma*, 2 vols., Boston, 1907.

Jardine, John, *Notes on Buddhist Law*, Rangoon, 1882.

Laurie, W.F.B., *Our Burmese Wars*, London, 1885.

Marks, E., *Forty Years in Burma*, London, 1917.

Mitton, G.E., *Scott of the Shan Hills*, London, 1936.

Nisbit, J., *Burma Under British Rule and Before*, 2 vols., London, 1901.

Noetling, Fritz, *Report on the Petroleum Industry in Upper Burma from the End of the Last Century to the Beginning of 1891*, Rangoon, 1892.

O'Conner, V.C. Scott, *Mandalay and Other Cities of the Past in Burma*, London, 1907.

   The Silken East: A Record of Life and Travel in Burma, London, 1905.

Phayre, Arthur, 'Private Journal of Sir Arthur Phayre' in Henry Yule, *Mission to the Court of Ava in 1855*, reprint, Kuala Lumpur, 1968.

Richardson, D., ed., *The Damethat or the Laws of Menoo*, Moulmein, 1847.

Sangermano, V., *A Description of the Burmese Empire*, reprint, London, 1966.

Scott, J.G., *Burma: A Handbook of Practical Information*, London, 1921.
  Burma: From Earliest Times to the Present Day, London, 1924.

Shakespear, L.W., *History of Upper Burma, Assam, and the Northeast Indian Frontier*, London, 1914.

Shway Yoe (J.G. Scott), *The Burman: His Life and Notions*, reprint, Edinburgh, 1989.

Smeaton, Donald MacKenzie, *The Loyal Karens of Burma*, London, 1887.

Stuart, J.M.B., *Old Burmese Irrigation Works, Being a Short Description of the Pre-British Irrigation Works of Upper Burma*, Rangoon, 1913.

Symes, Michael, *An Account of an Embassy to the Kingdom of Ava, Sent by the Governor-General of India in the Year 1795*, London, 1800.

Taw Sein Ko, *Burmese Sketches*, Rangoon, 1913.

Temple, Richard, *Thirty Seven Nats*, London, 1906.

Tha Aung and Mya Din, 'The Pacification of Burma: A Vernacular History' (edited H.R. Alexander), *Journal of the Burma Research Society*, 25 (1936), 80–136.

Trant, T.A., *Two Years in Ava: From May 1824 to May 1826*, London, 1827.

White, Herbert, *A Civil Servant in Burma*, London, 1913.

Winston, W.R., *Four Years in Upper Burma*, London, 1892.

Wood, W.A.R., *A History of Siam from the Earliest Times to the Year A.D. 1781*, Bangkok, 1859.

Yule, Henry, *Mission to the Court of Ava in 1855*, reprint, Kuala Lumpur, 1968.

Yule, Henry, and Burnell, A.C, *Hobson-Jobson*, London, 1903.

Newspapers

The Burma Gazette, 1888.
The Times, 1885–6.

Secondary sources

Unpublished secondary sources in Burmese

Ohn Kyi, 'Salin Thugaung Thamaing (Akyin)' in *Bama Thamaing* (Studies in Burmese History) by colleagues of Dr Thau Tun (mimeo.).

Published secondary sources in Burmese

Ba Lwin, *Abhisha Husseini Htayruppatti Kyan*, Mandalay, 1970.
Ba U, *Mandalay Centenary: History of Burmese Muslims*, Mandalay, 1959.

Myanma Okchokyay Pyinnya, Mandalay, n.d.

Chan Mya, 'Shay Hkit Pyinnashi Yway Pwe', in *Myanma-sa Pyiannya Padetha Sasaung*, 1 (1966), 250–85.

Maung Maung Tin, *Sadanmya*, Rangoon, 1975.

Shwenanthon Wawhara Abidan (Dictionary of Palace Terminology), Rangoon, 1975.

Ahmat-saya Pokko-mya, Rangoon, 1975.

Maung Tin (ed.), *Yaw Mingyi U Po Hlaing Attuppatti hnin Raza Dhamma Thingaha Kyan*, Rangoon, 1992.

Hmawbi Saya Thein, *Pyinnyashi Gyi Mya Akyaung*, Rangoon, 1966.

Myanma Wyngyi Hmugyi Mya Akyaung, Rangoon, 1967.

Saya O, *Kohkayaing Thaming-taw Attuppatti*, Mandalay, 1925.

Tin Ohn, *Yaw atwinwun U Po Hlaing*, Rangoon, 1969.

Government of Burma publications in English

Government of Burma, Economic and Social Board, Office of the Prime Minister, *A Study of the Social and Economic History of Burma (The British Period)*. Part V: *Burma Under the Chief Commissioners 1886-7 to 1896-7*, Rangoon, 1957.

Unpublished secondary sources in English

Croziet, Ralph Charles, 'Antecedents of the Burma Road: Nineteenth Century British Interest in Trans-Burma Trade Routes to China', M.A. dissertation, University of Washing, Seattle, 1960.

Koenig, William J., 'The Early Kon-Baung Policy, 1752–1819: A Study of Politics, Administration and Social Organization', Ph.D. dissertation, University of London, 1978.

Kyaw Thet, 'Burma's Relations with her Eastern Neighbours in the Konbaung Period, 1752–1819', Ph.D. dissertation, University of London, 1950.

Myo Myint, 'The Politics of Survival in Burma: Diplomacy and Statecraft in the Reign of King Mindon 1853–1878', Ph.D. dissertation, Cornell University, 1987.

Reynolds, Craig, 'The Buddhist Monkhood in Nineteenth Century Thailand', Ph.D. dissertation, Cornell University, 1973.

Thant Myint-U, 'The Crisis of the Burmese State and the Origins of British Rule in Upper Burma (1853–1900)', Ph.D. dissertation, Cambridge University, 1996.

Thaung, 'British Interest in Trans-Burma Trade Routes to China: 1826–1876',

Ph.D. dissertation, University of London, 1955.

Toe Hla, 'Moneylending and Contractual Thet-kayits', Ph.D. dissertation, Northern Illinois University, 1987.

Published secondary sources in English

Adas, Michael, 'Imperialist Rhetoric and Modern Historiography: The Case of Lower Burma before and after Conquest', *Journal of Southeast Asian Studies*, 3 (1972), 174–90.

  The Burma Delta: Economic Development and Social Change on an Asian Rice Frontier, 1852–1941, Madison, 1974.

  Prophets of Rebellion: Millenarian Protest Movements Against European Colonial Order, Chapel Hill, 1979.

  '"Moral Economy" or "Contest State": Elite Demands and the Origins of Peasant Protest in Southeast Asia', *Journal of Social History*, 13 (1980), 521–47.

  'From Avoidance to Confrontation: Peasant Protest in Precolonial and Colonial Southeast Asia', *Comparative Studies in Society and History*, 23 (1981), 217–47.

Akin Rabibhadana, *The Organization of Thai Society in the Early Bangkok Period, 1782–1873*, Ithaca, 1969.

  'Clientship and Class Structure in the Early Bangkok Period', in G. William Skinner and A. Thomas Kirsch, eds., *Change and Persistence in Thai Society: Essays in Honor of Lauriston Sharp*, Ithaca, 1975.

Allott, Anna, *The End of the First Anglo-Burmese War: The Burmese Chronicle Account of How the 1826 Treaty of Yandabo Was Negotiated*, Bangkok, 1994.

Allott, Anna, Herbert, Patricia and Okell, John, 'Burma', in Patricia Herbert and Anthony Milner, eds., *Southeast Asian Languages and Literatures: A Select Guide*, Whiting Bay, n.d.

Andaya, Barbara Watson, 'Religious Developments in Southeast Asia c. 1500–1800', in Nicholas Tarling, ed., *Cambridge History of Southeast Asia*, vol. I, Cambridge, 1993.

Anderson, Benedict, *Imagined Communities: Reflections on the Origin and Spread of Nationalism*, London, 1983.

Andrus, J. Russell, *Burmese Economic Life*, Stanford, 1948.

Aung-Thwin, Michael, 'Kingship, the *Sangha*, and Society in Pagan', in K.R. Hall and J.K. Whitmore, eds., *Explorations in Early Southeast Asian History: The Origins of Southeast Asian Statecraft*, Ann Arbor, 1976.

  'The Role of Sasana Reform in Burmese Economic History: Economic

Dimensions of a Religious Purification', *Journal of Asian Studies*, 38 (1979), 671–88.

'Prophecies, Omens and Dialogue: Tools of the Trade in Burmese Historiography', in David Wyatt and Alexander Woodside, eds., *Moral Order and the Question of Change: Essays on Southeast Asian Thought*, New Haven, 1982.

'Athi, Hkyun-daw and Hpaya-kyun' in Anthony Reid, ed., *Slavery, Bondage and Dependency in Southeast Asia*, London, 1983.

'The British "Pacification" of Burma: Order Without Meaning', *Journal of Southeast Asian Studies*, 16 (1985), 245–62.

Aung Tun Thet, *Burmese Entrepreneurship: Creative Responses in the Colonial Economy*, Stuttgart, 1989.

Aye Hlaing, 'Trends of Economic Growth and Income Distribution in Burma, 1870–1940', *Journal of the Burma Research Society*, 47 (1964), 57–108.

Ballhatchet, Kenneth, *Race, Sex and Class under the Raj: Imperial Attitudes and Policies and their Critics, 1793–1905*, London, 1980.

Battetto, W.L., *Mindon*, Rangoon, n.d.

Baruah, S.L., *A Comprehensive History of Assam*, New Delhi, 1985.

Bayly, C.A., *Indian Society and the Making of the British Empire*, Cambridge, 1988.

Imperial Meridian: The British Empire and the World, 1780–1830, London, 1989.

Information and Empire: Intelligence Gathering and Social Communication in India, 1780–1870, Cambridge, 1997.

Bennett, Paul J., *Conference under the Tamarind Tree: Three Essays in Burmese History*, New Haven, 1971.

Bose, Sugata and Ayesha Jalal, *Modern South Asia: History, Culture and Political Economy*, London, 1997.

Brailey, Nigel, *Two Views of Siam on the Eve of the Chakri Reformation*, Whiting Bay, 1989.

Breuilly, John, *Nations and the State*, Manchester, 1993.

Bruce, George, *The Burma Wars: 1824–1880*, London, 1973.

Cady, John, *A History of Modern Burma*, Ithaca, 1958.

Cameron, Rondo, *A Concise Economic History of the World*, New York, 1993.

Carey, Peter, 'Waiting for the Just King: The Agrarian World of South-Central Java from Giyanti to the Java War 1825–30', *Modern Asian Studies*, 20 (1986), 59–139.

Charnvit Kasetsiri, *The Rise of Ayudhaya*, Kuala Lumpur, 1976.

'Thai Historiography from Ancient Times to the Modern Period', in Anthony Reid and David Marr, eds., *Perceptions of the Past in Southeast Asia*,

Singapore, 1979.

Cheng Siok-Hwa, *The Rice Industry of Burma (1852–1940)*, Kuala Lumpur, 1968.

Chew, Ernest C.T., 'The Fall of the Burmese Kingdom in 1885: Review and Reconsideration', *Journal of Southeast Asian Studies*, 10, Singapore (1979), 372–81.

Cohn, Bernard S., 'Representing Authority in Victorian India', in Eric Hobsbawm and Terence Ranger, eds., *The Invention of Tradition*, Cambridge, 1983.

Corley, T.A.B., *A History of the Burmah Oil Company: 1886–1924*, London, 1983.

Damrong Rajanubhab, *Journey Through Burma in 1936*, Bangkok, 1991.

Desai, N.S. *Deposed King Theebaw of Burma in India*, Delhi, 1968.

Dobby, Eugene, *Southeast Asia*, London, 1950.

Donnison, F.S.V., *Public Administration in Burma: A Study of Development During the British Connection*, London, 1953.

Evans, Brian L., 'The Panthay Mission of 1872 and its Legacies', *Journal of Southeast Asian Studies*, 16 (1985), 117–29.

Ferguson, John, 'The Quest for Legitimation by Burmese Monks and Kings: The Case of the Shwegyin Sect (19th and 20th Centuries)', in B.L. Smith, ed., *Religion and the Legitimation of Power in Thailand, Laos and Burma*, Philadelphia, 1978.

Foster, R.F., *Lord Randolph Churchill: A Political Life*, London, 1987.

Furnival, J.S., *An Introduction to the Political Economy of Burma*, Rangoon, 1931.

'The Fashioning of the Leviathan', *Journal of the Burma Research Society*, 24 (1939), 1–137.

Colonial Policy and Practice: A Comparative Study of Burma and Netherlands India, Cambridge, 1948.

Geertz, Clifford, *Negara: The Theatre State in Nineteenth-Century Bali*, Princeton, 1980.

Ghosh, Lipi, *Burma: Myth of French Intrigue*, Calcutta, 1994.

Gombrich, Richard, *Theravade Buddhism: A Social History from Ancient Behares to Modern Colombo*, London, 1988.

Guyot, James, 'Bureaucratic Transformation in Burma', in Ralph Braibanti, ed., *Asian Bureaucratic Systems Emergent from the British Imperial Tradition*, Durham, NC, 1966.

Hall, D.G.E., *A History of Southeast Asia*, reprint, London, 1968.

Hall, D.G.E., ed., *Historians of Southeast Asia*, London, 1961.

Hao Yen-p'ing, *The Commercial Revolution in Nineteenth Century China: The*

Rise of Sino-Western Mercantile Capitalism, Berkeley, 1986.

Harrell, Stevan, *Cultural Encounters on China's Ethnic Frontiers*, Seattle, 1995.

Harvey, G.E., *History of Burma from the Earliest Times to 10 March 1824 – The Beginning of the English Conquest*, London, 1925.

  British Rule in Burma: 1824–1942, London, 1944.

Hla Pe, *Konmara Pya Zat: An Example of Popular Burmese Drama in the Nineteenth Century by Pok Ni*, London, 1952.

  Burma: Literature, Historiography, Scholarship, Language, Life and Buddhism, Singapore, 1985.

Hobsbawm, E.J., *Nations and Nationalism: Programme, Myth, and Reality*, Cambridge, 1990.

Hong Lysa, *Thailand in the Nineteenth Century*, Singapore, 1984.

Htin Aung, *Burmese Drama: A Study with Translations of Burmese Plays*, Oxford, 1937.

  'The Thirty-Seven Lords', *Journal of the Burma Research Society*, 39 (1956), 81–101.

  Burmese Law Tales, London, 1962.

  The Stricken Peacock: Anglo-Burmese Relations, 1852–1948, The Hague, 1965.

  Burmese Monks' Tales, New York, 1966.

  A History of Burma, New York, 1967.

  Lord Randolph Churchill and the Dancing Peacock, Delhi, 1990.

Huxley, Andrew, 'The Village Knows Best: Social Organisation in an 18th Century Burmese Law Code', *Southeast Asia Research*, 5 (1997), 1–32.

Hyam, Ronald, *Empire and Sexuality: The British Experience*, Manchester, 1990.

Kabui, Gangamumei, *History of Manipur*, vol. I: *Pre-Colonial Period*, New Delhi, 1991.

Kaung, 'A Survey of the History of Education in Burma before the British Conquest and After', *Journal of the Burma Research Society*, 46 (1963), 1–112.

Keeton, Charles, *King Theebaw and the Ecological Rape of Burma: The Political and Commercial Struggle between British India and French Indochina in Burma 1878–1886*, Delhi, 1974.

Keyes, Charles, 'Buddhist Economics and Buddhist Fundamentalism in Burma and Thailand', in Martin Marty and R. Scott Appleby, eds., *Fundamentalisms and the State: Remaking Politics, Economics and Militancy*, Chicago, 1993.

Khin Maung Kyi and Tin Tin, *Administrative Patterns in Historical Burma*, Singapore, 1973.

King, Winston, *A Thousand Lives Away: Buddhism in Contemporary Burma*, Berkeley, 1964.

Koenig, William J., *The Burmese Polity, 1752–1819: Politics, Administration, and Social Organisation in the Early Konbaung Period*, Ann Arbor, 1990.

Kyan, 'King Mindon's Councillors', *Journal of the Burma Research Society*, 44 (1961), 43–61.

'Village Administration in Upper Burma', *Journal of the Burma Research Society*, 52 (1969), 67–81.

Langham-Carter, R.R., 'Lower Chindwin Nats', *Journal of the Burma Research Society*, 23 (1933), 97–106; continued *Journal of the Burma Research Society*, 24 (1933), 105–12.

'The Kinwun Mingyi at Home', *Journal of the Burma Research Society*, 25 (1935), 121–9.

'Maha Bandula at Home', *Journal of the Burma Research Society*, 26 (1936), 122–31.

'Burmese Rule on the Toungoo Frontier', *Journal of the Burma Research Society*, 27 (1937), 15–33.

'The Burmese Army', *Journal of the Burma Research Society*, 28 (1937), 254–77.

'Four Notables of the Lower Chindwin', *Journal of the Burma Research Society*, 30 (1940), 336–43.

Leach, Edmund, *Political Systems of Highland Burma: A Study of Kachin Social Structure*, London, 1954.

Lee, James, 'Food Supply and Population Growth in Southwest China', *Journal of Asian Studies*, 41 (1982), 711–46.

Lehman, F.K., *The Structure of Chin Society: A Tribal People of Burma Adapted to a Non-Western Civilization*, Urbana, 1963.

Lieberman, Victor, 'Ethnic Politics in Eighteenth-Century Burma', *Modern Asian Studies*, 12 (1978), 455–83.

Burmese Administrative Circles: Anarchy and Conquest, c. 1580–1760, Princeton, 1984.

'How Reliable is U Kala's Burmese Chronicles? Some New Comparisons', *Journal of Southeast Asian Studies*, 17 (1986), 236–56.

'Secular Trends in Burmese Economic History, c. 1350–1830, and their Implications for State Formation', *Modern Asian Studies*, 25 (1991), 1–31.

'Local Integration and Eurasian Analogies: Structuring Southeast Asian History c. 1350–1830', *Modern Asian Studies*, 27 (1993), 475–572.

Luce, G.H., 'Chinese Invasions of Burma in the Eighteenth Century', *Journal of the Burma Research Society*, 15 (1925), 115–29.

'Mons of the Pagan Dynasty', *Journal of the Burma Research Society*, 36

(1953), 1–19.

'Social Life in Burma AD 1044–1287, *Journal of the Burma Research Society*, 41 (1958).

'Old Kyauksè and the Coming of the Burmans', *Journal of the Burma Research Society*, 42 (1959), 75–110.

Old Burma – Early Pagan, 3 vols., New York, 1969.

Phases of Pre-Pagan Burma: Languages and History, Oxford, 1985.

McCrae, Alistair, *Scots in Burma*, Edinburgh, 1990.

McCrae, Alistair and Prentice, Alan, *Irrawaddy Flotilla*, London, 1978.

Marr, David G., *Vietnamese Anti-Colonialism, 1885–1925*, Berkeley, 1971.

Maung Maung, *Burma in the Family of Nations*, Djambatan, 1956.

Law and Custom in Burma and the Burmese Family, The Hague, 1963.

Maung Maung Gyi, *Burmese Political Values: The Socio-Political Roots of Authoritarianism*, New York, 1983.

Maung Maung Tin and Morris, Thomas Owen, 'Mindon Min's Development Plan for the Mandalay Area', *Journal of the Burma Research Society*, 44 (1966), 29–34.

Maung Shein, 'Burma Railways 1874–1914', *Journal of the Burma Research Society*, 44 (1961).

Maung Tha Aung and Maung Mya Din (H.R. Alexander, ed.), 'The Pacification of Upper Burma: A Vernacular History', *Journal of the Burma Research Society*, 25 (1935), 80–136.

Mendelson, E.M., *Sangha and State in Burma: A Study of Monastic Sectarianism and Leadership*, Ithaca, 1975.

Mi Mi Khaing, *The World of Burmese Women*, London, 1948.

Moscotti, Albert, *British Policy and the Nationalist Movement in Burma 1917–1937*, Honolulu, 1974.

Mukerjee, Aparna, *British Colonial Policy in Burma: An Aspect of Colonialism in South-East Asia 1840–1885*, Delhi, 1988.

Mya Maung, *The Burma Road to Poverty*, New York, 1991.

Mya Sein, *The Administration of Burma: Sir Charles Crosthwaithe and the Consolidation of Burma*, Rangoon, 1938.

Naquin, Susan and Rawski, Evelyn, *Chinese Society in the Eighteenth Century*, New Haven, 1987.

Nash, Manning, *The Golden Road to Modernity: Village Life in Central Burma*, New York, 1965.

Ni Ni Myint, *Burma's Struggle Against British Imperialism: 1885–1889*, Rangoon, 1983.

Nobuyoshi Nishizawa, *Economic Development of Burma in Colonial Times*, Hiroshima, 1991.

Owen, Norman, ed., *Death and Disease in Southeast Asia: Explorations in Social, Medical and Demographic History*, Singapore, 1987.

Owen, Roger, *Cotton and the Egyptian Economy 1820–1914*, London, 1969.

'Egypt and Europe: From French Expedition to the British Occupation', in Roger Owen and Bob Sutcliffe, eds., *Studies in the Theory of Imperialism*, London, 1972.

Pearn, B.R., 'The Commercial Treaty of 1862', *Journal of the Burma Research Society*, 27 (1937), 33–53.

History of Rangoon, Rangoon, 1939.

Pemberton, R.B., 'Journey from Munipoar to Ava, and from Thence Across the Yooma Mountains to Arraccan', *Journal of the Burma Research Society*, 43 (1960), 98–103.

Penzer, *The Mineral Resources of Burma*, London, 1922.

Pointon, A.C., *The Bombay Burma Trading Corporation Limited 1863–1963*, Southampton, 1964.

Pollack, Oliver, *Empires in Collision: Anglo-Burmese Relations in the Mid-Nineteenth Century*, Westport, 1979.

Ramirez, Fransisco O., ed., *Rethinking the Nineteenth Century: Contradictions and Movements*, New York, 1988.

Rajat Kanta Ray, *Asian Capital in the Age of European Domination: The Rise of the Bazaar, Modern Asian Studies*, 29 (1995), 449–555.

Reid, Anthony, 'Low Population Growth and Its Causes in Pre-Colonial Southeast Asia, in Norman Owen, ed., *Death and Disease in Southeast Asia: Explorations in Social, Medical and Demographic History*, Singapore, 1987.

Southeast Asia in the Age of Commerce 1450–1680, vol. I: *The Land Below the Winds*, New Haven, 1988.

Reid, Anthony, ed., *The Last Stand of Asian Autonomies: Responses to Modernity in the Diverse States of Southeast Asia and Korea 1750–1900*, London, 1997.

Ricklefs, M.C., *Jogjakarta under Sultan Manguukubumi, 1749–1792*, London, 1974.

A History of Modern Indonesia, London, 1981.

Robinson, Richard and Willard Johnson, *The Buddhist Religion: A Historical Introduction*, London, 1997.

Robinson, Ronald, *Africa and the Victorians: The Official Mind of Imperialism*, London, 1961.

'Non-European Foundations of European Imperialism: Sketch for a Theory of Collaboration', in Roger Owen and Bob Sutcliffe, eds., *Studies in the Theory of Imperialism*, London, 1972.

Robinson, Ronald and Gallagher, J., 'The Imperialism of Free Trade', *Economic History Review*, 6 (1953), 1–15.

Rodrigue, Yves, *Nat-Pwe: Burma's Supernatural Sub-Culture*, Edinburgh, 1992.

Saimong Mangrai, *The Shan States and the British Annexation*, Ithaca, 1965.

  The Padaeng Chronicle and the Jeng Tung State Chronicle Translated, Ann Arbor, 1981.

SarDesai, D.R., *British Trade and Expansion in Southeast Asia, 1830–1914*, Delhi, 1977.

Sarkisyanz, E., *Buddhist Backgrounds of the Burmese Revolution*, The Hague, 1965.

Scholch, A., *Egypt for the Egyptians: The Socio-Political Crisis in Egypt 1878–1882*, London, 1981.

Scott, James C., 'The Erosion of Patron–Client Bonds and Social Change in Southeast Asia', *Journal of Asian Studies*, 32 (1972), 5–37.

  The Moral Economy of the Peasant: Rebellion and Subsistence in Southeast Asia, New Haven, 1976.

  Domination and the Arts of Resistance: Hidden Transcripts, London, 1990.

Sesser, S., *Lands of Charm and Cruelty: Travels in Southeast Asia*, New York, 1993.

Shein, *Burma's Transport and Foreign Trade (1885–1914)*, Rangoon, 1964.

Silverstein, Joseph, *Burma: Military Rule and the Politics of Stagnation*, Ithaca, 1977.

Singer, Noel, *Burmese Dance and Theatre*, Oxford, 1995.

Singhal, D.P., *British Diplomacy and the Annexation of Upper Burma*, Delhi, 1981.

Smith, Donald E., *Religion and Politics in Burma*, Princeton, 1965.

Spate, O.H.K., 'The Burmese Village', *Geographical Review*, 3(4) (1945), 23–43.

Spiro, Melford, *Burmese Supernaturalism*, Philadelphia, 1967.

  Buddhism and Society: A Great Tradition and its Burmese Vicissitudes, London, 1971.

  Marriage and Kinship in Burma: A Cultural and Psychodynamic Analysis, Berkeley, 1977.

Stargardt, Janice, *The Ancient Pyu of Burma*, vol. I: *Early Pyu Cities in a Man-Made Landscape*, Cambridge, 1990.

Steinberg, David I., *Burma's Road Toward Development: Growth and Ideology Under Military Rule*, Boulder, 1981.

  Burma: A Socialist Nation of Southeast Asia, Boulder, 1982.

  ed., *In Search of Southeast Asia: A Modern History*, Singapore, 1985.

Stivens, Maila, ed., *Why Gender Matters in Southeast Asian Politics*, Monash, 1991.

Tambiah, S.J., *World Conqueror and World Renouncer: A Study of Buddhism and Polity in Thailand Against a Historical Background*, Cambridge, 1976.

Tarling, Nicholas, ed., *Cambridge History of Southeast Asia*, 2 vols., Cambridge, 1993.

Taw Sein Ko, 'A Study in Burmese Sociology', *Journal of the Burmese Research Society*, 10 (1920).

Taylor, Robert, *An Undeveloped State: The Study of Modern Burma's Politics*, Monash, 1983.

The State in Burma, London, 1987.

Tet Htoot, 'The Nature of the Burmese Chronicles', in D.G.E. Hall, ed., *Historians of Southeast Asia*, London, 1961.

Than Tun, 'Administration under King Thalun (1629–1648)', *Journal of the Burma Research Society*, 51 (1968), 173–89.

Essays on the History and Buddhism of Burma, Edinburgh, 1988.

Thaung, 'Burmese Kingship During the Reign of King Mindon', *Journal of the Burma Research Society*, 49 (1966), 1–22.

Tin Ohn, 'Modern Historical Writing in Burmese', in D.G.E. Hall, ed., *Historians of Southeast Asia*, London, 1961.

Tinker, Hugh, *The Union of Burma: A Study of the First Years of Independence*, Oxford, 1961.

Trager, Frank, *Burma: From Kingdom to Republic: A Historical and Political Analysis*, London, 1966.

Trocki, A., 'Political Structures in the Nineteenth and Early Twentieth Centuries', in Nicholas Tarling, ed., *The Cambridge History of Southeast Asia*, vol. II, Cambridge, 1993.

Tun Wai, *Economic Development of Burma from 1800 till 1940*, Rangoon, 1961.

Burma's Currency and Credit, Bombay, 1962.

Turrell, Robert Vicant, 'Conquest and Concession: The Case of the Burma Ruby Mines', *Modern Asian Studies*, 22 (1988), 145–63.

Turwiel, B.J., *A History of Modern Thailand, 1767–1942*, St Lucia, 1983.

Twitchett, Denis and Fairbank, John K., eds. *The Cambridge History of China*, vol. II: *Late Ch'ing, 1800–1911*, part 2, Cambridge, 1980.

Vandergeest, Peter, 'Hierarchy and Power in Pre-National Buddhist States', *Modern Asian Studies*, 27 (1993), 843–71.

Woodman, Dorothy, *The Making of Burma*, London, 1962.

Woodside, Alexander, *Community and Revolution in Modern Vietnam*, Boston, 1976.

Wyatt, David, *A Short History of Thailand*, New Haven, 1984.

Studies in Thai History, Chiangmai, 1994.

Wyatt, David and Woodside, Alexander, eds., *Moral Order and the Question of Change: Essays on Southeast Asian Thought*, New Haven, 1982.

Yeager, Moshe, *The Muslims of Burma: A Study of a Minority Group*, Wiesbaden, 1972.

Yi Yi, 'Life at the Burmese Court under the Konbaung Kings', *Journal of the Burma Research Society*, 44 (1961), 85–129.

Index